The Chronic Pain Control WORKBOOK

SECOND EDITION

A STEP-BY-STEP GUIDE FOR COPING WITH AND OVERCOMING PAIN

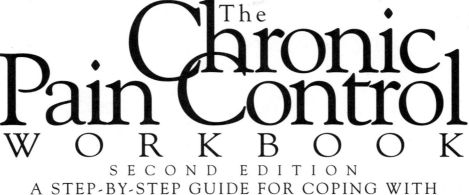

ELLEN MOHR CATALANO, M.A.
& KIMERON N. HARDIN, Ph.D.

With Introductions by Harold Carron, M.D., and Dennis C. Turk, Ph.D.

*and contributions from Robert W. Allen, M.D., Douglas DeGood, Ph.D.,
Catherine Geiser, R.D., Richard Gevirtz, Ph.D., William Stewart, Ph.D.,
Dorothy Waddell, M.D., Stephen Wegener, Ph.D., and Christine Zampach, M.Ed., P.T.*

New Harbinger Publications

Copyright © 1996 by Ellen Mohr Catalano and Kimeron N. Hardin
New Harbinger Publications, Inc.
5674 Shattuck Avenue
Oakland, CA 94609

Cover design by SHELBY DESIGNS AND ILLUSTRATES.
Text design by Tracy Marie Powell.

Distributed in U.S.A. by Publishers Group West; in Canada by Raincoast Books; in Great Britain by Airlift Book Company, Ltd.; in South Africa by Real Books, Ltd.; in Australia by Boobook; in New Zealand by Tandem Press.

Library of Congress Catalog Card Number: 96-67938

ISBN 1-57224-050-4 paperback

99   98   97

10   9   8   7   6   5   4   3   2

Acknowledgments

I would like to thank the following people who have graciously given their time and energy in the production of this second edition: John Rowlingson, M.D., Director, University of Virginia Pain Management Center; Lee Adams, LPC and Biofeedback Therapist, University of Virginia Pain Management Center; and Dr. Martha Brown Menard and Betty Seignor, Massage Therapists. And last, eternal thanks go to my husband Glenn for his consistent emotional support and our daughter Rubina, who has taught me a great deal lately about patience in managing life's changes.

—EMC

I would like to thank my good friends Ranjan Sharma, M.D., for his technical advice, Rob Allen, M.D., for his editorial help, and Randy Callahan, for his leadership and humor. I would also like to acknowledge my parents, Norman and Martha Hardin, for their excitement and encouragement about this project. Finally, a loving thanks for William Watson, who is an infinite source of inspiration, support, music, and strength, and who made wonderful editorial contributions and theoretical critique.

—KH

We would both like to thank Pat Fanning, Matthew McKay, Kirk Johnson, Farrin Jacobs, Lauren Dockett, and the rest of New Harbinger Publications for their patience, support, and enthusiasm for this project.

This book is dedicated to the memory of Nowell Bryant, Ph.D.,
who cared enough to make a difference and was an uplifting example to others.

About the Contributing Authors

Christine Zampach, M.Ed., P.T., is the Team Leader for Rehabilitation Services at the University of California at San Francisco / Mount Zion Medical Center and is a Clinical Specialist in chronic pain in physical therapy.

Catherine Geiser, R.D., is a Clinical Dietician at University of California at San Francisco / Mount Zion Medical Center and has a degree in kinesiology from UCLA.

Robert W. Allen, M.D., is Medical Director of the Pain Management Center at the University of California at San Francisco / Mount Zion Medical Center. He is an Assistant Professor of Anesthesiology with board certification in both anesthesia and pain management.

Dorothy Waddell, M.D., is an Associate Clinical Professor at the University of California at San Francisco in the Department of Medicine, and is in private practice. She is the former Chief of the Musculoskeletal Clinic at San Francisco General Hospital.

Douglas DeGood, Ph.D., is Director of Psychology, Pain Management Center at the Department of Anesthesiology, University of Virginia Medical Center.

Richard Gevirtz, Ph.D., is a Professor at the California School of Professional Psychology in San Diego, and is in private practice at the Biofeedback Institute of San Diego.

Stephen T. Wegener, Ph.D., is an Associate Professor as well as the Chief of Psychology in the Department of Physical Medicine and Rehabilitation at Johns Hopkins University School of Medicine.

William Stewart, Ph.D., works in Behavioral Medicine Services at the Dean Medical Center, Madison, Wisconsin.

Contents

Introduction

Pain has been experienced since the earliest recorded time. Yet, for many people pain remains recalcitrant to the best efforts, despite the advances in understanding of basic anatomy and physiology and increasingly sophisticated medical and surgical treatments that have occurred.

It is for the individuals who experience chronic pain that the persistence of noxious symptoms becomes an unending nightmare. They have been exposed to a multitude of diagnostic assessments, medical workups, and a plethora of treatments, but all to no avail. With increasing frustration on the part of health care professionals, these pain sufferers are often given the message that they will have to "learn to live with it [the pain and accompanying problems]." This is an especially demoralizing message since the sufferer does not want to be told that there is nothing that can be done, that their pain is chronic and, therefore, interminable. These people do not want to learn to live with the pain since they have been living with it for some time; rather they want to live *without it.*

The presence of pain affects all domains of the pain sufferer's life—familial, occupational, social, and recreational, as well as physical. The situation seems hopeless, health care providers from whom they have come to expect relief appear to have given up on them, and the sufferer feels helpless. Unremitting pain becomes the central focus of these people's lives. Its presence is felt 24 hours a day, 365 days a year, and there is no end in sight. These people's lives, as one patient noted, have "collapsed." It should come as no surprise that they experience a range of negative emotions—frustration, anger, anxiety, and depression.

When people with chronic pain complain, they are told they will have to learn to live with "it"; the implication is that it is their responsibility. Often, however, minimal information or assistance is provided to help the sufferer learn "how to live with it." The primary missions of this volume are to do just that.

The objectives of the text include: (a) helping people with chronic pain to move out of the passive patient role to become active and resourceful men and women, to no longer view themselves as patients or sufferers; (b) teaching these individuals how they can take charge to improve the quality of their lives; (c) teaching them what they can do to alleviate some of the problems created by the presence of pain; and (d) teaching them practical methods that they can use to help reduce to severity of the pain they experience.

The objectives of this volume are accomplished by the provision of basic information about the physical aspects of pain and its impact on people's lives and on their families, conventional treatments, and specific strategies that the patients can use in their daily lives. Information is essential, as knowledge can reduce the added stress of ambiguity and the uncanniness of the unknown associated with unremitting pain. Things always seem worse when they are vague and poorly understood. Information can provide a basis for people (notice I did not use the terms patient or sufferer) to accept greater responsibility for their lives. For people with chronic pain, information is essential but may not be sufficient.

Beyond basic information, this volume provides useful self-management strategies that, if adopted by the individual, can reduce both the emotional and physical distress that accompanies chronic pain. Moreover, some of the techniques included may actually lead to reduction in the degree of pain experienced. The added benefit is that as the individual accomplishes greater control his or her self-esteem will be elevated. Thus, the emphasis of the volume is not only on teaching people how to live with pain but how to take charge of their lives, how to grow as individuals, and ultimately how to regain their self-respect.

This volume has much to offer people with chronic pain, but the benefits will not occur without their effort. People who have chronic pain need to accept responsibility, to take charge. They must use the information provided and be active and resourceful. Some of those with chronic pain problems may be able to make use of the information contained in the text on their own, others will benefit from using the book in collaboration with a health care provider. Family members and significant others may benefit from the insights provided about different pain syndromes, treatments, and self-care methods.

This workbook can be used flexibly by the health care provider and person with pain working collaboratively with the ultimate goal being that of improvement in physical and emotional functioning. Health care providers may find it useful to suggest a specific chapter as a complement to treatment.

The information about pain syndromes and impact along with the specific self-help strategies included in the original edition of this volume have proven to be of great benefit to a large number of people who experience chronic pain. This extensively revised and expanded edition provides updated information and continues to include a set of self-management strategies that have a proven track record. As a result, this new edition should be an invaluable resource for health care providers as well as for those who need to learn how to live with diverse chronic pain syndromes.

Dennis C. Turk, Ph.D.
Pain Evaluation and Treatment Institute
University of Pittsburgh Medical Center

Introduction

(to the First Edition)

Pain is a personal experience. Usually initiated by injury or disease, the discomfort it produces on movement or at rest is amplified by the patient's emotional response to the meaning, persistence, intensity, and debilitating aspects of the experience. Most acute pain is limited in duration, amenable to treatment, and usually can be cured. But for reasons unknown to medical science, pain may persist following healing and despite the absence of any demonstrable pathology. This kind of chronic pain is poorly understood by both the patient and the treating professional.

With its demands and commands for rest, chronic pain leads to the additional hardships of muscle weakness and atrophy, tendon and ligament shortening, and joint immobility. Normal physical activities then become painful, further limiting the sufferer's ability to function. With no relief in view, many patients fall into the traps of doctor shopping in search of a cure, overdependence on medication, depression, and social withdrawal. Family and sexual relationships are also commonly damaged by the sufferer's unrelenting pain.

This text is designed for the chronic pain sufferer, but offers health professionals at all levels a rational approach to understanding chronic pain and its management. Throughout, it emphasizes the key point that the patient must take responsibility for carrying out his or her own treatment, a responsibility that can be accomplished by setting realistic goals and learning specific skills.

While there are few controlled studies on the management of any chronic pain syndrome—nor even a confluence of opinions as to the value of any specific therapeutic intervention—this workbook is based on many years of experience by specialists in the management of patients with chronic pain. The programs outlined reinforce the fact that chronic pain is seldom cured, and that one must "learn to control the pain rather than let it control him" as an alternative to disability. The text covers the development of coping skills through stress management and relaxation training and examines approaches to physical rehabilitation through appropriate exercise programs and use of body mechanics to avoid further injury.

Several chapters are devoted to the more common pain problems, of which back and neck pain lead the list. Also covered in depth are headache, temperomandibular pain, arthritis, abdominal pain, and the neuralgias. A final section is devoted to a description of pain clinics and their role and that of governmental agencies in rehabilitation.

This text is pragmatic in its approach. The reasons for particular self-help treat-ments are explained, the steps to take are detailed, and additional supportive measures that will enhance the patient's response to treatment are explored. The book should serve as a useful tool for health professionals working with chronic pain patients. And in this volume, many pain patients will find answers to their questions and a better understanding of chronic pain and its control.

Harold Carron, M.D.
Clinical Professor of Anesthesiology
Pain Consultant
Georgetown University Medical Center and N.I.H.
Washington, DC

1

Learning to Cope

This workbook may have caught your attention because you have chronic pain or you know someone who does. You know, then, that chronic pain can be terribly difficult to manage, both physically and emotionally.

The Chronic Pain Control Workbook is designed to help you assess your particular situation, learn methods of managing chronic pain, and try out some new options that you may not have considered before. Most importantly, each chapter encourages you to look at how your pain affects you as a whole person. Most pain sufferers go into treatment viewing their pain as a separate problem, unrelated to the rest of their lives. But a real ability to cope with your pain begins when you learn to see it as a complex interweaving of your own unique physical and emotional reactions.

Physically, as the pain drags on, you often begin to avoid even the smallest movement for fear of reinjury. You hold your breath and tighten your muscles in anticipation of the pain, as if that stiffness and constriction would keep it from returning. The pain wakes you up in the middle of the night, so it's a chore to get out of bed in the morning, and you frequently feel groggy and half-alert during the day. The pain interferes with your work and your home life; it is on your mind almost constantly. Often your friends and family can't understand it, since there are no visible broken bones or torn muscles and you still look like you used to look. But you look in the mirror and see the bags under your eyes and the pale, gaunt look of a face that is fighting pain.

The physical hardships of chronic pain may force you to withdraw from friends and family. This further contributes to your feelings of frustration, isolation, and loneliness. People say, "Try hot tubs . . ." "Exercise . . ." "Use ice . . . ." And you do try, but at the first sign of pain you're not sure how much is too much and you stop for fear of doing any more damage. You hold yourself very still and wait, hoping that someone will come along who has a cure, or at least a definite answer, so that you can get off this vicious pain cycle.

Emotionally, those of you who suffer from chronic pain may feel depressed about your prospects for recovery. You think to yourself, "This will never get better," and sometimes you despair that you will never again be your old self, able to enjoy, able to be spontaneous. Sometimes you feel plain scared. You imagine the pain continuing until you are overwhelmed or crazy, until everything you love or count on is lost. You may feel resentful that this is happening to you, that your pain is making you weak, unacceptable, useless. Or you may lash out at others, blaming them for not helping you or for putting you in a difficult situation.

As a result, your family and work relationships suffer. Your family wants you to get well but feels helpless. They might try to be supportive, but can turn on you or sulk when you get angry or complain. Children in the family may get confused about the change of pace at home—why is Mom staying home from work? Or perhaps the children and spouse begin to feel neglected and strained because your pain has taken up so much time, attention, and money. Those of you who live with or counsel chronic pain sufferers are probably well aware of the frustrations in helping someone adapt to the major life disruptions that pain causes. You may feel manipulated, stuck, or discouraged in your efforts to help the person cope.

When you're wrapped up in your pain, it's hard to make decisions like you used to. If you've stayed out of work for a while, you may find it increasingly difficult to imagine returning. If you do go back, you know that you will have to face the boss and request certain changes so you can continue to do your job; you're not sure what his or her reaction will be. On top of it all, you consult with several different doctors or health care professionals about your condition, only to find that you get widely varying opinions. No one agrees on how to treat your pain, or how and when you can resume work.

Traditionally, doctors have excelled at treating symptoms, curing acute problems, researching and prescribing drugs, and perfecting diagnostic techniques. But chronic pain frequently falls through the cracks of modern medical science. A pain symptom that may be diagnosed as one thing in clinic A is diagnosed as another in hospital B. Doctors sometimes fail to clearly communicate with one another or with their patients. It's not uncommon to find a chronic pain sufferer who takes one drug prescribed by one physician and another drug prescribed by another, and the doctors may have no idea that their patient is getting conflicting drug treatments. Often, one doctor cannot diagnose your problem and refers you to another doctor, who refers you to another department, which, in turn, refers you somewhere else, until you begin to feel like a hot potato being passed from hand to hand. If you were hoping that the doctors would know what to do, you feel mounting frustration as you realize that you're not going to be fixed or cured and the doctor whom you trusted really has no answers at all. The doctors who see, or at least sense, your frustration react in various ways—some try harder and harder to help you, others get defensive, and others prescribe still more drugs because it makes them feel bad to see you in pain.

With the traditional medical model, the doctor has the burden of control. He or she must *do something* to remedy your situation. But this traditional approach to chronic pain management is rapidly being replaced by a newer and more effective strategy. This strategy involves working with the *whole* person, not just the symptoms. Methods are being developed that attempt to return control of pain to you, the patient. Pills are replaced with skills—stress management, self-hypnosis, biofeedback, and exercise, among many others. You can internalize these skills—that is, learn them so well that they become natural to you. With them, you can learn to effectively manage your pain.

These approaches are *not* designed to replace your doctor. They are presented here as alternatives you should include as part of a full treatment plan—a plan that you and your doctor can work out together. In the process, you will come to depend less on doctors and more on yourself. You will find that most medical professionals prefer to work with patients who are informed about their condition and willing to take a variety of treatment approaches, and who have chosen to take responsibility for their own pain management.

Although the enormous scope of this subject necessitates simplified and brief explanations of the various techniques, this book will provide a comprehensive overview that will help you pick and choose among the available pain management options. You will be in a better position to ask educated questions of your doctor or health care professional, as well as design a treatment program that meets your needs. Suggested readings at the end of each chapter will help you pursue the topics that interest you most.

This book covers four basic areas:

1. Physical management of pain, including medical interventions, exercise, and stress management

2. Psychological management of pain, including examination of attitudes and beliefs about chronic pain

3. Information that can help you cope with the pain and pain-related changes in your life such as sleep hygiene, nutrition tips, and support groups

4. Techniques for managing specific pain conditions, with basic information about current medical treatments and medications

Most people find it helpful to begin with physical management. When pain is constantly reminding you of its presence, it can be extremely difficult to concentrate on anything else. This section is designed to teach you valuable exercises and relaxation skills to get you through your difficult times so that you can move on to other aspects of coping. First read chapter 2, which acquaints you with medical terms and current practices in treating chronic pain. Chapters 3 and 4 on exercise and basic stress management skills are indispensable and need to be read carefully. The passive stretches and strengtheners in chapter 3 and the basic relaxation techniques of breathing and progressive relaxation in chapter 4 complement each other and lay a firm foundation for the rest of the skills you will learn in the book. When you feel comfortable with relaxation, you will be ready to try out the advanced relaxation techniques in chapter 5 and move on to the psychological management section of the book.

Chapters 6 and 7 examine some common attitudes and beliefs about chronic pain and teach you effective skills for dealing with pain-related situations. In chapter 6, you will first learn to identify your internal messages and responses to pain by examining your negative thoughts and how they may be obstacles to progress. In chapter 7 you will learn to productively handle many of the interpersonal situations that pain sufferers face through assertiveness training and conflict management.

Chapters 8 and 9 will help motivate you to use resources available to you, such as pain centers, support groups, your state's vocational rehabilitation system, and other programs designed to assist you in making career decisions and getting well. We've added new chapters to this second edition to cover specific problem areas for most people with pain including sleep habits, chapter 10, and diet, chapter 11.

The second part of the book is devoted to specific chronic pain conditions. You can pick the chapters here that address your unique questions. The last chapter is a "pep talk" for you as you learn these new skills.

A pep talk is appropriate here also. Think of pain management as learning a new skill. Do you remember learning to ride a bicycle? You wanted to ride off down the street with the big kids. You knew the time had come to graduate from your tricycle, but the two-wheeler looked ominous. As you clumsily tried to balance yourself on the seat while searching for the pedal with your foot, you wondered if you would ever learn. You may even have considered forgetting the whole thing. But you remembered your basic goal: to ride with the big kids. So you tried, and from clumsy motions and awkward falls came a sense of balance. Your body finally learned to harmonize with the wheels and frame underneath. You worked hard to get there, but you knew it was worth it.

There is a close analogy between managing chronic pain and the learning process you went through with your bicycle. At first your pain looks like an insurmountable obstacle, and the time it will take to "fix it" seems astronomical. You may feel like giving up before you start. The exercises may feel awkward to you, or the slightest bit of exercise may aggravate your pain to the point that you have to stop. You may feel too distracted to try stress reduction exercises, or feel just plain silly doing them. Or maybe you don't know how to fit it all into your lifestyle. But you have your basic goal in mind. You want to get better. And so you persevere.

A crucial step in pain management is to formulate clear, realistic goals and keep them in your mind at all times. Realistic goals are reachable and appropriate, ones you know you can strive for and achieve. Don't tell yourself that you'll be a marathon runner one year after your injury, when you never ran before. If you promise yourself that you'll become *totally* pain free, that pain will never bother you again, you are setting yourself up for disappointment. But if you promise yourself that you will stick to the program, not give up at the first flickering of pain, and realize that you will have occasional relapses that you can manage . . . You'll have realistic goals and will be more likely to succeed.

Three overall goals for anyone who is suffering from chronic pain and is seeking help are:

1. Get basic information about the best methods of controlling your pain.

2. Decrease the level of pain you are experiencing while also decreasing the inappropriate use of medical interventions.

3. Work toward a return to full or partial functioning.

The first goal starts with reading this book and creating a pain control plan with your doctor or a pain clinic. Your second goal is to help yourself feel less pain by using specific medical and psychological interventions. For example, by working with your doctor, you can implement a treatment plan where you use a combination of nerve blocks, appropriate medications, exercise, and stress reduction strategies to help you cope with the pain and move on to your other goals. In order to pursue this goal efficiently, it is important for you to decrease the amount of time you spend going from doctor to doctor in search of the perfect cure. The inappropriate use of medical interventions, or doctor shopping, wastes a lot of time and energy on your part—time better spent accomplishing goals two and three. Finally, you can accomplish your third goal by making use of available resources, such as physical therapy and vocational rehabilitation, to help you return to partial, if not full, activity.

As with all major goals, you will find it helpful to formulate some mini-goals to help you accomplish your overall agenda. Mini-goals are tasks or activities that are laid out chronologically and have a specific time frame. For example, in order to satisfy your second overall goal, to decrease the level of pain you are experiencing, a mini-goal could be to take several deep, diaphragmatic breaths each time you begin to experience the pain. Another mini-goal might be to allow yourself to take this process step by step, go at the pace your body allows, and not force yourself to go faster than you are ready to go.

Remember though that requiring yourself to perform perfectly is one point where chronic pain management and learning to ride a bike are *not* similar. Stubborn perseverence paid off when you were a kid. But with chronic pain, trying too hard to control your pain is like saying to yourself, "Hurry up and relax." Pushing yourself too hard is counterproductive. Instead, adopt a "passive perseverance" attitude, one that allows you to experience the control *in time.* Gradually, all the pieces will fall into place, and parts of the puzzle will fit together. But the change will take some time, patience, and open-mindedness on your part. You will also need a plan to accomplish your goals.

Following a written plan of action can be a useful tool in getting started. Unless you have already had experience managing pain, you may not be ready to actually sit down and formulate a plan. As you go through this workbook, jot down ideas that you might want to pursue in your plan. We suggest that you read through the workbook once, pick out the sections that you would like to work on, and then write out a contract for yourself using the following format.

Sample Chronic Pain Action Plan

Goal 1. Get information about best methods for controlling pain

Activity 1.   *What:*   Look for a pain clinic or institution that specializes in pain management. Research the available clinics in my area. Ask friends. Locate one within a reasonable distance. Arrange for at least one or two follow-up visits.

   When: Call this week for the next available appointment. Do not put it off.

Activity 2.   *What:*   Set up an appointment with my regular doctor to discuss my concerns and learn about available pain management resources in my area.

Activity 3.   *What:*   Find out where I can learn stress management, self-hypnosis, biofeedback, or related techniques to help manage pain. Make an appointment and give it at least two or three tries.

Goal 2: Decrease level of pain—physical management

Activity 1.   *What:*   Start the special back exercise program

   When: Right after morning shower

   Where: On the soft bedroom carpet

Activity 2.   *What:*   Take the anti-inflammatory medication prescribed by my doctor

   When: Four times a day

Activity 3.   *What:*   Use the TENS unit

   When: Two hours after lunch when pain is the worst

   Where: Home or office

Goal 3: Decrease level of pain—relaxation training

Activity 1.   *What:*   Progressive muscle relaxation (PMR)

   When: Once in the morning, once in the afternoon or evening

   Where: In easy chair in den

Activity 2.   *What:*   Self-hypnosis

   When: Right after PMR

   Where: In easy chair

Goal 4: Decrease level of pain—psychological management

Activity 1.   *What:*   Learn to handle my anger and frustration by confronting negative thoughts and remembering coping thoughts

	When:	Every time I'm aware of growing anger
Activity 2.	*What:*	Learn to handle my anxiety by confronting any catastrophic thinking
	When:	Every time I start to feel anxious about my back
Activity 3.	*What:*	Learn to say no and set limits
	When:	People ask me to go beyond my limits
	Where:	At the physical therapist's office, at home when my spouse asks me to do certain tasks, and when negotiating with my boss about returning to work

Goal 5. Get back to partial functioning

Activity 1.	*What:*	Arrange to return half-time within four weeks
	When:	Now
Activity 2.	*What:*	Arrange modified duties: no travel, no carrying during first two months
	When:	Now
Activity 3.	*What:*	Explore permanent reassignment to a "desk job" at the plant
	When:	Now

Your Plan

Goal 1. Get information about best methods for controlling pain

Activity 1.	*What:*	_____
	When:	_____
	Where:	_____
Activity 2.	*What:*	_____
	When:	_____
	Where:	_____
Activity 3.	*What:*	_____
	When:	_____
	Where:	_____

Goal 2. Decrease level of pain—physical management

Activity 1.	*What:*	_____
	When:	_____
	Where:	_____
Activity 2.	*What:*	_____

	When:	_____
	Where:	_____
Activity 3.	What:	_____
	When:	_____
	Where:	_____

Goal 3. Decrease level of pain—relaxation training

Activity 1.	What:	_____
	When:	_____
	Where:	_____
Activity 2.	What:	_____
	When:	_____
	Where:	_____
Activity 3.	What:	_____
	When:	_____
	Where:	_____

Goal 4. Decrease level of pain—psychological management

Activity 1.	What:	_____
	Wben:	_____
	Where:	_____
Activity 2.	What:	_____
	When:	_____
	Where:	_____
Activity 3.	What:	_____
	When:	_____
	Where:	_____

Goal 5. Get back to partial functioning

Activity 1.	What:	_____
	Wben:	_____
	Where:	_____
Activity 2.	What:	_____
	When:	_____
	Where:	_____
Activity 3.	What:	_____

When: _____

Where: _____

Once you have drawn up a plan, show your desired contract to a doctor or health care professional who you feel can give you helpful feedback and assist you in setting realistic goals. It can also be helpful to share your contract with a spouse or friend who can give you support and encouragement.

A Final Note

Don't give up! The information presented here has been gleaned from hundreds of chronic pain sufferers who have learned to stick with it, bolster themselves when things get tough, and design for themselves a workable plan for coping. After applying some or all of the principles laid out in this workbook, they tell us that they have learned these things:

- To put the pain in perspective

- To relax away some or all of the pain

- To make new decisions based on changes the pain has caused in their lives

- To set realistic goals

- To minimize the disruption the pain has caused

Humans are skeptical by nature. It may be tempting at this point, to say, "You may have interviewed hundreds of people in pain, but they probably don't have the kind of pain I have." Or you may automatically say, "Nothing in this book is likely to apply to me." Being wary is a natural by-product of stressful situations. But put aside your disbeliefs for awhile and consider reading this book as a possibility for change in your life.

Further Reading

Bresler, D. 1986. *Free Yourself From Pain.* New York: Simon and Schuster.

Caudill, M. A. 1995. *Managing Pain Before It Manages You.* New York: Guilford Press.

Kabat-Zinn, J. 1991. *Full Catastrophe Living: Using the Wisdom of Your Body and Mind to Fight Stress, Pain and Illness.* New York: Dell Publishing/Bantam Doubleday.

Kane, J. 1991. *Be Sick Well.* Oakland, CA: New Harbinger Publications, Inc.

Klein, R. A., and M. G. Landau. 1992. *Healing the Body Betrayed.* Minneapolis: Chronimed Publishing.

Kushner, H. 1983. *When Bad Things Happen to Good People.* New York: Avon Books.

Pollin, I., and S. Golant. 1994. *Taking Charge: Overcoming the Challenges of Long-Term Illness.* New York: Times Books, Random House.

Marcus, N., and J. Arbeiter. 1994. *Freedom from Pain.* New York: Simon and Schuster.

Wall, P. D., and M. Jones. 1991. *Defeating Pain: The War Against a Silent Epidemic.* New York: Plenum Press.

2

Theories of Pain

A biofeedback patient with a painful neck problem once came to Ellen to learn about pain management. At the beginning of her program Ellen told her that she would keep her discussion of the theories of pain short and simple. "Good," the patient replied. "This pain wears me down. I'm too exhausted to hear any long explanations."

This chapter is about theories of pain, kept short and simple. But no simplification can avoid the fact that pain is an extremely complex interaction of the mind and body. Among the many theories and suggested treatments for chronic pain, one basic rule stands out:

When you have chronic pain, your mind as well as your body is involved.

First, understand the following five basic concepts:

1. Acute pain is a signal to the body that it has been or is being damaged in some way. It is an alarm that requests immediate attention. The sensation of acute pain protects you from getting too close to a flame or from walking on a fractured foot. Burns and broken bones are examples of acute pain.

2. Acute pain is different from chronic pain. The word *acute* comes from the Latin word meaning "needle" and basically means "sharp." When acute pain occurs as a result of a wound, a broken bone, or a bite, it requires immediate attention because of the tissue damage. When treated with the appropriate medical care, the wound heals, the bone mends, and usually the pain goes away. The word *chronic* is derived from a Greek word for "time." Chronic pain is persistent pain that tends to be constant rather than intermittent and can become a pattern of painful sensations that persist long after the initial injury. A chronic illness hangs around for months or years. You can usually get decisive medical care for your acute pain, but treating chronic pain can become a maze of misunderstanding and misdiagnosis.

3. Chronic pain is real. All pain is real, whether it is acute or chronic. Your pain may not be obvious to someone else, but you know when you hurt.

4. Pain is a subjective experience. Everyone is a unique individual, and everyone handles pain in different ways. You have probably seen some people cry out loudly at what seems to be a minor injury, while others are stoic and keep a "stiff upper lip." These variations in pain reaction will be examined in the following chapters from a physical, as well as emotional, perspective.

5. Chronic pain is influenced by your environment. Because it involves far more than tissue damage and a physical disability, chronic pain is not a simple problem. Chronic pain can be affected adversely or positively by your family, your job, and your world in general. The environmental and emotional factors in diagram 2.1 can frustrate the treatment efforts and confuse and depress not only the sufferer, but his or her family and the health care professional as well.

Diagram 2.1

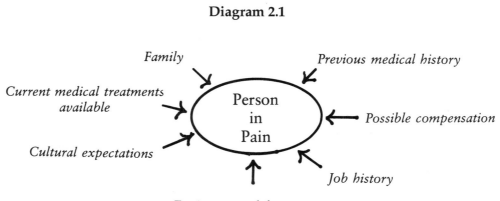

Beyond the Physiology Of Pain

Pain has been the subject of study and controversy for centuries, but only in the last several decades has careful research revealed illuminating new concepts about our perception of and reaction to pain. In 1956, a researcher named Beecher compared the reactions to pain of soldiers in battle with the reactions of a comparable number of civilians about to undergo an operation. Amazingly, he found that soldiers who had severe wounds complained less of pain and required less medication than did the civilians. To the soldiers, their severe wounds meant an end to battle and a return to the safety of the hospital. To the civilians, their wounds meant removal from the safety of home to the anxiety of being in the hospital and facing surgery. According to Dr. Beecher, the soldiers perceived less pain because they had reduced anxiety. This classic study showed that there is more to pain than mere sensation. A painful war wound means an end to battle and a quick ticket home. The pain of surgery means disease and an uncertain future. The meaning of pain affects the experience of pain.

Specificity Theory

Until recently, pain has been regarded as a straightforward mechanism—an individual gets hurt and that message is relayed directly to the brain. This simple stimulus-response concept, known as the *specificity theory*, is still taught in some medical schools. The theory assumes that the intensity of the pain is directly proportional to the amount of damage. In other words, if you have an obvious injury, you are expected to hurt; an unseen injury cannot hurt as much. This theory supposes that if surgery or medication can eliminate the cause of the pain, the pain should disappear. But when the pain drags on and there seems to be no obvious medical answer for it, this stimulus-response concept of pain is clearly an inadequate explanation.

A Broader Approach

More recent theories have shown that the experience of pain is not a simple cause-and-effect relationship between the body and the brain. Rather, it is a complex web of pain signals, chemical messengers, emotions, and thoughts involving several different pathways of pain. These pathways can transmit the pain signal either at lightning speed or slowly and continuously. Often, the pathways can continue to transmit a pain signal after the injury has supposedly healed, or even when an injured site has been entirely removed (as in the case of phantom limb pain). Imprinting, a fairly recent concept, may serve as the explanation here. The nervous system gets "conditioned" to transmit certain pain messages. In other words, for some reason the pain gets "stamped" onto the pain pathways, inducing the central nervous system to retain the memory of the pain for a while. The theory supposes that one way the nervous system gets stamped or stays turned on to the pain may be through a disruption in the balance of neurochemical transmitters relaying the pain messages. As a result of the imprinting theory, researchers have become absorbed in spinal cord research for the treatment of both acute and chronic pain.

Sometimes the pain sensation is transformed along its pathway so that when it reaches the brain it is perceived as something other than pain, or the brain sends messages back to the injured area to stop the pain sensation. In other words, there is continuous feedback motion from pain to brain and back again.

This fluid and constantly changing motion can be prevented or relieved by surgery and medications. You can have a surgeon sever a nerve in hope of cutting off the transmission of pain, or you can take drugs to try to block the pain. But more often than not, the pain is somehow regenerated even after surgery. As the drug effect wears off, you find you have to take higher and higher drug dosages. Since drugs and surgery are costly, in most cases you are left with what is usually offered as the last, but is actually the best, alternative—internally changing that fluid motion of pain to brain by changing *your attitude toward the pain*. You can change the way your pain feels by changing how your body and your brain feel. In order to do this, you will find it helpful to know specifically what happens to those pain sensations from a physiological viewpoint so that you know why pain sensations can be changed internally. The following simplified descriptions of pathways for pain transmission show how your attitudes can make a difference and explain how such therapies as nerve blocks, acupuncture, and nerve stimulators can work. To understand the phenomena of pain in your body, we'll look more closely at the physiology of pain.

Pain Pathways—Going Up and Down

Going up: fast and slow pain. Pain starts with a physical event—a cut, burn, tear, or bump. Nerve endings, or *pain receptors,* in the periphery of your body (limbs and organs) pick up the pain. The receptors send the pain information from one bunch of nerve fibers to another to cells in the spinal cord, where the message is then relayed to the brain. This pathway is called the *ascending tract.*

This process can happen at different rates of speed because the nerve fibers that transmit the pain messages come in different sizes. Large diameter A-beta nerve fibers transmit pain quickly along the cable network. This is commonly known as "fast pain." You know it as the kind of pain that feels like *pressure.* Two smaller diameter A-delta and C nerve fibers transmit pain information at a slower rate of speed. You know the A-delta pain as a *sharp and stabbing* pain you feel from a cut or burn. The C fiber pain is *dull and aching* and is typically called "slow pain" or secondary pain. As someone with chronic pain, you are all too familiar with C fiber slow pain—the dull aching sensation usually associated with chronic problems.

The spinal cord is the central concourse along which all pain messages travel to and from the brain. When you stub your toe and your peripheral nerves register alarm, the pain is immediately relayed along the nerve fibers of your foot and leg to a special area within the dorsal horn of the spinal cord called the *substantia gelatinosa.* The cells within the substantia gelatinosa relay this "fast pain" message along the pain tract, or the *neospinothalamic* pathway. The trip ends at specific locations in the brain, namely the *thalamus* and the *cortex.* The cortex is the portion of the brain where most of your thought processes take place. A pain message arrives and the cortex prompts you to say "ouch!" and begin rubbing the afflicted area.

By contrast, chronic pain tends to move along a different, slower tract called the *paleospinothalamic* pathway. This "slow pain" tends to be dull, aching, burning, and cramping. Initially it travels the same route as the fast pain through the dorsal horn of the spinal cord. Once there, however, the slow pain message separates in the brain stem area to turn toward final destinations in a different portion of the brain, the *hypothalamus* and *limbic structures.* The hypothalamus is the gland responsible for instructing the pituitary gland to release certain stress hormones. It is sometimes referred to as the central clearinghouse of the brain. The limbic structures are the place where your emotions are processed. Their involvement in the process helps to explain how your feelings can influence your pain. For more on pain pathways, refer to chapter 12.

Going down. Just as there is a "pain to brain" motion, there is also a "brain to pain" motion that attempts to counteract the pain message trying to make its way up. You have probably heard about athletes who sprain or strain something during a game but continue to play seemingly unaffected until the game is over. Or recall the study mentioned earlier in this chapter about soldiers wounded in battle who did not complain of pain because they were so relieved to be off the battlefield. In both of these cases, the brain instructs the body not to register, or pay attention to, the pain until later, if at all.

This downward pathway from the brain is called a *descending tract;* the brain uses it to send chemical substances and nerve impulses back down to the cells in the spinal cord to act against the pain message sent up by the pain receptors. Dr. John Rowlingson, Director of the University of Virginia Department of Anesthesiology Pain Management Center, notes that although not as much is known about these descending systems, they are largely chemical in nature and can be described as acting centrally to modify the pain messages coming into the spinal cord and brain. This might explain why therapies that act primarily in the brain, such as hypnosis, biofeedback, and brain stimulation, work so well to control pain.

Neurotransmitters

Another essential link needed to forge the chain of pain events is the presence of chemical substances within each cell of the nerve tract. These substances are called *neurotransmitters;* they can either pass the pain message on its way or make sure that the pain message is stopped. Neurotransmitters can act as painkillers or pain producers. A commonly known neurotransmitter is *serotonin,* one of the most important chemicals involved in pain relief.

A group of neurotransmitters believed to be the body's own natural painkillers are called *endorphins* and *enkephalins.* These substances are produced in the brain and can have the same powerful effect as morphine or heroin. New research indicates that different people produce different amounts of these natural painkillers, which may explain why some people experience pain more than others do. For example, when an athlete is performing with an injury, he or she may be producing enough endorphins to override the pain message.

The Gate Control Theory

Have you ever bumped your shin and then instinctively rubbed it to make it feel better? You probably noticed that when you did, the shin seemed to ache a little less. Why is this so?

In 1965, Drs. Melzack and Wall proposed that there were "gates" on the bundles of nerve fibers on the spinal cord that can either open to allow pain impulses through to your brain or close to cut them off. The Gate Control Theory proposes that a sufficient amount of stimuli can close the gate to the pain sensation. Specifically, the large diameter nerve fibers close the gate to the small diameter fibers, so that A-beta pain supersedes the pain of the A-delta and C fibers. This gating mechanism can also be influenced by other factors, such as messages sent from the brain instructing certain gates to close to the pain sensation.

The rubbing that you do after you bump your shin is a fast pain sensation transmitted quickly over the large fibers; it cancels out the sharp pain of hitting your shin, slowly transmitted by the small fibers. The result is that you feel the rubbing rather than the sharp pain. This mechanism explains why stimulators and acupuncture can be so effective in managing pain—they operate on the gating mechanism to close out slower pain sensations.

Many studies have attempted to prove the Gate Control Theory, but none have shown conclusively that all facets of the theory are valid. Still, the importance of this theory should not be underrated, since it has served to stimulate much thinking on the subject of pain and helped us come to the conclusions we have today about effective treatment of chronic pain.

Pain Treatment Strategies

Every day you can read in newspapers and magazines about some new technique for managing chronic pain. Some of these techniques have just appeared on the scene, while others have been around for centuries. Some are conservative in nature, while others strain your imagination as to their connection to pain control. You can be massaged by a masseuse, whirlpooled in a jacuzzi, operated on by a surgeon, medicated by a medical doctor, exercised by a physical therapist or exercise physiologist, manipulated by a myotherapist, hypnotized by a hypnotherapist, analyzed by a psychiatrist, behaviorally modified by a psychologist, or rehabbed by a social worker. The possibilities are mind-numbing, and explanations are so confusing and conflicting, that you may feel like giving up before you start.

To guide you through this maze, this section discusses techniques usually associated with a medical setting, such as nerve blocks and electrical stimulators. The next chapter deals with physical techniques, such as exercise, and the four chapters after that deal with psychological techniques such as relaxation and assertiveness training.

Take time to discuss with your doctor any of the techniques described in this book that you would like to use. Try to educate yourself as much as possible about each technique, so that you know what you are getting into. Don't be afraid to ask questions! If your doctor is too rushed to explain, or doesn't know something, go get another opinion. This book is designed for you to become better informed, and to motivate yourself to take charge of your healing process.

Also, be aware that not all techniques work for everyone. What works for your best friend may not be the key to your recovery. You may know instinctively that a certain technique is not for you, while you can adapt to others quite readily. Or you may need to try everything once to get a feel for it. In any case, this process of pain management takes time. Explore all your options and decide which works best for you. Most importantly, keep an open mind, be patient, and be persistent.

Electrical Stimulators

If you have gone to a pain clinic you may have been prescribed an electrical stimulator for pain relief. One common type of stimulator is a small box-shaped device known as a *transcutaneous* (across the skin) *electrical nerve stimulator* (TENS). The small box is a transmitter which can be carried in the pocket or worn around the waist hanging on your belt. It transmits electrical impulses through wires to electrodes that are taped to the skin surrounding the painful area. When the unit is turned on, most people feel an electrical buzzing or tingling sensation, the intensity of which can be controlled by a dial on the transmitting box.

The device is designed to work on the principle of the Gate Control Theory, discussed earlier. An electrical impulse is transmitted over the large nerve fiber tracts, which in turn inhibit the small nerve fiber tracts from transmitting pain. In other words, you feel a tingling sensation rather than a pain sensation. You can increase or decrease the intensity of the tingling sensation as your pain increases or decreases.

TENS also works in two other ways. First, in addition to inhibiting the pain sensation, the tingling sensation also helps to distract you from it. Second, some researchers feel that TENS stimulates the release of endorphins in the brain and spinal cord. As noted above, endorphins are your body's own natural painkiller.

Some people find that brief periods of stimulation can provide hours, days, or weeks of pain relief. Others find that they need to wear the device regularly in order to feel some relief. Daily stimulation sometimes provides gradually increasing pain relief over periods of weeks or months. A great advantage of a TENS unit is that once you locate the point on your body that provides you with the greatest amount of pain relief, you can use this method at home or work as needed, giving you a significant measure of control over your own pain therapy.

TENS units are simple and easy to use and can be purchased through most medical supply offices. Some people may find that they develop a skin irritation from the unit's electrode paste or tape. Check with your doctor for types of nonallergenic paste and nonabrasive tape. These devices are safe and are found to have virtually no significant side effects even with continuous use. Although, be aware that you may want to provide periodic, rather than continuous, daily stimulation so that your body will not adapt to the message. Discuss this issue with your doctor.

TENS units are found to be most useful as an adjunct to other forms of therapy commonly found in multimodal pain clinics, such as exercise, physical therapy, appropriate medication use, and relaxation techniques.

A further development in the concept of TENS is spinal cord and brain stimulation to hyperstimulate the nervous system from different locations. This can be provided with implanted, permanent electrodes, much like a pacemaker for regulating cardiac rhythms.

Acupuncture

Acupuncture is an ancient and time-tested method of pain and disease control discovered in China as early as 3000 B.C. Chinese folklore says that a warrior discovered the principle of acupuncture during a battle. He was pierced by an arrow in his leg, and found that the wound from the arrow made another wound in his shoulder feel better.

Acupuncture works on the principal of *meridians*, or imaginary lines, drawn on the body that represent internal organs and the torso. Points on these lines are thought to connect different parts of the body. For example, a point on the skin between the thumb and index finger connects to various parts of the head for control of headaches; a point on the leg is specified for control of gastric disorders.

When one of these points is stimulated by an acupuncture needle or deeply massaged (acupressure), a headache or stomachache can be relieved. In practice, a thin metal or gold needle is inserted at the acupuncture point and gently twirled. The round tipped needle simply spreads the skin rather than puncturing it, thereby reducing the chance of infection. Some needles are twirled for brief periods of ten to twenty minutes and then removed; others are left in over a longer period of time.

Remember the Gate Control Theory? Here is another direct application of it. The stimulation of the needles is thought to set off a series of electrical impulses that travel the large nerve fiber tracts, cutting off the more painful sensations sent along the small fiber tracts. With acupuncture you feel a pleasant, tingling, warm sensation, much like the sensation you get from a TENS unit.

There are three other explanations for the effectiveness of acupuncture. First, acupuncture has been shown to stimulate better circulation to tissues; often the effects of poor circulation to an injured area can increase pain and retard the healing process. Second, acupuncture can release tension in the muscle surrounding the acupuncture point. Third, recent research suggests that acupuncture stimulates the production of endorphins, the natural painkiller, in the brain and spinal cord.

A related acupuncture method has served to further awaken Western interest in the field. Electroacupuncture involves stimulation of body tissues through needles hooked up to batterydriven stimulators. In modern China, this method is used to produce intense analgesia during surgery. "Films of such operations are extremely dramatic, and the feeling arose that if acupuncture could produce sufficient analgesia for surgery, it must surely be effective for chronic pain of all kinds." (Melzack and Wall, 1982)

Consult your doctor for help in contacting trained and licensed acupuncture specialists.

Trigger Points

When a trigger point is pressed, it causes a great deal of pain, sometimes reproducing an exact chronic pain sensation. Trigger points in muscles or ligaments can also be identified by muscle spasms or contractions. They are known to lie above or near the point in the muscle where the motor nerves are firing most intensely (thereby producing pain).

Although the exact mechanism of trigger points is unknown, they are probably caused by a direct stress to your muscle such as trauma (tear during an injury), chronic tension, abnormal posture, or muscle fatigue. Sometimes trigger points lay dormant for many years after recovery from an injury. You may not have chronic pain complaints, but instead are accumulating unsuspected latent trigger points. These can be activated by chronic strain from sedentary living habits, minor stresses from daily living, anxiety, or overstretching or fatigue of your muscles.

Trigger points are thought to be similar to acupuncture points in location. A study done by Melzack, Stillwell, and Fox (1977) showed that every trigger point has a corresponding acupuncture point and that there is a close correlation between the pain syndromes associated with each point. In other words, the Western medical world labels these points differently from the Eastern medical world, but they represent the same underlying nerve mechanisms. However, acupuncture points aren't supposed to produce pain when pressed, so they are dissimilar to trigger points in that respect.

Trigger points are often injected for pain relief. These trigger point injections are a form of nerve block. See chapters 14 and 15 for more on trigger points.

Nerve Blocks

When you have chronic pain, you are tempted to tense your muscles in an attempt to brace yourself against the pain. This common and automatic response can lead to a *pain-spasm-pain cycle*.

As a result of this response, your muscles remain in a tense or contracted state, blood flow is decreased to the muscle, and your posture can become abnormal. In other words, your muscles become immobile and inflexible, which further contributes to your pain.

Local anesthetic nerve blocks and trigger point injections can interrupt this cycle. An anesthesiologist specially trained in the area of pain management injects a local anesthetic solution into the painful area, causing the nerve fibers to become numb or anesthetized and to stop sending pain signals. You should feel an alleviation of your pain immediately following each injection. This is a good time to do gentle stretching exercises to improve your mobility and relax your muscles and to return to normal posture. Sometimes the mere insertion of the doctor's needle can aid in pain relief, as an acupuncture needle would do.

If you have acute pain, the effect of the nerve block will often outlast the duration of the painful stimulus from your injury or surgical incision. However, local anesthetic blocks for chronic pain often do not produce long-term benefits. An exception to this is the repeated use of blocks for causalgia (burning pain) or causalgia-like symptoms such as in complex regional pain syndrome, where permanent pain relief can often be achieved, if treated early. Refer to chapters 12, 13, and 20 for more information on nerve blocks.

Heat and Cold Therapy

Getting you back to full or at least freer movement is an important goal of chronic pain management. The pain-spasm-pain cycle discussed in the previous section reinforces immobility—you brace yourself against the pain and hold your muscles stiffly for long periods of time, which further contributes to your pain and makes even menial activity a chore. A physical therapist or an exercise physiologist can help you reverse this process by gradually increasing your mobility through strength and flexibility exercises. Exercise is such an important part of pain management that all of chapter 3 is devoted to it.

Other forms of physical therapy can be useful as adjuncts to a multimodal approach to pain management. Both heat and cold therapy reduce muscle tension or spasm. If you try heat, the physical therapist will usually apply hot packs for twenty minutes under six to eight layers of towels. Cold packs are also applied for twenty minutes, but under two layers of towels. An ice block massage involves lightly rubbing the painful area with a cake of ice for at least ten minutes or until numbness occurs. In one study, the ice block massage was considered more effective than the cold pack because it provided more intense stimulation to the painful area; the cold pack cooled tissues more slowly.

Both heat and cold therapy reduce muscle spasms and swelling from an injury or inflammation. Both also decrease the number of nerve impulses from the painful area to the spinal cord, which means that less small fiber input (carrying the pain message) is available to open the pain gate.

You can decide for yourself which temperature provides more relief. Both are considered equally effective methods of pain reduction.

Massage

Massage can be a relaxing and revitalizing experience and an excellent addition to a pain management program. Its therapeutic effects include soothing aching muscles and benefitting emotional well-being.

Its benefits are gaining widespread acceptance in the medical community as growing research reveals the healing power of massage for both acute and chronic pain. Martha Brown

Menard combines her Ph.D. in educational research with a practice in massage. Her study of the effects of massage on postsurgical hysterectomy patients produced several significant findings: First, after four days of a daily forty-five minute massage, patients in the massage group produced not quite half the level of urinary cortisol of patients in the nonmassage group. Cortisol, produced by the adrenal glands, is one of the hormones your body produces in response to stress. The massage group patients also reported reduced pain and stress. Equally important, for the four weeks following their discharge, the massage group patients had no additional physician visits.

Massage can stimulate blood flow and release toxins from muscles and tissues. It can also help to break the pain-spasm-pain cycle by relaxing muscles that are tight or in spasm, increasing circulation, improving oxygen and nutrition flow to the painful area, increasing range of motion, and finding and relaxing trigger points. Systematically working with each muscle in your body, your massage therapist may use a light stroke or deep kneading action, depending on what he or she thinks is right for you and your comfort level. Trigger points, which often recur in the same places, are relieved through sustained pressure. As you find out which ones contribute to your pain you can learn to massage them yourself to help decrease your pain.

Often, you start to lose muscle tone in as little as three weeks after an injury. For people who have to be inactive due to injury, illness, or age, massage can help compensate for lack of exercise and muscular contraction. In other words, massage is not intended as a substitute for exercise, but can help prevent or reduce muscular atrophy in the interim.

Perhaps most important, however, is that massage acts on an emotional level. As Dr. Menard sees in her practice and research, people who are in pain often have significant feelings of loneliness and isolation. Massage can become a way to help a person vent about what has been going on in their lives and feel that they are being cared for. Massage helps to create feelings of acceptance, safety, nurturing, and trust.

A well-trained therapist will take a medical history from you to determine the acute or chronic nature of your problem, extent of medication use, and other pertinent information. A massage is usually contraindicated (not suggested) in cases of inflammation, edema (swelling), herniated discs, fever, and other conditions that require you to wait until the acute nature of those conditions has subsided.

You can do massage for yourself, especially for neck and headache pain. This will help when you're feeling tense; but for a more relaxing and effective experience, try letting your spouse, trusted friend, or massage therapist give you a massage. Make sure, however, that they listen to your feedback and do not massage spasms or painful areas too heavily when they hurt. You want your massage to be a pleasant experience.

To locate a trained massage therapist in your area, ask for referrals from other health care providers or write to:

American Massage Therapy Association
820 Davis Street, Suite 100
Evanston, IL 60201-4444
(708) 864-0123
Fax: (847) 864-1178

National Certification Board for Therapeutic Massage and Bodywork
1735 North Lynn Street, Suite 950
Arlington, VA 22209

(703) 610-9015
Fax: (703) 524-2303

Your Internal Resources

This chapter covered medical approaches to the problem of pain, from the basic foundation of pain anatomy to the current medical technology of nerve blocks and TENS units. These methods can be considered "external" approaches—you have something done to you, such as an ice massage or a nerve block. These, of course, are extremely important elements in any pain control effort.

But there is an even more important element in pain control—that of managing your "internal" resources. In the following chapters you will read about identifying and making use of your own internal resources to reduce pain through relaxation and exercise.

To show how these approaches can be applied, return to the woman with the neck problem described in the opening of this chapter. She can make sure she is not unconsciously bracing against her neck pain and contributing to the pain-spasm-pain cycle by holding her neck, shoulder, and arm stiffly. She can use a TENS unit or a nerve block to gain some pain relief so she can begin to gently stretch her muscles and increase her circulation and flexibility. She can take certain medications prescribed by her doctor specifically for pain relief. Or she can send soothing, pain-free messages to her painful area by distracting her attention from the pain and focusing on something pleasant with the aid of relaxation training or self-hypnosis. All of these are valid and effective means of reducing pain. They can be used alone or in combination with each other. If you maintain an open mind to them, you can find which approach works best for you.

Further Reading

Aronoff, G., ed. 1992. *Evaluation and Treatment of Chronic Pain.* 2nd ed. Baltimore: Williams & Wilkins.

Claire, T. 1995. *Bodywork: What Type of Massage to Get and How to Make the Most of It.* New York: William Morrow and Co., Inc.

Goleman, D., and T. Bennett-Goleman. 1986. *The Relaxed Body Book.* Garden City, NY: Doubleday.

Hendler, N. 1993. *How to Cope with Chronic Pain.* Rev. Ed. Boca Raton, FL: Cool Hand Communications, Inc.

Horay, P., and D. Harp. 1991. *Hot Water Therapy: How to Save Your Back, Neck & Shoulders.* Oakland, CA: New Harbinger Publications, Inc.

Krieger, D. 1992. *The Therapeutic Touch.* New York: Simon and Schuster.

Lidell, L., et al. 1984. *The Book of Massage.* New York: Simon and Schuster.

Melzack, R., and P. Wall. 1991. *The Challenge of Pain.* Rev. Ed. New York: Penguin Books.

Menard, M. B. 1993. "Massage Therapy for Chronic Pain: An Overview of Research and Practice." Unpublished paper presented to the Virginia Psychological Association Fall Convention, October 15, 1993.

Raj, P. P., ed. 1992. *Practical Management of Pain.* 2nd ed. St Louis: Mosby Year Book.

Ruhnke, A., and A. Wurzburger. 1995. *Body Wisdom: Simple Massage and Relaxation Techniques for Busy People.* Boston: Charles Tuttle Co.

Sternbach, R., ed. 1986. *The Psychology of Pain.* 2nd ed. New York: Raven Press.

Woolf, C., and M. Chong. 1993. "Preemptive analgesia-treatment postoperative pain by preventing the establishment of central sensitization." *Anesthetic Analgesia,* 77: 362–379.

3

Exercise

By Ellen Mohr Catalano, M.A., and Christine Zampach, M. Ed., P.T.

Exercise has become quite a fad in America, with booming marketing campaigns for the right clothes to wear, the right kind of place to do it, and the right companion to meet while you're there. With so many facts and opinions flying around, it is no wonder that people are confused about the right way to exercise. In fact, it may seem like such an arduous task to wade through the facts and figures (no pun intended) that you are tempted not to start exercising in the first place. Throw in the burden of a chronic pain condition, and the uncertainty about what to do for your condition is perfectly understandable.

But amid all the many research theories, Hollywood promotions, and magazine suggestions, one thing is obvious—exercise is extremely important. If you have chronic pain, exercise should be an integral part of your life.

Research has shown that people who gradually introduce exercise into their daily routine after an injury, sprain, or strain (a) return to a more normal lifestyle faster and (b) maintain a pain-free existence more consistently. Gradual stretching and strengthening exercises help recondition your muscles, a benefit which in turn aids in healing and rehabilitation, prevents reinjury, and relieves the stress of chronic pain.

Take stock of your exercise habits. Do you lead a sedentary life? If you have chronic pain, have you made a commitment to yourself to move your muscles at least a little every day?

Some people find that honestly evaluating their exercise habits helps motivate them to begin a regular program. Record your exercise activities for the past week on the chart on the following page. Be sure to include your attitudes toward exercise. Sometimes automatic negative thoughts can become obstacles to starting something new. It will be helpful for you to uncover them early in your exercise program, and learn to dispel them so that you can avoid discouraging yourself. Examples of negative thinking about exercise are:

- "My parents were fat, so I'll be fat."

- "I'll never learn to cope with this much pain—exercise will make it worse."

- "I don't have time."

For more about the effects of negative thinking on chronic pain, refer to chapter 6. For now, jot down your activities and your thoughts on the chart, and share it with a friend or relative who exercises regularly. Chances are that person has had the same or similar thoughts before and can lend a sympathetic ear.

Pre-Exercise Chart for the Past Week

Day	Physical Activity	Attitudes

When to Start Exercising

Because movement can sometimes make the pain feel worse, the natural reaction for most people in pain is to brace or guard their muscles against the pain, holding them in a rigid position. In fact, during the initial stages of an acute pain condition, inactivity and bracing serve a useful purpose. Vigorous movement during an early stage may further aggravate a torn muscle, ligament, or bulging disc through increased swelling and inflammation, which can interfere with the healing process. However, when the pain has gone into the chronic stage, the natural acute-stage guarding habit no longer serves a useful purpose. At this point you will have to relearn how to move without guarding if more normal movement patterns are to be established, and if your pain is going to be decreased.

To allow maximum healing to take place, the key is a program of gentle movement of the body, including the injured area. Athletes are able to get back on the field or court in a short period of time partly due to the gentle motion exercises they go through under the guidance of a physical therapist, athletic trainer, or exercise physiologist. Movement allows for the injured tissues to heal at the proper length and increases the blood flow to the injured area, which can promote quicker healing. Bed rest, elevation of an injured limb, and ice can all help with acute pain, especially in the first twenty-four to forty-eight hours. A doctor-recommended anti-inflammatory or analgesic may also be helpful. Heat can be used after the forty-eight-hour period to decrease pain.

If the pain has become chronic (after approximately three months), it is even more important to move and exercise the painful area to increase your mobility, flexibility, and circulation. Movement is key to getting you back on the road to healthy functioning. Before you start increasing your activity level and exercising, follow these suggestions:

1. Check with your doctor before beginning any exercise program. He or she may refer you to a physical therapist, exercise physiologist, or certified athletic trainer to assist you in getting started safely.

2. If you were a regular exerciser before your injury, do not expect yourself to be able to immediately resume the same strenuous exercise. Have patience and gradually build up your strength and tolerance. The healing and coping process takes time, and you may reinjure yourself if you push too hard.

3. Educate yourself. Learn about your muscles and how they work to move or support the body. It has taken you this long to learn how your body responds to pain and stress; now give yourself some time to learn how to move and exercise and to incorporate this knowledge into your daily life.

Some Basic Muscle Anatomy

A muscle is a strong type of body tissue that can contract and relax when instructed by nerves to help your body move and to help your joints maintain stability. A *muscle spasm* is a muscle that is continually contracted due to tension or trauma (injury). You can create a muscle spasm by making a fist and holding your hand and arm tightly for as long as you can. Eventually your hand and arm begin to tremble and you feel a cramping, burning sensation. This discomfort may also be felt in the shoulder, shoulder blades, and neck. Because you are squeezing the muscles, oxygen and blood cannot move through the muscle to remove a build-up of waste, in the form of lactic acid. The acid produces pain when it accumulates in the tissue, causing the burning and cramping. Muscles that are chronically in spasm, or contracted because of guarding, become short and weak. They hold the tension without the ability to completely relax, release, and let go of pain.

When a muscle is *strained*, it is usually overstretched due to overexertion. A *sprain* actually refers to a partial tearing of ligaments, the tough fibers that hold the bones together at the joints. Both sprains and strains tend to go away spontaneously in a few days or weeks with rest, gentle non-weight bearing movement of the injured muscle or joint, ice for the first twenty-four to forty-eight hours with the switch to heat, if desired, and gentle massage.

A healthy muscle can stretch or contract and then return to a normal resting state. An injured or spasming muscle is *shortened* or *weak*. A shortened muscle is not able to withstand much movement or bear much weight. Its energy is gone because its blood supply is actually squeezed out. An *overly stretched* muscle is also weak and unable to provide necessary support to the spine and joints. For example, people with large bellies have overstretched and weak abdominal muscles. Their other back muscles are forced to compensate to hold the torso erect and may in turn spasm or become fatigued. Stretching a shortened muscle helps to lengthen it and increase its blood supply. Strengthening an overly stretched muscle to the proper length can help build fiber strength, which assists in movement and support. This is why a balanced exercise program includes both stretching and strengthening, done with proper posture, to help contracted muscles become more flexible and overly stretched muscles become stronger and return to normal length.

Proper Posture

Poor posture is a major culprit contributing to lower and upper back and neck pain. Poor posture is often learned in childhood, when it's popular to order children to "Stand up straight—stick out your chest and hold your stomach in!" Both commands can put your spine into unnatural positions that fatigue and strain the back's muscles and joints.

Your spine is out of balance whenever it loses its natural curves—the cervical curve and the lumbar curve. Poor posture distorts these natural curves by unevenly distributing pressure along the spine, causing stress to the vertebrae, joints, and muscles.

You can test your posture by standing with your back against a wall. Put your hand in the small of your back. You should feel only minimal space between your back and the wall. People with poor posture either slouch forward, slumping their shoulders and rounding their backs, or they overly arch their backs, sticking out their chests and buttocks. Both postures unbalance the spine and stress the muscles and joints. As you are standing at the wall, tuck your pelvis into a posterior pelvic tilt position (see diagram 3.1) and feel how the lumbar curve in your back is partially reduced. This is proper, balanced posture.

Here are five simple, commonsense rules to follow to correct poor posture. You'll be surprised at how much they help relieve a backache and help you prevent further problems.

1. Slightly tuck in your chin.

2. Relax your shoulders and arms.

3. Tuck in your stomach (into the posterior pelvic tilt position).

4. Tighten your buttocks.

5. Slightly bend your knees.

If you commit these rules to memory, it will become a habit for you to tuck your tummy instead of slump. You can practice good posture anywhere, but pay special attention to it while you're at your job, especially when sitting or standing in one position for a long time. If you have to stand awhile, prop up one foot on a low box or stool.

Exercises

Stretching properly and sufficiently is a critical part of any exercise program. Many injuries or reinjuries occur during exercise because the muscle is "cold," and not at its proper length. Your muscles also need to be warmed up before they are asked to do fast or heavy work. Your body is like a car; it needs to be warmed up before you drive it too fast.

If your muscles have not been physically active, they become atrophied—small and weak. Stretching and strengthening help the muscles to return to a more normal size, increasing their endurance and enabling them to withstand more twisting, turning, and sudden movement.

Proper stretching involves a "static stretch." This means a stretch that is slow, gentle, and continuous, with only minor discomfort experienced at any given time. No quick bounces. Bouncing only tears muscle fibers, which creates more pain. Have you ever suddenly sprinted for the bus, and felt a sharp cramp in your calf or foot? Your leg was not ready for action, which resulted in a spasm. Even muscles that are in good shape can cramp or spasm if subjected to a sudden shock such as twisting or sprinting. But conditioned muscles will withstand the shock better, and return to a normal state faster than muscles that are out of shape.

Diagram 3.1
Posterior Pelvic Tilt

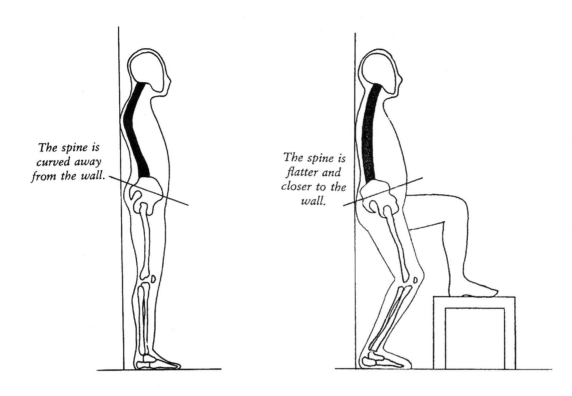

The spine is curved away from the wall.

The spine is flatter and closer to the wall.

Unbalanced pelvic position

Balanced posterior pelvic tilt

1. Stand with your back and buttocks against a wall.

2. Place your hands between the hollow of your back and the wall.

3. Place one foot on a chair seat in front of you.

4. note that your pelvis is tilted up and your back is straighter and closer to the wall than it was when both feet were on the ground.

You are now in the pelvic posterior tilt position.

5. Tighten your stomach and buttock muscles to keep your back in this position.

6. Hold this balanced pelvic position as you lower your leg to the floor.

7. Walk around the room holding this position.

From Dr. David Imrie's *Goodbye Back Ache* (Toronto: Prentice-Hall/Newcastle Publishing, 1983).

Stretch for at least five to ten minutes before you begin your conditioning exercises. If you are a new stretcher, hold each stretch for twenty seconds. Stretch to the point of gentle resistance, *not pain.* As you become familiar with the stretches and your body's responses, increase the stretch time gradually to between thirty and sixty seconds. Sometimes it is helpful to stretch lightly and easily first, ease up, and then repeat the stretch, holding for a longer period and pushing slightly beyond the first stretch. In his popular *Stretching* workbook, Bob Anderson reminds us that the object of stretching is to reduce muscular tension and promote freer movement—not to force yourself to attempt such extreme flexibility that you risk overstretching and injury. The key is regularity and relaxation.

Ten Rules For Proper Stretching

1. The object of stretching is to regain the flexibility lost due to inactivity or injury.

2. Do static stretches—no bouncing.

3. Start slowly and gently. Move twice as slow as you think you should. Do ten minutes of slow stretching before starting any strengthening exercises.

4. Hold stretches at least twenty seconds.

5. Stretch to the point of gentle resistance, not pain. At the slightest pain, back off the stretch.

6. Don't throw your head or body around. Move slowly and carefully even when getting into position for the next exercise. Proper posture and body alignment are key to not injuring yourself.

7. Keep breathing during stretches. Begin and end exercise sessions with five to ten deep and slow diaphragmatic breaths.

8. Avoid exercise entirely right after acute injury.

9. Many short sessions are better than a few long sessions. It's better for your body to do six stretches, six times a day than to do thirty-six stretches all at once.

10. Consult your doctor if soreness persists more than two days, or if your symptoms are worse immediately after exercise and don't get better the next day.

The following stretches and strengtheners have been chosen from the recommendations of experts in the field for overall body strength and flexibility. However, it is always wise to consult with your doctor, physical therapist, or athletic trainer before you attempt any of these exercises. Professional expertise will tell you whether you have a specific problem that needs special attention, or the garden variety of musculoskeletal pain that responds well to these types of exercises.

A safe way to begin is on the floor with gentle stretching *only,* until you and your doctor feel you are ready to move on to strengthening exercises. You should do strengthening exercises only after you are warmed up from the stretching. As you become familiar with these exercises and feel your strength and flexibility increasing, add repetitions to your daily workout.

Consult chapter 13 for more information about how to exercise.

Remember, if you are unaccustomed to exercise, you will probably feel some tightness and soreness at first. This is the normal microscopic tearing and rebuilding of muscle fiber associated with any exercise. However, if the soreness persists for more than two days, or if your symptoms are much worse immediately after exercising and remain worse the next day, consult with your fitness professional. Back off a bit from your exercise routine and decrease the number of repetitions of each exercise. But do not quit altogether. Keep moving, if only gently and gingerly. The movement will help you decrease the pain and stress and keep healing oxygen and blood nutrients circulating throughout your body. With relaxed persistence, in time you will be able to move about again more freely.

The following exercises are designed to be done in the sequence presented, but, after consulting your health professional, you are encouraged to add, delete, or modify the exercises based on your needs and your body's reactions. The sequence will take approximately twenty minutes at the beginning, but will lengthen somewhat as your stretches increase above twenty seconds each. Make sure you do your exercises at least once a day.

I. Leg Stretches

1. *Ankle and calf stretch* (seated or lying). Rotate ankles slowly, with feet relaxed, first clockwise, then counterclockwise, eight times in each direction.

2. *Hamstring stretch.* Place your left foot against your right inner thigh. Slightly bend your outstretched leg, keeping your knee pointing toward the ceiling. Bend forward at the hips until you feel the stretch in the back of your legs (hamstrings). Hold for twenty seconds. Repeat three times on each side.

3. *Hip flexor stretch.* Lace your hands under your knee. Pull your leg toward your chest, keeping your lower back on the floor and your other leg slightly bent. Hold for twenty seconds. Repeat three times on each side. *Advanced hip flexor stretch:* To increase your workout, raise your head and shoulders slightly when doing the hip flexor stretch, tucking your chin to meet your bent knee and tightening your stomach muscles. Hold for five seconds to begin and gradually increase.

4. *Quadricep stretch.* (Note: IF YOU HAVE BACK OR KNEE PROBLEMS, TAKE CARE AS YOU GET INTO THIS POSITION.) Sit with your right leg bent backwards and your left leg bent with your foot touching your right knee. *Slowly* lean straight back until you feel the stretch in the muscle on top of the leg bent backwards (quadricep). Hold for twenty seconds. Repeat three times on each side. Keep your neck muscles relaxed as you perform this exercise.

II. Lower Back Stretches

1. *Cross leg rotation stretch.* (Note: IF YOU HAVE DISC PROBLEMS, CHECK WITH YOUR DOCTOR BEFORE DOING THIS EXERCISE.) Place your left leg on top of your right leg and gently pull left towards the floor. Feel the stretch in your lower back, sides, and the top of your hips. Hold for twenty seconds. Repeat twice on each side, pulling in the direction of the knee on top.

2. *Lower back stretch and roll.* (Note: IF YOU HAVE DISC PROBLEMS, CHECK WITH YOUR DOCTOR BEFORE DOING THIS EXERCISE.) With your hands laced under your knees, pull both knees to your chest, keeping your lower back flat on the bed or floor. Hold for twenty seconds. Keep breathing. Now rotate your knees slowly to the right, gently twisting as far as you feel comfortable. Keep your shoulders on the bed or floor. Hold for twenty seconds. Breathe. Slowly roll to the left and hold for twenty seconds. Repeat the sequence three times.

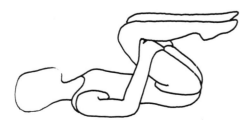
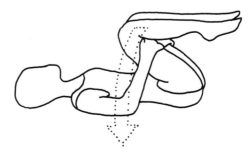

3. *Press-ups.* (Note: IF YOU HAVE DISC PROBLEMS, CHECK WITH YOUR DOCTOR BEFORE DOING THIS EXERCISE.) Lie on your stomach with your arms bent at the elbow. Press up slowly, keeping your elbows bent. Keep your pelvis and legs relaxed. Repeat ten times.

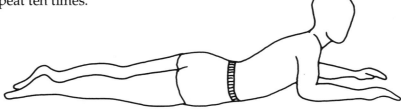

Advanced press-ups: As you are pressing up, slowly straighten your arms and lift your torso as far as feels comfortable.

III. Upper Back, Chest, and Neck Stretches

1. *Middle-upper back stretch.* Raise your right arm and hold it below the elbow with your left hand. Pull your right elbow gently toward your left shoulder until you feel the stretch. Hold for five seconds. Repeat for the other side.

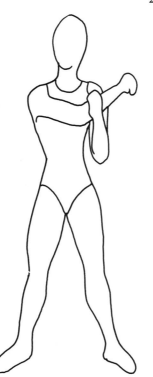

2. *Pectoral stretch.* Lace your hands behind your neck and press your elbows back as far as you can. Hold for five seconds. Return to your starting position, then drop your arms and relax. Repeat.

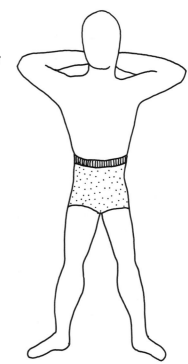

3. *Arm circles.* Stand with your feet shoulder-width apart. Inhale and cross both arms in front of your body, feeling the stretch in your upper back. Uncross your arms and raise them over your head. Exhale slowly while lowering both arms in an arc behind your body, feeling the stretch in your chest. Do the entire exercise as if in slow motion. Breathing is a very important part of this exercise. For this reason, it is an excellent warmup and cool-down exercise. Repeat five to ten times.

4. *"Yes-no-maybe."* First stretch your head forward with your chin tucked, then stretch it from side to side, and at last at an angle on each side (the "maybe" position). Hold each stretch for ten seconds and repeat three times.

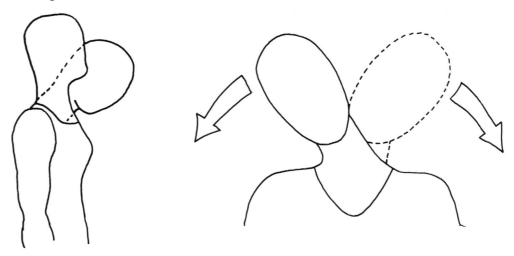

5. *Advanced neck stretches.* While seated, pull your neck forward (as shown, from the top of your head), and then to each side 30 to 35 degrees. Pull your head until you feel a slight stretch in the back of your neck and your upper back. Hold the stretch for twenty to thirty seconds.

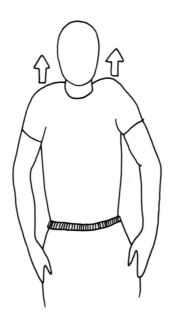

6. *Shoulder shrugs.* Pull both shoulders upward (but do not hunch your neck downward) simultaneously for ten seconds. Do this three times in a row. Gradually increase the time for each shrug.

7. *Neck Strenghtener.* Lie down. Raise your head off the bed or floor and hold for five seconds. Lower your head slowly and press it into the bed or floor for five seconds. Repeat three times.

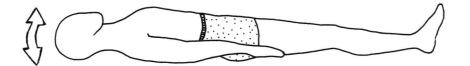

IV. Overall Body Stretches

1. *Chair stretch.* Place your feet wide apart on the floor. Drop both hands between your knees and slowly bend over to the point where you feel a stretch. Hold for twenty seconds. Relax and breathe.

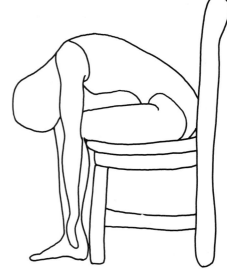

2. *Spinal twist.* (Note: DO NOT DO THIS EXERCISE IF YOU HAVE DISC PROBLEMS. CHECK WITH YOUR DOCTOR FIRST.) Bend your left leg over your outstretched right leg. Your left foot should rest on the outside of your right knee. Rest your right elbow on the outside of your upper left thigh. With your left hand behind you, slowly turn your head to look over your left shoulder, rotating your upper body toward your left arm and hand. Hold for twenty seconds. This is a good stretch for your upper and lower back, hips, and ribcage.

V. Back Strengtheners

1. *Lower back flattener (pelvic tilt).* Flatten the curve in your lower back by flattening against the floor with your lower abdominal muscles. Hold for at least five seconds. Start with only a few repetitions, but repeat many times during the day. Stop if you feel pain. This is one of the best exercises for lower back injuries and good exercise for practicing a correct pelvic tilt and strengthening the gluteus and abdominal muscles.

2. *Abdominal curls (curl-ups).* Lie down and bend your knees with your feet flat on the floor. While maintaining a pelvic tilt, slowly curl your head, shoulders, and upper back off the floor toward your knees. With your chin tucked, hold this raised position for a count of five. Slowly lower yourself back to the starting position. Repeat five times.

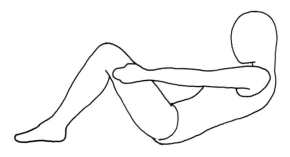

3. *Curl-backs.* (Note: This exercise should be tried only after you feel comfortable and stronger during curl-ups.) Start by sitting tilted slightly back, with a *C* curve in your spine. Keep your arms folded, your knees bent, and your feet flat on the floor. Lean back one third to one half of the way to the floor, leaning back very carefully and only as far as you feel safe. Pull forward to your original position. Repeat five times. (Caution: When doing curl-backs, do not anchor your feet under a chair or bed. This causes you to use muscles other than your abdominals to lower yourself. Also, be sure to keep your chin tucked and your neck relaxed. Do not throw your head back.)

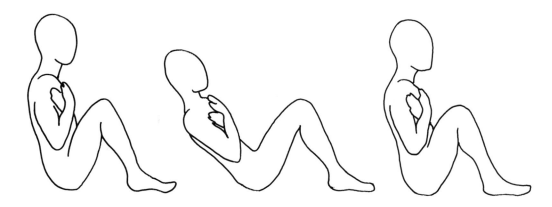

A Case for Exercise

"The worst thing about chronic pain for me was the loneliness, the isolation. There was nothing to look forward to."

These are the words of Mary Jo, a normally active mother of four who was totally unprepared for the disruption in her life that a riding injury caused. But when she was interviewed a year and a half after her accident, she was up and moving around her kitchen, busy fixing iced tea, wrestling with stuck kitchen windows, and tending to a sick child. Looking back at her progress, she was sure that doing consistent exercise was a major factor.

Horseback riding had always been one of Mary Jo's favorite activities. Although she was an expert horsewoman, a tree branch struck her in the shoulder one day on a cross-country ride. Nothing was broken, but she felt a severe burning pain ("It felt just like a branding iron") spreading down her arm.

Several weeks later, she couldn't use her arm and hand, and her fingers were numb. A doctor put her on complete bed rest with traction and a ten-day series of steroid medications. The medications relieved the burning sensation, but Mary Jo found herself nearly immobilized.

"I couldn't drive, cook, brush my teeth, or wash my hair. I would struggle to get up in the mornings to have coffee with my family, but the pain would drive me back to bed after fifteen or twenty minutes."

After three months in this situation, Mary Jo felt desperate. A doctor had prescribed more bed rest, with possible surgery, but Mary Jo realized that she would have to start moving to get better. She had a friend drive her to the physical therapy department of a local hospital. There she was given massages, whirlpool baths, and a series of exercises to do daily to begin loosening up her tense shoulder and neck muscles. After their many months of inactivity her muscles were weak, inflexible, and unable to withstand much movement before they were thrown into painful spasms.

She tried the easy exercises first—gentle shoulder shrugs, "yes-no-maybe" exercises, and neck stretches (all described earlier in this chapter). She did her exercises first thing in the morning, again after she had a hot shower and her muscles were more relaxed, and once more in the evening. At first she did only a few repetitions of each exercise, because her muscles would tire easily. As she got stronger, she increased the repetitions.

Mary Jo had also gone to a pain clinic, where the exercise therapist showed her how to strengthen her muscles by using gentle resistance exercises (see chapter 13) and arm circles with jelly jar weights. She was also given a TENS unit, which provided so much pain relief that she was able to greatly increase the time spent exercising.

"I began to exercise in earnest, doing more vigorous neck, shoulder, and arm exercises three times a day and after a hot shower. Instead of searing pain, all I felt during and after exercise was heat in my muscles.

"These days I still do a lot of shoulder shrugs, deep breathing, and neck exercises to loosen my neck and shoulders. I remember to drop my shoulders and let my arms and hands hang loose and heavy. I check the points in my body where I know I tense up. I still have some pain, but I know that exercise has really helped me get moving again and back into my life."

Further Reading

Anderson, B. 1980. *Stretching.* Bolinas, CA: Shelter Publishers.

Davis, M., E. R. Eshelman, and M. McKay. 1995. *The Relaxation & Stress Reduction Workbook,* 4th ed. Oakland, CA: New Harbinger Publications.

Imrie, D. 1983. *Goodbye Backache.* Toronto: Prentice-Hall/Newcastle Publishing.

Online Information Can Be Found At:

http://www.healthychoice.com/trainer/html/CustomExerciseProgram.htm

4

Pain and Basic Stress Management

Paulette suffered from a combination of tension and migraine headaches for years. At first her headaches seemed manageable, but then they grew worse and began to seriously disrupt her work and home life. She decided that she had to do something about them.

After visiting several different doctors, she reluctantly agreed to go to a pain clinic for biofeedback and stress management. She politely listened to the therapist's explanations of the program, with her face frozen into a smile, all the while thinking to herself that the therapist—and the other doctors—must all think her crazy. She finally blurted out, "What does stress management have to do with my pain? I'm not making this up. And anyway, I don't have time to learn anything new because my headaches take so much of my energy."

Many people have these same concerns. If you've been sent from one doctor to the next and given different explanations for your pain each time, then it's reasonable to begin to wonder if they really think that you're fabricating your pain—or that you're truly crazy.

Odds are that you're not crazy or faking. However, you do have an understandable amount of stress in response to a difficult situation—coping with chronic pain. And health professionals are often tempted to pin a label on you when they don't know what else to do. In your frustration, you may even begin to doubt yourself, thinking that your pain is all in your head and there's nothing you can do about it.

Self-defeating behavior (behavior that adds to or keeps you in pain) and negative thinking are what this and the next three chapters are all about. In this chapter, we will examine ways to counteract self-defeating pain behavior by practicing relaxation strategies. You will learn to deal' with the pain in your life much as you deal with other stressors. After all, your chronic pain drains your energy much like the stress of a demanding job or a nagging family problem.

When you have chronic pain, life stressors seem like insurmountable obstacles in your path. Your family harmony is affected, sexual relations with your spouse can be reduced or stop altogether, and your ability to do your job or chores around the house can be severely curtailed, perhaps leading to financial worries.

When pain flares up, it feels like it will never go away, which can make you feel depressed and angry. You find yourself facing not only your physical pain, but mental anguish as well. You feel helpless and alone. Sometimes you feel that your hopes for recovery are being chiseled away with every ache and throb. As Paulette said, "I feel like I use all my energy doing battle with the pain—I have no stamina or joy left over for important things in my life, like my family and job."

Ease Your Pain by Managing Your Stress

When you're in pain, you need to learn and practice stress management for two simple reasons. First, chronic pain is itself a stressor. It reduces your ability to function, to cope, and to feel good. If you can't function, you feel useless. If you can't cope, then other stressors begin piling up. Second, you tense your muscles in response to pain and its by-products. You grit your teeth in anticipation of the pain. You hold your shoulders rigidly to brace against the pain. This increases your body's overall tension level, which only makes your pain worse.

Begin by realizing that there is a stress component to your pain. Physical tension and mental anxiety can make coping more difficult. You can minimize the domino effect of stress and pain by learning to manage the tension component in your life. Learn to identify stress in your body and its interplay with your pain.

Understanding the Stress Response

When your body is physically tense because of pain or other stressors, it usually reacts with what is termed the *stress response*. You may also know it as the "fight-or-flight" response. In his popular book *The Relaxation Response* (1992), Dr. Herbert Benson suggests that the fight-or-flight response, which is controlled by the sympathetic nervous system, had important evolutionary significance for human survival. We inherited this response from our ancestors, who put it to good use in the face of extreme physical danger. Among other things, their hearts pumped blood faster to their muscles and lungs, enabling them to strike harder or run faster than they normally would. But now, although you have the same physical response, your world seldom requires or even permits you to fight or run. For example, you cannot run away from or hit your boss when he or she yells at you. The same ancient physical response is turned on, but it doesn't benefit you in the same way. You don't have an appropriate outlet or release valve for the stress.

This doesn't mean that all stress is bad. The natural stress response can help you react quickly to protect yourself or give you a charge so that you think more quickly and clearly. The adrenaline that's suddenly pumped into your blood stream helps you swerve out of the path of an oncoming car. Similarly, a challenging project at work can motivate you to work harder. But when the adrenaline that gave you a quick reaction continues to course through your bloodstream for months or years, its effects are not so positive.

The danger of a prolonged stress response is its wear and tear on your body. And when stress is coupled with chronic pain, the wear and tear you experience is multiplied. Twenty years of a demanding job or six months of pain will both take a toll on your body. You may end up with circulation problems from decreased blood flow, or the chronic secretions in your stomach may eventually contribute to an ulcer. Or the shoulder, neck, and head muscles that you tense to brace against the pain may lead to tension headaches or temporal mandibular joint syndrome, a problem of the jaw resulting in part from chronically clenched teeth.

Here is what usually happens to the human body under stress and what you can feel:

- Your heart rate increases.   You feel your heart pounding in your chest.

- Your blood pressure increases.   (Not detectable unless measured.)

- Your sweat level increases.   Your skin feels cold and clammy.

- Your respiration rate changes.   Your breathing becomes shallow or you breathe in gulps.

- Adrenaline, and other hormones are released into the blood stream, causing vasoconstriction in the periphery and increase in muscle tone. Blood flows away from the periphery (hands and feet) to the heart, lungs and muscles.

Your muscles contract; your hands and feet become cold.

- Certain acids are secreted in the gastrointestinal tract.

You feel "butterflies," or nausea or discomfort, in your stomach.

Other organs such as the liver and spleen are also affected by stress, and some processes shut down altogether, such as digestion and sexual functioning.

You can help yourself by learning to identify your typical unhelpful stress patterns and by beginning to eliminate them from your daily routine. This can be done with regular and consistent daily practice of one or more of the techniques discussed in the rest of this chapter and in chapter 5. These techniques have different names and use different processes, but they are all designed to do virtually the same thing . . . to relax your body so that you can cope with your pain and stress better.

You can also manage your pain and stress levels by attending to your thoughts and feelings—that is, by identifying the negative self-talk which is part of your belief system. This highly important part of your coping repertoire will be discussed in chapter 6. For now, you'll find it easier to branch out into other coping methods once you begin to take care of your immediate problem— your aching body. After that, you will have more energy to devote to other aspects of chronic pain management.

Deep Breathing

Deep breathing is one of the easiest, most effective ways to release tension in your body. Yet it's easy to take this important function for granted, and when you are stressed or in pain, you are likely to forget to take this essential relaxation step.

Think for a moment about the last time you sat in a theater engrossed in a movie—you probably did not move or breathe deeply for a good part of two hours. That's why you stretched when you rose from the seat—your muscles had been deprived of oxygen and your circulation slowed, and stretching is a natural reflex to rejuvenate the muscles. Now think about the last time you had a bout with your pain. You probably sucked in your breath, clenched your teeth, and hunched your shoulders, as if doing these things would ward off the pain. In fact, these responses only make as your situation worse, because you now have your pain *plus* tense muscles, a headache, and insufficient oxygen. As a muscle relaxer, deep breathing can help to release tension in the abdomen, neck, and shoulders, which are common places where people brace against the pain.

Deep breathing helps to make sure there is a sufficient amount of oxygen in your body. Oxygen is a nutrient carried in the blood, and it is necessary for metabolism in healthy tissues. Internal organs and muscles, as well as injured areas, need a sufficient daily amount of oxygen to survive, and a great deal more to heal.

Some people use deep breathing as their only relaxation exercise. Some use it as a cue to signal the start of their tension-relieving regimen. However you choose to use it, it is quick, pleasant, and readily available.

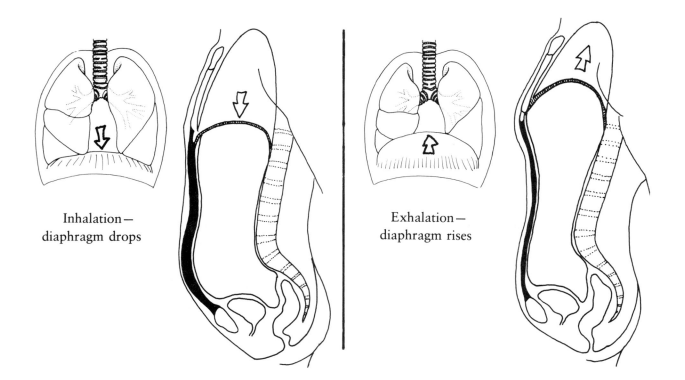

Inhalation—
diaphragm drops

Exhalation—
diaphragm rises

1. Breathing awareness

a. Lie down on a rug or blanket on the floor with your legs uncrossed and slightly apart. Allow your arms to relax comfortably at your sides. Close your eyes.

b. Bring your attention to your breathing and place your hand on the spot that seems to rise and fall the most as you inhale and exhale. Note that if this spot is in your chest, you are not making good use of the lower part of your lungs. People who are nervous tend to breathe many short, shallow breaths in their upper chest.

c. Place both of your hands gently on your abdomen and follow your breathing. Notice how your abdomen rises with each inhalation and falls with each exhalation.

d. Allow yourself to breathe through your nose. Clear your nasal passages before doing breathing exercises.

e. Is your chest moving in harmony with your abdomen, or is it rigid? Spend a minute or two letting your chest follow the movement of your abdomen.

f. Scan your body for tension, especially in your throat, chest, and abdomen.

(Adapted from *The Relaxation & Stress Reduction Workbook.*)

2. Abdominal breathing—sitting or lying on your back

Abdominal breathing can be practiced anywhere—in the office, riding the bus, driving, at home, before bedtime—while sitting, standing, or lying. But become comfortable with the technique, it is recommended that you first focus your attention on abdominal breathing while lying on your back. After abdominal breathing has become automatic for you, it will take only seconds to use it anywhere, anytime, to help relieve tension and pain.

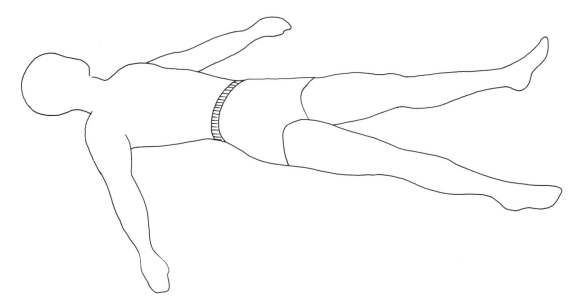

a. Lie on your back, place one hand on your chest, and the other on your abdomen. Uncross your legs, allowing them to spread comfortably apart or bend at the knees with your feet flat on floor.

b. Inhale slowly through your nostrils.

c. Feel the breath move through your chest, raising the hand on your chest slightly. As the breath reaches your stomach push your abdomen upwards toward the ceiling, while completing your inhalation. Allow the hand on your abdomen to raise slightly higher than the hand on your chest.

d. Hold for a second and then reverse the process, allowing the breath to pass back out through your chest and nostrils. As you exhale, feel your muscles let go of tension. Allow your jaw to unclench as you exhale.

e. Focus on this breathing process twice each day, for a period of ten to twenty minutes each time. Your body will tell you when you are comfortable with this breathing, and you will soon be able to apply it automatically when your body tenses up from pain and stress.

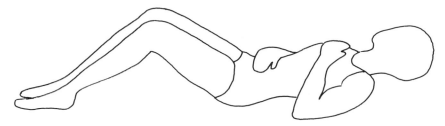

3. Abdominal breathing—on your stomach

This is an excellent exercise for practicing abdominal breathing, especially if you have difficulty feeling the movement of the diaphragm while breathing in a sitting or lying down position.

a. Lie on your stomach, placing your legs a comfortable distance apart with your toes pointed outward. Fold your arms in front of your body, resting your hands on your biceps. Position your arms so that your chest does not touch the floor.

b. As you inhale, feel the abdomen pressing against the floor. As you slowly exhale, feel the abdominal muscles relaxing. It is easy to feel the diaphragmatic motion while in this position.

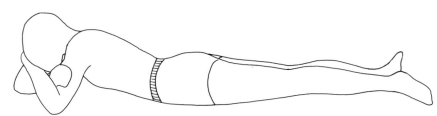

4. Deep breathing and imagery

As you become comfortable with deep breathing exercises, you can begin experimenting with imagery to combat pain in combination with your breathing.

a. When you notice the first twinges of pain, begin to calm your body by spending a minute or two doing three to four deep, natural breaths.

b. With the fourth or fifth breath, as you exhale, feel the muscles that are beginning to tighten and sink down into the rug or chair. Use imagery to represent the muscles relaxing. Imagine them as knotted ropes slowly loosening and becoming limp, or picture warming blood flowing into the muscles, making them heavy. Refer to the section on imagery in chapter 5 for other ideas.

c. Focus specifically on the area that is hurting. With each inhalation, assign an image to represent the hurting area. You might see it as a bright red pulsating light. With each exhalation, see the image change to a more pleasant and relaxing image. For example, see the bright light change to a dim, cool blue or green light.

d. Keep one hand on your abdomen and move the other hand to a point on your body that hurts. As you inhale, imagine energy coming in and being stored in your abdominal area. As you exhale, imagine the energy flowing to the spot that hurts. Inhale more energy, and when you exhale, imagine the energy driving out the pain. Imagine this process clearly, as you alternately send energy to the spot that hurts, and then drive out the pain.

(Adapted from *The Relaxation & Stress Reduction Workbook.*)

Points to remember about deep breathing:

• Deep breathing can be extremely useful in combating daily stress, including the daily stress of pain. Deep breathing can serve as a preventative tool to help you guard against a buildup of tension levels. Monitor yourself throughout the day. At the first signs of stress or twinges of pain, take a few moments to do five or six breaths. You can do this anywhere, anytime, sitting or standing. Simply close your eyes and focus on your breathing, slowing it and deepening it. Do this as many times during the day as necessary to help calm yourself. With persistence, you'll begin to notice an accumulation of calm by the end of the day, rather than a buildup of pain and stress.

• Develop the ability to "passively concentrate" on your deep breathing. The concept of passive concentration or passive volition is well known to Eastern philosophy, but less understood in Western culture, where striving for perfection is emphasized. Passive concentration means focusing on what you are doing, but in such a way that you are observing yourself comfortably. In other words, *allow* yourself to breathe deeply, rather than *force* yourself to breath "just right" like the book says. A common problem with ambitious achievers who are attempting to relax is that they expect themselves to relax perfectly on schedule and on command. When stray thoughts of business or pleasure interrupt their task, they get frustrated and try to force the thoughts away. They work too hard. If you feel that you have to do the deep breathing and the other exercises in this chapter "just right" in order to be successful, then consider that "forcing" yourself to relax can only be counterproductive. Repeat to yourself over and over, "I am *allowing* myself to relax." Watch your extraneous thoughts pass through your mind; observe them and let them go. Give yourself permission not to do it "just right" all the time.

Progressive Muscle Relaxation

Progressive muscle relaxation (PMR) was developed by Edmund Jacobson in the 1930s, when he discovered that his hypnosis patients kept a good deal of tension in their muscles while attempting to relax. He taught his patients to release this residual tension by tightly contracting their muscles group by group and then releasing the tension slowly. He felt that deep muscle relaxation would help his patients replace the habit of tensing their muscles in response to stress with the habit of releasing muscle tension.

PMR can be an effective way to learn about the amount of muscle tension in your body and to feel the sharp contrast between tensed muscles and relaxed muscles. It's possible to walk around with clenched teeth or fists all day and not even realize it until the evening, when a tension headache or sore shoulder lets you know what you've been doing. Or you may think that you have relaxed your muscles even though they are still tightly contracted. Your unawareness of what state your muscles are in can lead to muscle fatigue, poor circulation, cramping, and stiffness. Chronic muscle tightness can lead to exacerbation of your pain condition. Inflexible muscles are more prone to spasming, which sets off the pain-spasm-pain cycle discussed in chapter 2.

One word of caution about progressive muscle relaxation: If you feel pain when you first try this exercise, take care! Avoid over-tensing your injured area and the muscles surrounding it. Some people even find that they cannot relax with this type of PMR because it increases the pain too much. You may find that a "letting go" version of this exercise, where you don't tense, but you concentrate on *letting the tension go* in each muscle, is better for you (see also "Autogenics" in chapter 5). Whichever version you choose, we recommend that you ease into this exercise slowly and do not strain yourself.

Progressive muscle relaxation is a more "active" exercise than the others described in this chapter. You physically tense and relax your muscles, pushing up the tension in order to feel the upward limit of your muscle contraction. If you are hooked up to a biofeedback machine, you will notice that the needle registers more muscle activity as you continue tensing the muscle group being monitored. These factors make PMR a valuable way to learn about the tension in your body and a good exercise for beginning relaxers, but also mean that it may not be as conducive to deep relaxation as other relaxation exercises. Experiment with PMR and the other exercises in this chapter; after you get to know your own responses, pick the ones that work best for you. The following exercise has been adapted from *The Relaxation & Stress Reduction Workbook* and from *The Relaxation Training Program* by Thomas Budzynski.

We will be focusing on four major groups of muscles in the body:

1. Hands and arms

2. Feet, calves, thighs, and buttocks

3. Chest, stomach, and lower back

4. Shoulders, neck, throat, face, and head

Spend at least twenty minutes per day for two to three days on each muscle group. Most beginners find it helpful to follow along with a tape at first. You can order a prerecorded tape, or make one yourself by recording the instructions given here.

Begin by lying down or sitting in a comfortable chair with your head supported. Take several deep breaths, releasing each breath slowly. Let the deep and natural breathing be your cue to begin your relaxation session.

a. Focus on the first group of muscles—your right hand, arm, and bicep. Make a fist, clenching as hard as you can. Hold that tension, feeling it creep up your arm towards your shoulder. Hold it till you begin to feel a slight cramping, burning sensation.

b. Now relax, feeling the muscles go limp. Feel the warming blood flow through your arm into your hand and fingers. Notice the contrast between what your muscles felt like when they were tense, and what they feel like now that they are relaxed.

c. Repeat this procedure twice more. Remember to pay attention to your breathing as you tense and relax. Does your breathing begin to get shallow? Make sure you are not unconsciously holding your breath.

d. Now notice how your right arm and hand feel in comparison to your left arm and hand. Now focus on your left hand, arm, and bicep and repeat the exercise three times.

After two to three days on the first muscle group, move on to the second group: feet, calves, thighs, and buttocks. Repeat the same procedure as above, alternating sides of your body.

a. Focus on your right foot and calf. Tighten them as hard as you can. You can either pull your foot upward, or stretch your foot outward by pointing your toe. Hold the tension, feeling it creep up your leg toward your torso. Hold the tension till you begin to feel a slight cramping, burning sensation.

b. Now relax, feeling the muscles go limp. Feel the warming blood flow through your calf and foot. Notice the contrast between what your muscles felt like when you were tense, and what they feel like now that you are relaxed.

c. Repeat this procedure twice more. Remember to pay attention to your breathing as you tense and relax. Does your breathing begin to get shallow? Make sure you are not unconsciously holding your breath.

d. Now notice how the right calf and foot feel in comparison to the left calf and foot. Focus on your left calf and foot and repeat the exercise three times.

e. Now focus on your right leg again. Tense your thigh and buttocks as you tense your foot and calf. Tense as hard as you can, until you begin to feel a slight cramping and burning sensation.

    f. Now relax, feeling all the muscles in your right leg go limp. Feel the warming blood flow through your buttocks, thigh, calf, and foot. Notice the contrast between what your leg felt like when it was tense, and what it feels like now that it is relaxed.

    g. Repeat this procedure twice more. Remember to do relaxed and natural breathing. Notice how your right leg feels in comparison to your left leg.

    h. Now focus on your left leg, tensing your buttocks and thigh as you tense your left foot and calf. Repeat the exercise three times.

Spend the next two to three days of your practice on the third group: chest, stomach, and lower back. Remember to breathe deeply and exhale slowly as you release the tension in your stomach. (Note: If you have lower back pain, proceed cautiously with the tensing of your back muscles. Contract the muscles as much as you can, but do not strain or overdo it.)

    a. Focus on your chest, stomach, and lower back. Tense those areas, lightly pushing your lower back into the bed or chair as you contract your abdominal muscles and shrug your shoulders. Hold the tension until you begin to feel a slight cramping, burning sensation.

    b. Now relax, feeling the muscles go limp. Feel the warming blood flow through your lower back, stomach, and chest. Notice the contrast between how these areas felt when they were tense, and what they feel like now.

    c. Repeat this procedure twice more. Remember to do relaxed and natural breathing.

For the next two to three days, focus on your shoulder, neck, face, and head muscles. Pay special attention to the facial muscles, since they are extremely sensitive to stress and anxiety. You may be tensing the powerful muscles in your jaw all day without realizing it. Follow this script:

    a. Focus first on your shoulder muscles. Do a "shoulder shrug" by raising your shoulders as close to your ears as possible. Hold it. Feel the knots begin to form in the trapezius muscles and back of your neck. Now relax your shoulder muscles. Feel the difference when they are at rest and smooth, rather than creeping up toward your head.

    b. Now turn your attention to your head. Wrinkle your forehead as tight as you can. Now relax and smooth it out. Let yourself imagine your entire forehead and scalp becoming smooth and at rest. Now frown and notice the strain spreading throughout your forehead. Let go. Allow your brow to become smooth again. Now close your eyes and squint them tightly closed. Feel the tension. Relax your eyes. Let them remain closed gently and comfortably. Now clench your jaw, bite hard, and notice the tension throughout your jaw. Relax your jaw. When your jaw is relaxed, your lips will be slightly parted. Let yourself really appreciate the contrast between tension and relaxation. Now press your tongue against the roof of your mouth. Feel the ache in the back of your mouth. Relax. Now press your lips together and purse them into an "O." Relax your lips. Notice that your forehead, scalp, eyes, jaw, tongue, and lips are all relaxed.

Differential Relaxation. Differential relaxation is a variation of progressive muscle relaxation. You tense and relax as you would with PMR, but you focus on diagonal muscle groups at the same time. For example, when working with the first and second muscle groups, you tense your *right* arm and hand and *left* leg and foot at the same time. You also release both sides simultaneously. As you tense, you also pay attention to the sides of your body that you are not tensing (your left arm and hand and your right leg and foot).

The purpose of differential relaxation is to introduce you to a slightly more complex exercise that more closely resembles your daily activity. For example, when people drive, they often unconsciously clench their teeth and jaw in response to traffic or the normal tensions of driving. But no one ever wants to relax *all* of his or her body while driving. Of necessity, any driver needs to keep a leg and foot tense and alert on the accelerator pedal. Differential relaxation takes this kind of situation into account and teaches you to tense one part of the body while keeping another relaxed.

As you practice this exercise, be sure to pay attention to the feelings of tension on the tense side *and* the feelings of relaxation on the relaxed side. By holding both awarenesses simultaneously, you are encouraging your brain to develop a capacity for staying alert and relaxed at the same time. This exercise will also help you to adapt other forms of relaxation to your everyday activity.

Remember not to rush through each muscle group while practicing PMR or differential relaxation. Allow yourself the luxury of a full week per muscle group.

You may also find it useful to subvocalize these expressions while releasing your muscle tension:

- Let go of the tension.

- Relax and smooth out the muscles.

- Let the tension dissolve away.

- Let go more and more.

Further Reading

Alman, B., and P. T. Lambrou. 1993. *Self-Hypnosis: The Complete Manual for Health and Self-Change.* London: Souvenir.

Kirsta, A. 1986. *The Book of Stress Survival.* New York: Simon & Schuster.

Davis, M., E. Eschelman, and M. McKay. 1995. *The Relaxation & Stress Reduction Workbook.* 4th ed. Oakland, CA: New Harbinger Publications, Inc.

Mason, L. J. 1985. *Guide to Stress Reduction.* Berkeley, CA: Celestial Arts.

Swami Rama, R. Ballentine, and A. Hymes. 1981. *Science of Breath: A Practical Guide.* Honesdale, PA: The Himalayan International Institute of Yoga Science and Philosophy.

Cassette Tapes

Budzynski, T. H. 1981. *Relaxation Training Program.* Rev. Ed. New York: BMA Audiocassettes Publications.

Budzynski, T. H. 1985. *Stress Control.* Futurehealth, Inc., Distributed by MED Associates.

Miller, E. E. 1980. *Letting Go of Stress.* San Rafael, CA: Sound Rx.

Online Information Can Be Found At:

http://www.stress.org.uk/

5

Advanced Stress Management
Techniques

Autogenics Training

The word *autogenics* means "self-generated." In the 1930s, two physicians named Johannes Schultz and Wolfgang Luthe found that they could help their patients reduce fatigue and tension by teaching them to generate feelings of heaviness and warmth in their extremities.

Autogenics can be an especially helpful exercise for chronic pain sufferers for several reasons. First, there is no physical activity involved with this exercise—no physical tensing and releasing as there is with progressive muscle relaxation. Particularly when you're hurting a lot, it often feels better to relax passively rather than actively with a physical exercise. Second, the phrases used in autogenics encourage the flow of blood to the extremities. When you brace against pain and hold your muscles in a rigid position, you are actually inhibiting the healing circulation of blood. Autogenics can help to reverse this by allowing your hands and feet to be warmer because of better blood flow, and thus help you feel more overall relaxation.

After you have tried the standard autogenics phrases below and felt your body responding to them, you can make the phrases more specific to your particular pain problem. For example, you might first warm your hands and then move them to your stomach if you have an abdominal disorder. In this way, your hands would be acting like a hot-water bottle. Samantha, a migraine sufferer, often experienced cold hands and feet before she began her stress management and biofeedback training. When she first started training, her finger temperatures measured seventy-two degrees (normally warm fingers measure in the nineties) and her hands felt cold and clammy. She began to use the autogenic phrases, and then shortened them to create her own "warmth mantra" that she could use anywhere, at any time. This exercise would take her approximately thirty seconds. She would often combine her phrase with the image of sitting on warm rocks in the sun by a stream. After about ten weeks of practice, her finger temperatures rarely dipped below ninety degrees. She also had great success warming her feet—even though the bulk of her training took place in the winter! Samantha found that her headaches decreased from a bad one each week to a minor one each month.

You will focus on the same four muscle groups as you did with progressive muscle relaxation.

1. Hands and arms

2. Feet, calves, thighs, and buttocks

3. Chest, stomach, and lower back

4. Shoulders, neck, throat, face, and head

Spend at least twenty minutes per day on each muscle group and set aside approximately two to three days of practice for each group. Beginners often find it helpful to follow along with a tape at first. You can order a prerecorded tape, or make one yourself by recording the instructions given here (adapted from *The Relaxation Training Program* by Thomas Budzynski).

Begin autogenics by lying down or sitting in a comfortable chair with your head supported. Take several deep breaths, releasing each breath slowly. Let the deep and natural breathing be your cue to begin your relaxation session.

1. Focus on the first muscle group—your right hand and arm. Repeat these phrases to yourself:

My right hand is heavy.
My right hand is heavy and warm.
My right hand is letting go.

My right arm is heavy.
My right arm is heavy and warm.
My right arm is letting go.

Repeat each set of phrases twice, then move to your left hand and arm.

My left hand is heavy.
My left hand is heavy and warm.
My left hand is letting go.

My left arm is heavy.
My left arm is heavy and warm.
My left arm is letting go.

2. After several days on the first group, move on to the second group—your feet, calves, thighs, and buttocks. Repeat these phrases to yourself:

My right leg is heavy.
My right leg is heavy and warm.
My right leg is letting go.

My left leg is heavy.
My left leg is heavy and warm.
My left leg is letting go.

My right thigh is heavy.
My right thigh is heavy and warm.
My right thigh is letting go.

My left thigh is heavy.
My left thigh is heavy and warm.
My left thigh is letting go.

My buttocks are heavy.
My buttocks are heavy and warm.
My buttocks are letting go.

3. Now move on to the third group—your stomach, chest, and lower back. Focus on each area separately, and repeat these phrases to yourself:

My stomach is heavy.
My stomach is heavy and warm.
My stomach is letting go.

My chest is heavy.
My chest is heavy and warm.
My chest is letting go.

My lower back is heavy.
My lower back is heavy and warm.
My lower back is letting go.

4. Next focus on the fourth group—your shoulders, neck, throat, face, and head. Repeat these phrases to yourself, focusing first on your shoulders, then on your neck and throat, then on your head and face:

My shoulders are heavy.
My shoulders are heavy and warm.
My shoulders are letting go.

My neck and throat are heavy.
My neck and throat are heavy and warm.
My neck and throat are letting go.

My head and face are heavy.
My head and face are heavy and warm.
My head and face are letting go.

As you become comfortable with and adept at using the phrases, you can add additional instructions, such as "My right arm is loose and limp." Remember to check your breathing periodically to make sure that you are breathing deeply, slowly, and regularly.

Autogenics and imagery. Imagery can be used effectively in combination with your autogenics work. Imagine a warm sun beating down on your hands and arms or the tingling sensation of settling into a warm bath. Some people like to imagine that they are sitting by their cozy fireplace or wood stove in the wintertime. To reinforce heaviness, imagine yourself under layers of comfortable, warm blankets that feel so snug and secure over you that you don't want to move. Or imagine that your arms and legs are like heavy objects that are pleasant to you, such as tree limbs or your Aunt Ethel's fruit cake.

These additional expressions may be used while you repeat the autogenic phrases or at the end of your session (from *The Relaxation and Stress Reduction Workbook*):

- I feel quiet.

- My mind is quiet.

- I withdraw my thoughts from the surroundings and I feel serene and still.

- My thoughts are turned inward and I am at ease.

- I feel an inward quietness.

- Deep within my mind, I can visualize and experience myself as relaxed and comfortable and still.

Remember to adopt an attitude of passive concentration while practicing your autogenic techniques. Do not force yourself to concentrate. Rather, *allow* yourself to focus on the exercises. When extraneous thoughts intrude on your concentration, simply allow them to pass through your mind. Eventually, with practice, these thoughts will become less numerous and intrusive.

Imagery

Imagery is one of the most powerful tools you can use to relieve pain. Imagery lets your mind communicate directly with your body, instructing it to heal itself or feel better.

Imagery practices have been used extensively in ancient and modern tribal communities as part of the groups ritual. For example, American Indian medicine men call up the image of a spiritual guide receiving the pain of a patient in order to reduce illness and discomfort.

You are probably affected by imagery during your daily activity more than you realize. When you think about the traffic you'll have to face on your way home from work, you unconsciously clench your jaw. Then you remember that your spouse is cooking your favorite meal, and you relax a little and think pleasant thoughts in anticipation. But while the imagery that comes up in daily life can be either positive or negative, this section focuses on using positive imagery to give you that extra boost you need to effectively manage your pain.

There are many different ways to use imagery for pain control. Perhaps the simplest is to pick an image that represents your pain, put yourself into a relaxed state, and then imagine the image of your pain changing into a pleasant sensation or disappearing altogether.

Jeanne Achterberg, a psychologist who has worked extensively with imagery and chronic pain conditions, takes two approaches to imagery, using it as both diagnostic tool and a therapeutic tool. Dr. Michael Samuels, who works with cancer patients as well as pain patients, uses a similar approach, but he terms his dual imagery work "receptive" and "programmed" visualization.

During a basic diagnostic or receptive imagery session, you relax and allow spontaneous images depicting your pain to spring up in your mind. These images can help to clarify your pain and give you a starting point from which to work. For example, Helen, a migraine sufferer, described her pain image as "hundreds of tiny pins pricking my skin." Harry, who suffers from shoulder pain, imaged a bright yellow-red light burning at the point of his pain.

Therapeutic imagery or programmed visualization is the healing component of imagery. This is where you change the symbol you have selected to represent your pain into a more tolerable, even pleasant, visualization. Or you distract yourself away from your pain symbol by replacing it with another pleasant image. Helen imagined the tiny pins regrouping to form a splendid silver crown sitting atop her head. Harry visualized the yellow-red light in his shoulder changing into a cool blue light. Other healing images suggested by Dr. Samuels include making hot areas cool, releasing pressure from tight areas, and bringing blood to areas that need nourishment or cleansing.

Four-Step Imagery

The following four-step process will help you use effective pain relief imagery.

1. Learn to relax deeply by regularly practicing some form of relaxation exercise for at least ten minutes daily. Arrange a conducive setting for relaxation. (If your living room is usually as busy as Grand Central Station, it will probably not be a conducive setting.)

2. After you have relaxed, conjure up an image that represents your pain. You may want to draw a picture of the symbol you choose to help you visualize it. Make the image fit the pain.

3. Now visualize the therapeutic image or process that you have chosen to release your pain. Watch the knotted ropes of your aching muscles go limp and melt away. Or let the tiny pins grow smaller and smaller until they are simply dots, and watch the dots then disappear altogether, leaving only the color gray.

4. Visualize the positive benefits of your pain control. See yourself coping well, moving freely, smiling, and laughing. See yourself growing stronger and stronger, doing more and more. Create an active and positive image of yourself filled with energy and good health.

As you gain experience, change your images to depict your pain and its release more accurately. Make sure that the approaches you select are appropriate and that your images of success are strong. When Helen first started using imagery, she could only visualize vague color changes. Now, with practice, she can visualize the constriction of individual blood vessels to keep her head from throbbing when she feels a migraine coming on.

Suggested Imagery

The following is a representative sample of images collected from patients. This list is designed to get you started; you will find that the most effective imagery is the kind that you create yourself in your own mind.

Pain Imagery	**Relief Imagery**
For dull ache of tension headache pain:	
Band tightening around head	Band loosening, falling away
Vice gripping head	Vice disintegrating, fading in color
Muscles in head contracted	Muscles loose, limp
For sharp, throbbing vascular headache pain:	
Pins pricking around temples and eyes	Pins becoming tiny dots and disappearing
Pain like a razor's edge	Razor disintegrating or melting like a Salvador Dali painting
Hot, bright colors	Ice block cooling eyes and temples; snow-covered ground; cool colors
For dull, aching muscular pain:	
Bricks, heavy stones, or weights pressing on muscles	Bricks or stones dissolving, fading, falling away
Knotted ropes	Knots untying; ropes limp or becoming flowing water
For ripping, tearing, burning muscular pain:	
Ripping fabric	Fabric mended and strong

| Flames | Flames dying out or extinguished by water flowing over them; cool wind blowing out flame. |
| Knife cutting | Knife dissolving, cut healing |

For gastrointestinal discomfort:

Flames in abdominal and chest areas	Flames extinguished by cool water
Acid secretions in abdominal and chest areas	Secretions replaced by healing oxygen with each deep breath
Muscles tight and contracted	Healing blood, flowing in to warm and release muscle tension

Relax and allow your own images to flow. Don't be discouraged if you feel stuck and your mind seems blank: if you wait for them, the images will come. You can draw on any dream imagery that you have to serve as a catalyst to your daily, waking imagery. Post this simplified four-step program by your relaxation place to remind you of the structure of your image work.

1. Relax deeply.

2. Image your pain.

3. Image your pain relief.

4. Image the positive benefits.

Biofeedback

Biofeedback is a way for you to monitor your relaxation progress. Under stress, your body tends to contract your skeletal muscle groups, such as your shoulder and jaw muscles. Adrenaline is released into the bloodstream, causing the blood vessels in your extremities to constrict, making your hands and feet cold. Your heart beats faster and you sweat more. Biofeedback provides a measurement of the tension and changes in each of these areas. Electrodes hooked up to biofeedback machines and to parts of your body give you "feedback" about how tensed or relaxed your muscles are, how cold or warm your hands are, how much you sweat, and how fast your heart beats. All of these measurements are indications of your degree of physical relaxation.

Biofeedback can also help you to learn about your own unique response to your pain and stress. Some people automatically clench their teeth in response to pain, while others clench their fists, or hold their breath, or become overly active in an effort to ignore the pain. Samantha found that her hand temperatures reflected her typical response to stress. Whenever she became super-busy (and consequently super-anxious), she noticed that her hands would feel like ice. She calls her hands her "vulnerable place."

Placement of the electrodes varies depending on the pain problem and the preference of the person administering the biofeedback. One school of thought in biofeedback says that you can relax by focusing on a specific muscle group, while a second school believes that it is possible to focus on overall body relaxation. In the first approach, electrodes may be attached to specific muscle group sites such as the lumbar muscles of the lower back or the trapezius muscles of the shoulders. The frontalis muscles of the forehead are commonly used in the second approach as an electrode site for overall body relaxation. For both schools of thought, the general goal is to reduce your tension levels and replace anxiety with calm. This goal follows from the belief that a reduction in your anxiety level will in turn raise your level of tolerance for pain.

Electrodes placed on your muscle groups measure the muscle's electrical activity. As the muscle contracts, its electrical output increases. The needle on the biofeedback machine accordingly registers at a higher level, and a tone beeps at a louder volume to let you hear that your tension level is increasing. Conversely, as you relax, electrical output is decreased. The needle moves in the other direction, and the beeping sound diminishes to a quieter tone. The machine has no physical effect on you; the needle simply provides you and the therapist with a numerical value for your muscle tension. You use the readings that the machine provides as a guide to release your muscle tension, letting your muscles become limp, heavy, and warm, giving you an overall feeling of calm. Many biofeedback patients have remarked that they had no idea they could carry around so much muscle tension. Patients are surprised and pleased to learn that they can use the feedback of the tone and numbers to release even minute bits of muscle tension.

Electrodes placed on your fingertips tell you three things: (1) the temperature of your fingers, (2) the amount of sweat you produce, and (3) your heart rate. These measurements are all expressions of *autonomic* activity defined as "independent of volition," or not under conscious control, specifically referring to the autonomic system. As you tense up, the blood flows away from the hands and feet, causing your temperature to decrease. The palms of your hands produce more sweat, and your heart beats faster. A person doing biofeedback training with these measurements learns to increase the flow of blood to the periphery, to indirectly decrease the amount of sweat produced, and to slow down the rate that the heart beats.

Biofeedback can be helpful for managing all kinds of chronic pain conditions. An important benefit is its ability to teach you to avoid unnecessarily tensing your muscles. You can also learn to isolate your pain rather than have it spread to other parts of your body via muscle contractions and spasming. Mary Jo, a biofeedback client with a shoulder injury, learned that when she tensed her neck in reaction to the pain in her shoulder, she began to have painful neck muscle spasming as well. With the help of biofeedback, she learned to check herself regularly for unconscious bracing and to position her head and neck differently to avoid neck spasming. Kathy, a chronic tension headache sufferer, learned that she unconsciously clenched her jaw muscles regularly, so that by the end of the day she had a whopping headache. Through biofeedback, she learned to monitor her jaw clenching periodically throughout the day, thereby reducing the intensity of her headaches and sometimes preventing them altogether.

You can learn to provide good blood flow to all parts of your body by combining biofeedback with the heaviness and warmth phrases used in autogenics. This approach can be especially helpful to migraine sufferers who, like Samantha, have chronically cold hands and feet. Samantha found that raising her hand temperatures whenever she felt tense helped to decrease not only the intense pain of her migraine, but its frequency as well. She went from three to four migraines per month to one minor headache every five to six weeks.

Bob, who had been experiencing a daily combination of migraine and tension headaches for years, used biofeedback and autogenics tapes to learn how sensitive the muscles in his face were. "I've learned to avoid some of the daily buildup of muscular tension during the day. At home I lie outstretched on the floor, turn on an autogenics tape of the ocean, and just let my mind wander—let it drift off into a sort of pleasant daydreaming imagery. This whole process has sensitized me enough to know when I'm tense and when I'm relaxed. Before my daily twenty-minute session, I notice my shoulders becoming tense and riding up towards my neck, my jaw clamped shut, and my breathing getting shallow. After the session, I get up feeling refreshed and energized, and the feeling lasts all the rest of the afternoon. I believe this daily routine breaks my cycle of tension."

Biofeedback training usually lasts from eight to ten weeks, one or two sessions each week, with the sessions lasting approximately one hour. Ask your doctor for a referral to a local practitioner, or write to the following organization for a list of biofeedback resources in your area.

Association for Applied Psychophysiology and Biofeedback
10200 West 44th Avenue, #304
Wheat Ridge, CO 80033
(800) 477-8892

Relaxation Enhancers

A *temperature ring* can be particularly helpful when used to augment biofeedback training. Samantha regularly wears a ring that indicates temperature fluctuations and signals her to relax when her temperature drops. The ring has a temperature range of sixty-seven to ninety-four degrees, with little dots that light up at each point on the range. As a preventative tool, the ring functions as an early warning system: if you notice your temperature dropping, you can use this indication as a cue to take note of your situation. Are you feeling tense? Angry? Are you anticipating your pain? Or are you simply in a cold room?

For more information, the Futurehealth Thermometer Ring brochure can be ordered from

Futurehealth, Inc.
3171 Rail Avenue
Trevose, PA 19053
(215) 364-4445

Stress dots also provide you with a general idea of your temperature range. You peel the dot from a piece of paper and attach it to your hand. The dot changes color as your hands change from cool to warm. Stress dots can also be ordered from Futurehealth, Inc.

There are literally thousands of cassette tapes available right now, covering every imaginable pain and stress disorder. You can buy cassettes that use specific relaxation techniques, such as progressive muscle relaxation, or tapes that use a combination of techniques, such as music and self-hypnosis. Ask around for recommendations, borrow your friends' tapes, and experiment with the various possibilities to find the tape or tapes you like.

To get you started, here are some tapes that biofeedback patients have found to be effective.

Cassette tapes (and where to find them)

Relaxation Training Program

Thomas Budzynski, Ph.D.
Biofeedback Systems, Inc.
2736 47th Street   or
Boulder, CO 80301
(303) 444-1411

BMA Audio Cassettes
200 Park Avenue South
New York, NY 10003
(212) 431-9800

Three cassettes: Progressive Muscle Relaxation, Autogenics, Stress Management

Relaxation and Stress Reduction Cassette Tapes
Matthew McKay, Ph.D. and Patrick Fanning
New Harbinger Publications
5674 Shattuck Avenue
Oakland, CA 94609
(800) 748-6273

Multiple cassettes: Breathing and Progressive Muscle Relaxation, Autogenics and Meditation, Body Awareness and Imagery, Thought-Stopping,
Self-Hypnosis, and Pain Control

Dr. Pulos Seminars
Lee Pulos, Ph.D.
2nd Floor, 1260 Hornby Street
Vancouver, B.C. V6Z IW2
(604) 669-6979

Multiple cassettes: over thirty different visualization and self-hypnosis tapes covering a
wide range of subjects

Letting Go of Stress
Emmett Miller, with music by Steven Halperin
Source Cassettes
945 Evelyn Avenue
Menlo Park, CA 94025-4709
(415) 328-7171

One cassette: Progressive Muscle Relaxation, Autogenics, and Visualization

Sounds to Relax By
Syntonic Research, Inc.
Mail Order Department
175 Fifth Avenue
New York, NY 10010
(212) 517-8038

Eight cassettes: Sailing, Ocean Waves, Stream, Crickets, Wind in the Trees, Thunder-
storm, Heartbeats, English Meadow

Catalogs

New Harbinger Publications, Inc.
5674 Shattuck Avenue
Oakland, CA 94609
(800) 748-6273

BMA Audio Cassettes
A Division of Guilford Publications, Inc.
200 Park Avenue South
New York, NY 10003
(212) 431-9800

Futurehealth, Inc.
3171 Rail Avenue
Trevose, PA 19053
(215) 364-4445

Also, see the appendix to this book for advice on preparing your own personalized relaxation tape.

Self-Hypnosis

The feelings that you can get from practicing self-hypnosis are similar to the relaxed, refreshed feelings you get after a light nap, a good night's sleep, or a meditation session. Your body feels warm, heavy, relaxed, and refreshed. Through self-hypnosis, you can also explore ways of productively and positively managing your pain—ways that might not be readily apparent to you in a waking state. But self-hypnosis is unlike sleep in that you remain aware of your experience throughout an hypnotic trance.

The trance phenomenon has been used in various forms for centuries. In ancient Greece, priests used sleep temples to cure illness and disease through dreams and posthypnotic suggestions. An English surgeon named Esdaile, living in India in the early 1800s, performed numerous surgeries on patients under hypnotic analgesia. At the time, hypnosis was called a "mesmeric" process, after the Austrian physician Franz Mesmer who began by using magnets and seances to cure his patients of various emotional and physical ailments. Mesmer later found that he could "mesmerize" a person by simply talking to him or her and giving suggestions. Mesmer paved the way for the continuing use of hypnosis throughout the nineteenth century for treatment of neuroses and in operating rooms for dramatic surgeries performed with minimal or no anesthesia. But with the advent of anesthetic medications in the operating room, the popularity of hypnosis waned.

Unfortunately, popular books and movies have sensationalized the practice of hypnosis, encouraging the misconception that people under hypnosis can be made to do things against their will. In the original film version of *Dracula,* the Count was able to induce people to carry out his evil wishes by simply fixing a steely gaze on his unfortunate victims. The many movies that have used similar characters have done little to enhance the reputation of hypnosis. The very words "hypnotic trance" and "induction techniques" suggest mysterious goings-on, the presence of some magic spirit invading your soul aided by a power you cannot control.

But in recent years, people have begun to understand that hypnosis is a natural process, a simple shifting of consciousness from a waking state to a subconscious place which can be deeply therapeutic. You have total control over each step in a trance and cannot be made to do anything that you do not want to do. The new information that has appeared has sparked a renewed interest by the medical and psychological professions in using hypnosis and self-hypnosis as part of a wide variety of treatment programs. The healing powers of hypnosis have especially gained momentum in the medical world, where it has proven itself a viable tool for enhancing pain relief.

All hypnosis is essentially self-hypnosis. When hypnosis is practiced in a clinic or hospital, a trained therapist guides you through the steps, which you can then continue to use on your own. Many patients do find it useful to begin hypnosis practice under the guidance of a trained clinician who can introduce the techniques, guide you in their appropriate uses, and motivate you to follow through in your home practice.

You have probably experienced self-hypnosis without realizing it. Recall the last time you took a long drive and found yourself staring at the white lines on the highway. Or remember the times when you have been riveted to your seat during a good movie and have lost all sense of time. Even staring out the window and daydreaming is an example of a light hypnotic trance. In each of these cases, you became totally absorbed in thought and forgot for a period of time to pay attention to your environment. You can train yourself to deepen these trances and use them therapeutically to help manage your pain, much as you can use visualization or biofeedback.

But note that, as with the other relaxation strategies introduced in this and the previous chapter, self-hypnosis should never be used as the sole treatment of a health problem.

Simple Instructions for Self-Hypnosis

A key to inducing an hypnotic trance is to become as relaxed as possible. Relaxation helps you decrease muscle tension and calm your body in general, so that you can avoid distracting thoughts and feelings and focus entirely on changing your pain sensation.

The following six steps are the major components of a relaxation induction that takes you from awake and alert to a deep trance. These instructions and the sample inductions that follow are adapted from Hadley and Staudacher's book, *Hypnosis for Change*.

Step 1. Beginning the induction. The induction begins by focusing your attention on your breathing and inner sensations. As you do so, your awareness of external surroundings will decrease. By breathing deeply, you become aware of your internal sensations. You introduce your body to relaxation. Your pulse slows, your breathing slows, you begin to withdraw, and you can direct your attention to the suggestions that are given to you.

Step 2. Systematic relaxation of the body. As the induction directs you to concentrate on relaxing every muscle in your body, your mind will also become more relaxed. You will experience an increased awareness of internal functions and an increased receptivity of the senses.

Step 3. Creating imagery of deeper relaxation. The induction's image of drifting down deeper and deeper helps you to enter a deeper trance. Tension in your shoulders is released by an image of weight being lifted from your shoulders. Any difference in your bodily sensations will support the suggestion that a change is taking place. It does not matter whether the direction specified in the induction is upward or downward, so long as the image of rising or descending makes it possible for you to experience a change in your physical feelings.

Step 4. Deepening the trance. To help you deepen your trance, or "go down," you count backwards from ten to one. In order to return to full consciousness, or "come up," you count forward from one to ten. The induction uses the image of a staircase with ten steps, but you can substitute any image you like in order to enhance the feeling of going down. The image of an elevator descending ten floors is a popular alternative.

At this stage your limbs become immobile. Your attention will have narrowed, and your suggestibility will heighten. The surrounding environment will be closed out.

Step 5. The special place. The special place you choose to imagine will be one that is unique to you and your experience. It can be a place you have actually visited or one that you imagine. The place does not have to be real, or even possible. You can be sitting on a big blue pillow floating on the surface of a quiet sea. You can be stretched out in a hammock suspended in space. You can be in a cave of clouds. Your special place must be one in which you can be alone and it must produce a positive feeling in you. It is in this special place that you will have an increased receptivity to further suggestions. That is, once a peaceful feeling is established, you will be responsive to imagery which reinforces and supports posthypnotic suggestions.

Step 6. Concluding the induction. Before counting "up" from one to ten, a feeling of well-being should be suggested to avoid an abrupt return, which may cause drowsiness or a headache. Upon completion of the induction, you should feel relaxed and refreshed. You may walk around to make sure you are fully alert and congratulate yourself on doing a good job.

Recording Your Induction

Many people find it helpful to tape-record an induction to help guide them through each step. You may choose to record your own voice or the voice of a friend, or to use one of the many available prerecorded hypnotic induction tapes. Here are some suggestions for recording the sample induction that follows.

1. Read the induction aloud several times in order to become familiar and comfortable with its content. When recording, speak slowly and in a monotone, keeping your voice level and your words evenly spaced. You will need to experiment with tone and stress until you are satisfied with the way the induction sounds.

2. When you are comfortable with your voice and the length of time the induction will require, make sure that you have chosen a location free of any sounds that may be picked up by the tape, such as clocks, the television, the telephone, or the doorbell. You will also need to alert your family or roommates. Make sure they understand that you are not to be interrupted and that they are not to make any sounds that can be heard in the location where you will be recording.

3. Put on comfortable clothing and get in a comfortable position. You may want to lie down, sit in a rocking chair, or sit at your desk with your feet up. Whatever your preferred position, make sure it is one that will be comfortable throughout the entire recording session. If you are shifting around or feeling physically uncomfortable, this discomfort will be reflected in the tone and quality of your voice.

Going Down

Take a nice deep breath, close your eyes, and begin to relax. Just think about relaxing every muscle in your body from the top of your head to the tips of your toes. Just begin to relax. And begin to notice how very comfortable your body is beginning to feel. You are supported, so you can just let go and relax. Inhale and exhale. Notice your breathing; notice the rhythm of your breathing and relax your breathing for a moment. Be aware of normal sounds around you. These sounds are unimportant, discard them; whatever you hear from now on will only help to relax you. And as you exhale, release any tension, any stress from any part of your body, mind, and thought; just let that stress go. Just feel any stressful thoughts rushing through your mind, feel them begin to wind down, wind down, wind down, and relax. And begin with letting all the muscles in your face relax, especially your jaw; let your teeth part just a little bit and relax this area. This is a place where tension and stress gather so be sure and relax your jaw and feel that relaxation go into your temples and relax the muscles in your temples and as you think about relaxing these muscles they will relax. Feel them relax, and as you relax you'll be able to just drift and float into a deeper and deeper level of total relaxation. You will continue to relax and now let all of the muscles in your forehead relax. Feel those muscles become smooth, smooth and relaxed, and rest your eyes. Just imagine your eyelids feeling so comfortable, so heavy, so heavy, so relaxed and now let all of the muscles in the back of your neck and shoulders relax, feel a heavy, heavy weight being lifted off your shoulders and you feel relieved, lighter, and more relaxed. And all of the muscles in the back of your neck and shoulders relax, and feel that soothing relaxation go down your back, down, down, down, to the lower part of your back, and those muscles let go and with every breath you inhale just feel your body drifting, floating, down deeper, down deeper, down deeper into total relaxation. Let your muscles go, relaxing more and more. Let all of the muscles in your shoulders, running down your arms to your fingertips, relax. And let your arms feel so heavy, so heavy, so heavy, so comfortable, so relaxed. You may have tingling in your fingertips. That's perfectly fine. You may have warmth in the palms of your bands, and that's fine. And you may feel that you can barely lift your arms, they are so relaxed, they are so heavy, so heavy, so relaxed. And now you inhale once again and relax your chest muscles. And now as you exhale, feel your stomach muscles relax. As you exhale, relax all of the muscles in your stomach, let them go, and all of the muscles in your legs, feel them relax and all of the muscles in your legs, so completely relaxed right to the tips of your toes. Notice how very comfortable your body feels, just drifting and floating, deeper, deeper, deeper relaxed. And as you are relaxing deeper and deeper, imagine a beautiful staircase. There are ten steps, and the steps lead you to a special and peaceful and beautiful place. In a moment you can begin to imagine taking a safe and gentle and easy step down, down, down on the staircase, leading you to a very peaceful, a very special place for you. You can imagine it to be any place you choose, perhaps you would enjoy a beach or ocean with clean, fresh air, or the mountains with a stream; any place is perfectly fine. In a moment I'm going to count backwards from ten to one and you can imagine taking the steps down and as you take each step, feel your body relax, more and more, feel it just drift down, down each step, and relax even deeper, ten, relax even deeper, nine . . . eight . . . seven . . . six . . . five . . . four . . . three . . . two . . . one . . . deeper, deeper, deeper, relaxed. And now imagine a peaceful and special place. You can imagine this special place and perhaps you can even feel it. You are in [INSERT SPECIAL PLACE]. You are alone and there is no one to disturb you. This is the most peaceful place in the world for you. Imagine yourself there and feel that sense of peace flow through you and that sense of well-being and enjoy these positive feelings and keep them with you long after this session is completed, for the rest of this day and evening, tomorrow. Allow these positive feelings to grow stronger and stronger, feeling at peace with a sense of well-being, and each and every time that you choose to do this kind of relaxation you will be able to relax deeper and deeper. Regardless of the stress and tension that may surround your life, you may now remain more at peace, more calm, more relaxed, and allow the tension and stresses to bounce off and away from you, just bounce off and away from you. And these positive feelings will stay with you and grow stronger and stronger throughout the day as you continue to relax deeper and deeper.

Coming Up

Enjoy your special place for another moment and then I will begin to count from one to ten and as I count from one to ten you can begin coming back to full consciousness, and will come back feeling refreshed as if you had a long rest. Come back feeling alert and relaxed. Begin to come back now. One . . . two . . . coming up, three . . . four . . . five . . . six . . . seven . . . eight . . . nine, begin to open your eyes, and ten, open your eyes and come all the way back, feeling great. Very good.

Using a Self-Guided Relaxation Induction

Instead of taping your induction, you may prefer to rely instead on your internal voice and mental imagery. If so, change the "you" to "I" in the previous induction and then silently lead yourself through it, keeping the guidelines of the six basic key steps in mind.

Note that the effectiveness of either a self-guided or a recorded induction will depend on your personal preference. You may want to try the induction both ways to determine which type provides you with the most successful hypnotic experience.

Pain Control Suggestions

Once you have learned to use the relaxation induction to deepen your trance, you will be ready to begin experimenting with inserting specific pain control suggestions.

Dr. Joseph Barber, a leading practitioner of clinical hypnosis, has outlined five techniques for creating pain relief while you are in a trance.

1. *Reduce the pain sensation* (direct diminution). Reduce the feeling of your pain by making the discomfort gradually go away. Imagine turning down the "volume" of your pain as if you were turning a radio dial from unbearably loud to barely a whisper. Or dim the brightness of your pain, or cool the heat of your pain. Refer to the section on imagery in this chapter for other visualization suggestions.

2. *Change the pain sensation* (sensory substitution). Reinterpret your pain sensation by replacing it with another sensation, such as itchiness or tingling. The sensation that you substitute does not necessarily have to be pleasant. This technique has the advantage of allowing you to move gradually from pain to pleasure. Trying to shift abruptly from noxious pain to complete absence of pain can be frustrating and difficult—try substituting a sensation somewhere in between, like coldness or numbness. This technique also allows you to know that the pain is still there, in case you need to pay medical attention to it.

3. *Relocate your pain* (displacement). Put your pain somewhere else in your body. For example, move your abdominal pain from your abdomen to your finger. The relocation helps you to be less incapacitated by the pain and lets you choose the new location. Eventually, this technique can teach you to move your pain at will, or even to diminish it entirely.

4. *Numb your pain* (anesthesia). Make your painful area feel numb or tingling, with no pain sensation at all.

5. *Observe your pain* (disassociation). With this technique, you still perceive your pain, but you also see yourself removed from your pain. In other words, you distance yourself from

the pain, so that your body remains but your mind goes away on a vacation. The "special place" in the relaxation induction can help you achieve this distance by leading you to your favorite vacation spot or a quiet retreat.

The following are three entire pain control scripts (adapted from Hadley and Staudacher's *Hypnosis for Change*) which incorporate some of Dr. Barber's suggestions.

General Pain Control Induction

Now take pain and give it a shape and a form, make pain into a tunnel, a tunnel that you can enter and exit, now imagine yourself entering the tunnel. You are entering that tunnel and the intensity of your pain increases for a few seconds. As you begin to walk through the tunnel you can see the light ahead, every step now takes you away from the discomfort, the deeper into the tunnel you go, the less discomfort you feel, the light at the end of the tunnel grows larger and larger and you begin to feel better and better, every step reduces your discomfort, every step heals and strengthens your body, with every step you feel more comfortable, much more comfortable, very comfortable, and as you reach the light you feel relieved of any discomfort, you feel relaxed, stronger, comfortable, from now on each time you enter the tunnel, pass through the tunnel, watch the light at the end of the tunnel grow larger, you will be comfortable and as you exit the tunnel, you will grow stronger and stronger, heal, and feel better and better. The tunnel is yours, you control it, and can enter it anytime you like, anytime at all, and passing through it will always make you feel better.

Induction for Chronic Pain

Focus your attention on the part of the body that causes you discomfort. [INSERT THE BODILY AREA, "your shoulder," "your jaw," ETC.] Now recognize the pain and relax the muscles surrounding the area, relax the muscles all around that area, completely around the area. Feel these muscles relax and imagine the inflamed, sore area begin to reduce, cool, and heal. The inflamed, sore area will reduce, cool, heal, and feel comfortable, very comfortable. Now feel the discomfort drain out of the [INSERT BODILY AREA] and right out of your body. Feel it drain, drain away, now just imagine a cool sensation, like cool water flowing over your [INSERT BODILY AREA] and away. The cool water flows over that area washing away discomfort, washing away discomfort, completely away, and now soothe and relax this area, soothe and relax this area, and now you can begin to feel relief, relaxation, and mobility again. Your [INSERT BODILY AREA] feels normal, healed, relaxed, and mobile. From now on your subconscious will keep your [INSERT BODILY AREA] relaxed and stress-free.

Induction for Injury, Illness, Disease

Focus your attention on your pain, now imagine your discomfort to be a large red ball of energy, like the sun. Your discomfort is a large red ball. Now imagine and watch this bright red ball of energy become smaller and smaller, imagine the color of the ball beginning to lighten, beginning to change to a soft pink and reduce, reduce in size, as you watch the ball become smaller and smaller you will feel less and less discomfort. The ball grows smaller and you feel less and less discomfort, you begin to feel better and better, you feel better as you watch the ball become smaller, now watch the pale pink ball become tiny, tiny, smaller and smaller; watch the color change from faint pink to pale blue, it is now becoming a small blue dot, small blue dot, and now just watch it disappear and when it disappears you feel much, much better, you feel better, more comfortable, you feel better, more comfortable, very comfortable. You feel completely comfortable.

Posthypnotic Suggestions and Cues

One of the most important parts of practicing self-hypnosis is to carry over what you have learned in a trance state to your everyday activity. Posthypnotic cues can be words, or images, or even events that trigger a desired response after you have finished your self-hypnosis work. Dr. Brian Alman, who has worked extensively with hypnosis, says that posthypnotic suggestions and cues are a powerful extension of your self-hypnosis work.

For example, assume that you have picked Dr. Barber's relocation technique to practice while under self-hypnosis. You could begin by giving yourself the posthypnotic suggestion that whenever you begin to feel pain, you will automatically place your finger on the spot that hurts. As you become practiced at self-hypnosis, you can suggest to yourself that the pain will flow out of your body and into your finger. Eventually you can train yourself to transfer the pain from your finger to another part of your body.

You can make use of another kind of posthypnotic cue by fixing your gaze on something while inducing your hypnotic trance. This can be a familiar object that you see regularly, such as the face of a watch, or a chair. Whenever you see that object, you will associate with it your feelings of relaxation and calm almost immediately. (You will find that eventually even the relaxation tapes you use and the recorder you play them on will elicit relaxed feelings.) Pick an object in your home or office that you know will remind you of the pain-relief work you do under trance.

Obstacles to Self-Hypnosis

When you have a great deal of pain, it is often difficult to even think about relaxing or distracting yourself from your discomfort. Dr. Alman provides two suggestions for dealing with this problem.

- Pick a time when the pain has subsided a bit to practice self-hypnosis. Dr. Alman suggests that a good time might be when you are in a whirlpool, having heat therapy, or under cold packs. The brief moments when you have even the tiniest bit of pain relief can be expanded to longer and longer stretches of time as you become more practiced with self-hypnosis.

- Use your pain as a focus for your trance. If you are experiencing all-encompassing pain and are not able to distract yourself from it, then turn all of your attention to it. Examine it carefully. Assign images to it. As you focus totally on your pain, and nothing else, you will find you have greater control over it and will be able to change it to less noxious images.

A young girl named Maggie was practicing biofeedback and self-hypnosis for debilitating menstrual cramps. Before she started the program, her mother had taken her to the emergency room at the local hospital each month for a shot of Demerol to control the pain. While practicing self-hypnosis, she discovered that she could focus on each of her cramps. She imagined each cramp as a wave, crashing up on the shore, and then subsiding back into the sea. Maggie loved the ocean dearly, so this was actually a very pleasant image for her. Eventually the sea would grow calm. And when Maggie awoke from her trance, her cramps would be gone. Besides feeling proud of her accomplishment, she had no further need for the emergency room's services.

Further Reading

Imagery

Achterberg, J., B. Dossey, and L. Kolkneier. 1994. *Rituals of Healing: Using Imagery for Health and Wellness*. New York: Bantam Books.

Davis, M., E. Eschelman, and M. McKay. 1995. *The Relaxation & Stress Reduction Workbook*. 4th ed. Oakland, CA: New Harbinger Publications, Inc.

Fanning, P. 1994 *Visualization for Change*. 2nd ed. New Harbinger Publications, Inc.

Self-Hypnosis

Alman, B., and P. T. Lambrou. 1993. *Self-Hypnosis: The Complete Manual for Health and Self-Change*. London: Souvenir.

Bowers, K. S. 1983. *Hypnosis for the Seriously Curious*. New York: Norton.

DeBetz, B., and G. Sunnen. 1985. *A Primer of Clinical Hypnosis*. Littleton, MA: PSG Publishing Co.

Hadley, J., and C. Staudacher. 1987. *Hypnosis for Change*. New York: Ballantine Books.

Holzman, A., and D. Turk. 1986. *Pain Management: A Handbook of Psychological Treament Approaches*. New York: Pergammon Press.

6

Psychological Techniques for Managing Chronic Pain

The earlier chapters of this book have shown you how to practice pain control by exercising and reducing your stress levels. You have learned to manage your body's initial reactions to pain—muscle contraction and stress. By dealing with these responses effectively, you have overcome the first obstacles to getting better.

Perhaps you've already identified an obstacle that remains—an integral part of yourself that can make or break any endeavor. That last obstacle is your mind—your ability to accept new ideas, change old personal myths, examine your attitudes and beliefs, and peer into the part of you that forms your reflex reactions to the challenge of pain. Bringing your mind over to your side of the healing process is the final stage of pain management.

Consider Jean's case. She carefully followed her exercise and stress management regimen for back pain, but during the whole process she was also giving herself messages that were sabotaging her efforts. When she examined these messages with her counselor, she realized that she was telling herself she was a weak person for succumbing to the pain in the first place, and that she had better get back to her old self as quickly as possible. The rushed deadline demanded by the second part of this message was an unrealistic goal; when she couldn't meet it, she had her physical pain *and* the distressing feelings of letting herself down. The guilt she heaped upon herself for having pain to begin with only increased her anxiety levels, making it that much harder for her to cope and to follow her program. In counseling, Jean was able to identify perfectionistic tendencies like these in many areas of her life that played a part in her pain response. Eventually she learned to slow down, give herself some time and space, and talk back to the inner voice that kept pushing her so hard.

The crucial fact is that your mind can block effective coping. Maybe you have reached a plateau with your healing exercises. Or perhaps you have trouble concentrating on your stress management techniques. You may feel that your family situation or lifestyle doesn't reinforce your new coping behaviors. Whatever your situation, if you feel you have gone as far as you can with pain control and can't seem to go any farther, these next two chapters will be helpful to you.

This chapter is divided into two major subject areas: coping with your negative thinking and stress inoculation. Chapter 7 covers assertively dealing with your situation, handling conflict that arises around your pain, and decreasing your resistance to getting better. Read the following section on negative thinking first, because it is a foundation for understanding the remaining four subjects and it will help you make the most of the other sections.

Negative Thinking

It is easy to indulge in negative thinking when you have chronic pain. Your pain drags on, and a part of your reaction to that situation comes in the form of thoughts and feelings of fear and frustration. These negative thoughts can be so automatic that you may not be aware of how frequently they occur and how debilitating they are. You need to take the time now to examine your negative thinking and understand its effect on your ability to manage your pain.

Negative thoughts have the effect of *increasing* your anxiety and pain because they focus on catastrophe and resentment, creating a reality where the worst seems bound to happen and you are the helpless victim. Your body reacts by tensing with fear and anger. As your body tightens, your pain increases.

Right now try to recall some of your typical negative thoughts. See if they sound like any of these:

- I have no control over my pain.

- I'll never get better.

- This pain is a sign I'm getting old . . . I wish I was young again.

- This is going to get worse and worse until I go crazy.

- This should never have happened to me.

- I should have gotten better quicker than this.

- I'll never work again.

- No one else can ever really understand this pain.

- I'll never be able to enjoy life again.

- It's all my (job's, boss's, doctor's, family's, spouse's) fault that I'm in this mess.

- It's all *my* fault that I'm in this mess.

- I'm headed for a lifetime of pain.

Do any of these statements sound familiar to you? Note that these are only a few of an infinite variety of pain-related messages. You may have identified others of your own that are unique to your situation.

Dr. Aaron Beck, a founder of the field of cognitive therapy, describes negative thoughts as part of a "downward spiral" of depressed thinking. Once you get started, the momentum of your negative thoughts continues to carry you down and down, unless you do something to break out of the pattern.

Dr. Albert Ellis, also one of the developers of the field of cognitive psychology, argues that your thoughts *create* your emotions, and that your perception of a situation literally determines your reactions to it. What you think becomes what you feel. Through cognitive restructuring (for example, changing the way you think) you can learn to change the negative internal monologue that fuels your anxiety, depression, and anger and inevitably makes your pain worse.

A Little Theory

One way to break out of the "downward spiral" of negative thinking is to understand a little theory about the physiological effects of negative thinking.

Your brain takes in and processes all messages and emotions simultaneously. The part of the brain responsible for messages, or thoughts, is the *cerebral cortex,* the center of higher learning and cognition. The part responsible for emotions is an area called the *limbic structures.* It was once thought that these two parts operated independently of each other, but scientific theory now supports the belief that there is a great deal of neuronal interaction between all parts of the brain. Between the cortex and the limbic structures, messages flow freely back and forth through the *hypothalamus,* a pea-sized gland at the base of the brain. The hypothalamus is sometimes referred to as the brain's "central clearinghouse" because it is responsible for sending and receiving messages from brain to body and back again. The hypothalamus regulates the *pituitary gland,* which in turn activates certain stress hormones, such as *adrenaline.* You know from reading the chapter on basic stress management what happens to your body when the autonomic nervous system and adrenaline are kicking up.

The cortex represents thoughts, and the limbic structures represent feelings, with the hypothalamus acting as mediator. Here's an example of a mind-body interaction: The pain message travels up the spinal cord through the hypothalamus. You think, "I hate this pain," and you feel angry and depressed. Then you think, "What if I never get well," which causes you to feel afraid. The fear sends out a stress alarm via the hypothalamus, which in turn contracts your muscles in anticipation. The tight muscles fatigue and cramp, causing you more pain.

Because of this simultaneous processing, it is sometimes difficult to separate out which comes first—your negative thoughts, your negative feelings, or the pain. But it is safe to say that whenever you think negative thoughts about your pain, you will probably have a resulting negative physical reaction. Conversely, whenever you feel physical pain, you will probably think negative thoughts about it, setting off a vicious cycle, unless you take steps to reverse or prevent this reaction.

Consider Sally's case. Sally's boss has a deadline to meet, and Sally finds herself at the word processor furiously typing away. She skips lunch and breaks in order to try to get it all done. She feels her back strain from the buildup of pressure and from sitting in a rigid position. She clenches her teeth against the pain and thinks:

- "My boss should have planned ahead better."

- "If I ignore the pain, I can get this done now and relax later."

- "My back is killing me—I shouldn't have been so foolish that day at the gym when I showed off and tried to lift all that weight."

- "I can't afford to go slowly or take a break because my boss might think I can't do the job."

By the end of the day, Sally has not only an aching back, but also a pounding tension headache from gritting her teeth all day. She arrives home exhausted and collapses into bed.

Sally could have managed this situation better by controlling some of her negative thinking. Here's a different way to think about each one of those statements above:

- "Yes, it would have been nice if my boss had planned ahead better, but that didn't happen. My getting upset about that doesn't help me get through this work. I can manage this."

- "If I stretch and relax in short intervals throughout the day, the pain won't be so bad later."

- "For this hassle, I'll reward myself by stretching and doing an easy workout at the gym after work, or I'll relax in the sauna/jacuzzi."

- "Back injuries/strains happen to many people. My boss won't think less of me for having a back problem. We both know that I'm a good typist; I'll show that I can get the work done even better by relaxing and stretching as I do it."

What was your reaction when you read this second set of statements? Did you feel a sense of relief that Sally did not have to lock herself into a mindset that only leads to frustration and hopeless thinking? When you have pain, how do you typically think?

Getting to Know Your Negative Thinking

Take a few days to jot down all thoughts that occur to you concerning your pain. Note when and where these thoughts occur. Take an observer's stance while writing down your thoughts. In other words, try not to censor or debate your thoughts; simply write down all that come to you, whether they're about yourself or others. Remember that it takes practice to become familiar with your brand of negative thinking. Automatic thinking is lightning fast; if you can identify only one thought in a week, that's fine. In time, more thoughts will come to you. After the week, look back on your list of statements. Compare them to the following characteristics of typical negative thinking. Which of the following do you do most often?

Eight Styles of Negative Thinking

1. *Blaming.* You make someone or something else responsible for your pain. "My lousy boss is to blame for my job accident." "My family demands so much from me, I can't afford the time or money to take care of this pain." Blaming is a natural outgrowth of being tired, frustrated, and angry. But blaming only makes a situation worse, since you are not taking responsibility for what is happening to you, but rather expecting others to take the responsibility.

   Some people go too far in the other direction and focus all the blame entirely on themselves. "It's all my fault that this happened to me." If you continually put yourself down in this way, the insidious nature of self-blame can lead to lethargy and depression. This self-defeating stance can also serve as an excuse for inactivity. "Since I'm such a worthless person, getting better is hopeless. So why should I try?"

2. *"Should" Statements.* Albert Ellis states that "should" statements are one of the cornerstones of irrational thinking. The words *should, must,* or *ought* appear regularly in chronic pain negative thinking. Shoulds are usually a put-down, implying that you were stupid, foolish, or weak for not living up to some standard. "I *should* have thought of good body mechanics before I lifted that box." "I *shouldn't* have been in such a hurry when I slipped on the ice." "If only I hadn't been wearing those high heels—I *shouldn't* be such a slave to fashion." "I *must* keep up with all my responsibilities, pain or no pain." "I *shouldn't* react to pain like this."

   Should statements can sound a lot like blaming. You are admonishing yourself for not being perfect. But shoulds can also apply to others. You create a set of expectations for other people's performance that you *expect* will be met. "My spouse *should* provide consistent support and sympathy when I hurt."

3. *Polarized Thinking.* Everything is "black or white," "good or bad." There is no gray area in the middle for improvement. Chronic pain sufferers are often tempted to think, "If I'm not better by March, then that's it—either this particular program will work for me or I'm

a failure." Polarized thinking assumes things must go perfectly or else. If you have a pain relapse, then you're likely to think that the program you're using is no good or it's a sure sign of your ineptness.

This thinking can also be directed towards others, particularly medical professionals. "If they can't cure me, then they are useless." People attempting a pain management program for the first time can easily fall into this line of thinking by demanding rapid and total recovery instead of expecting a slow process of building pain control. Small steps toward feeling better are meaningless to these people, because progress is acknowledged only when they feel completely well.

This thinking leads to damaging overgeneralizations. You have one relaxation session where you are unable to decrease your pain, and you assume that you'll *never* be able to decrease your pain. Overgeneralizations are often couched in terms of absolute statements—cue words are *all, every, none, never, always, everybody*, and *nobody*. Absolute statements tend to limit your options and ignore any positive data that supports your efforts to change.

4. *Catastrophizing.* People who engage in this kind of thinking react to life situations by imagining the worst possible outcome and then reacting to their fear-provoking scenario as if it will surely come true. "I *know* that the only option left open to me is to have surgery. I'm sure I'll be laid up for months. What if the operation is a failure?" "What if" statements characterize this thinking, and greatly add to anxiety levels. "What if my pain *never* gets better, and I have to live like an invalid for the rest of my life? What if my spouse leaves me? What if I am unable to work?"

5. *Control Fallacies.* Some chronic pain sufferers see themselves as "externally controlled" by others, such as those in the medical profession. By assigning a doctor or a clinic total power over their fate, they make themselves helpless victims of their pain and of the system. In effect, they absolve themselves of any responsibility. Others may see themselves as powerless to change a dysfunctional family situation. "My spouse doesn't think I need to see a counselor for my pain, so I can't come to the session."

On the other hand, people who see themselves as "internally controlled" believe that they have complete responsibility for everything and everyone. "Everyone depends on me. The family will fall apart if I don't recover quickly from this mess." These people assume all of the responsibility, rather than allowing other family members to share some of the load. Some pain sufferers suspect they could be completely well—if only they wanted it enough. "Maybe I don't want to get better, that's why this has gone on so long."

6. *Emotional Reasoning.* This line of thinking assumes that what you feel *must* be true. If you feel guilty about needing time to heal, then taking the time must be wrong and needing the time must be your fault. If you're frightened that the pain will never stop, then you *believe* it will never stop. If you feel grief at the thought that you'll never run again, then you must be right—you won't run again. You let your feelings rule your reasoning ability. While it's usually helpful to get in touch with your feelings, what you feel may be quite unrealistic. The strength of the feeling creates conviction, but later things may seem different as the emotional storm dies down.

7. *Filtering.* Some people have a tendency to see their pain through tunnel vision, filtering out any potentially positive aspects. These people make things worse than they are by

focusing only on the pain and nothing else. Ted could not appreciate his spouse's genuine efforts at caring and support because he was so wrapped up in his pain. He failed to enjoy any aspect of this nurturing relationship.

The process of filtering can also be very selective. You may choose to remember only those things which support your angry feelings, thus pulling your negative memories out of context and isolating you from positive experiences. What you fear can be magnified to the point that it fills your awareness to the exclusion of everything else. Ruth was so obsessed with the possibility of another back attack, that she filtered out her doctor's advice on prevention and exercise.

8. *Entitlement Fallacy.* People often feel that they are "entitled" to a pain-free existence. They believe they shouldn't have to suffer pain or loss. They feel cheated, that life is being unfair. John felt that it was totally unacceptable that he couldn't play tennis because of his injury. He felt that his abilities had been "stolen" from him. His sense of entitlement and outrage kept him from considering new sports to replace his old one. People who harbor the entitlement fallacy feel that the luxury of ignoring or taking their bodies for granted is their right. And if they lose some capacity due to chronic pain, they feel that their life has been diminished.

All of these eight styles of thinking are related to each other. In fact, if you have a tendency towards one line of thinking, you will probably catch yourself doing several of the others. While the categories are a helpful way of showing how negative thinking works, don't be surprised if you have trouble labeling your own thoughts, since the boundaries between styles can blur. It's also quite possible to bombard yourself with a number of negative thoughts all at once in a lightening-fast mental shorthand. You rapidly heap negative thought upon negative thought until you feel overwhelmed and ready to give up. Be patient with yourself and allow yourself to gradually become familiar with your unique way of negative thinking.

Replacing Negative Thoughts

There are three ways of approaching the task of replacing your negative thoughts.

Step 1: Thought Stopping

This behavioral approach focuses on stopping negative thoughts cold. Devise for yourself a list of quick responses to use to replace those that are negative and unproductive. Do not spend any time wondering *why* you do the negative thinking that you do—simply choose positive thoughts that you commit yourself to use as soon as you notice yourself regressing into your characteristic negative thinking. Here are some suggestions to get you started.

Copy this list or cut it out and put it next to your sink, refrigerator, word processor, desk, or dashboard of your car—somewhere you will see it regularly. Breathe deeply first, then say:

- "I can cope."
- "Relax. I can manage the pain."
- "I have managed this situation before. I can do it again."
- "I am learning new coping skills everyday."
- "I am not a bad person because I have this pain."

- "The pain comes and goes. I know how to take care of it."

- "No one thinks less of me because I have this pain."

- "I am a good worker."

- "I am a loving person."

- "The pain comes in waves. Soon it will start to subside."

Add some positive thoughts of your own:

_____

_____

_____

_____

You can also substitute angry rebuttal statements for the negative thoughts. These are called *Howitzer Mantras*. The more angry and hostile you make your Howitzer Mantra the better. It may help to swear. Here are some examples:

- "Stop this negative shit."

- "Shut up with the negative stuff."

- "Stop this garbage."

- "To hell with this catastrophic crap."

- "Screw this blaming baloney."

- "No more of the helpless stuff."

Add your own:

_____

_____

_____

_____

Step 2: The ABCD Model

This model developed by Ellis, Beck, and others can be a useful tool in structuring your approach to understanding negative thinking about pain.

A is the "activating event" or stressor. In this case, let's make it a muscle spasm in your back that keeps you from fulfilling a commitment.

B is your "belief system," or your thoughts and attitudes about the stressful event. For example, you may think "Now I can't do what I said I would—they'll think I'm weak. I can't do anything anymore."

C stands for the "consequences" of the activating event, or basically, your feelings. When you think poorly of yourself, as in *B*, you *feel* guilty, frustrated, depressed.

D is a way to change the above sequence of events. *D* means "disputing" the negative thinking you discover in *B*, which can affect how badly you feel in *C*.

How to Use this Model

It takes a little getting used to breaking your thoughts and feelings down into this structured format. Once you do, however, you'll be more familiar with your own typical pattern and will be able to more automatically and rapidly dispute the negative thinking that gets in your way.

This model was originally designed for all types of stressors, but can be nicely adapted to fit the stress of chronic pain. For now, focus on your presenting problem of pain. It is helpful to work on step *A*, step *B*, and step *C*, before you begin to dispute any negative thinking in step *D*.

A: Write down a recent event that has caused your pain to flare up. Keep this event concise, rather than describing every single detail in lengthy pages.
Example: "I twisted in my chair while reaching for the phone and felt my back strain."
The fresher the event, the better able you will be to identify all thoughts and feelings. Keep the event pain related.

B: Skip for now.

C: Jot down, without censoring or debating, all feelings you had when the event occurred. A feeling is a word describing your emotions—a sentence that begins with "I think that..." is not a feeling sentence, but rather a thought or a statement. However, there may be some feelings hidden in the thought statement.
Example: "I felt fear, disgust, disappointment."
You do not necessarily need a page of feelings. Several will do.

B: Now go back to *B*. List all thoughts that occurred to you when *A* happened.
Example: I thought, "My back is going out again"; "I have to take up the slack and answer the phone for the other secretary who's always out sick"; and "I thought my doctor said this wouldn't happen if I exercised regularly."

Work this *A-B-C* process several times until you feel comfortable with it. Note your stress levels as you work it. Also note that *A* doesn't actually cause your negative feelings. *B* causes the feelings. *B* is your *perception of the event*, and determines your reaction to it. Negative thoughts and feelings also create a pain-making feedback loop. The more negative thoughts, *B*, the more negative feelings, *C*. Then as you feel more anxious, depressed, and so on, you start thinking how horribly anxious or depressed you are, and this only serves to intensify your negative feelings.

D: Move on to *D* when you feel ready to break out of the negative thought cycles you are identifying in the first three steps. Focus on *B* in one of your examples. Pick a thought or belief you had that is particularly upsetting, one that really "gets" you. Sometimes it is easier to work with "hot" thoughts because of the wealth of responses they can bring. To help you dispute and refute your negative thinking, here is the list again of the eight styles, with specific suggestions for coping.

1. Blaming

For *self-blame*, remind yourself that you have always made the best choice you could *at that particular point in time*. Based on your awareness at the exact moment of your choice, what you did seemed reasonable and for the best. Now, with the hindsight and the luxury of knowing how things turned out, you blame yourself. There was no way, however, back when you made the choice, that you could know the future. You made, what seemed *then,* the best decision.

Coping thoughts:

- "Forget blaming with hindsight."

- "I've made reasonable choices, based on my awareness at the time."

2. "Should" Statements

When you catch yourself saying the words "should," "ought," or "must," you are in effect putting yourself down, telling yourself that you are stupid for not doing things differently. The fact is, you did it the way you did it, and no amount of self-admonishment will make the situation any better or easier. "Should" statements only immobilize you, and contribute to an unrealistic expectation that you must be perfect.

Coping thoughts:

- "I do not have to be perfect."

- "I may get irritated when other people don't act according to my values, but other people may think differently than I do."

3. Polarized Thinking

If you persist in thinking in terms of black or white, you leave little room for the gray area of improvement. Any change effort takes time and steady work. If you expect yourself to be magically better overnight, you will be disappointed when you're not and discount your smaller efforts at progress. Watch out for absolute words like *all, every, none,* and *never.* And remember, *you always have options.*

Coping thoughts:

- "I wish I could be completely well, but I certainly have made some progress in certain areas. Even though it doesn't seem like much now, it will add up."

- "Sometimes improvement is not obvious at first. I'll give myself some time and patience."

4. Catastrophizing

When you catastrophize, you assume the worst and require proof for anything positive. The antidote is to start doing the opposite. Require stringent proof that your worst fear will take place. What evidence do you have that it will happen for sure—other than the fear itself? Is there any reason to believe it might not happen? List the reasons why it might not happen. (i.e. it never happened before, you have better coping skills than when you first got ill, etc.). When the catastrophic thoughts arise, firmly remind yourself that this is "what if" thinking without any *definite proof.* Also begin listing the reasons why the feared event may *not* happen. Ask yourself in all honesty, what is the percentage chance that my *worst* fears will come true—5 percent? 10 percent? .01 percent? Try to make a realistic assessment.

Coping thoughts:

- "I have no proof of this."

- "There are good reasons why _____ probably won't happen." (list the reasons)

- "I'll find a way to cope with whatever happens."

5. Control Fallacies

Whenever you catch yourself saying that "so and so" knows best, change it to "So and so has experience in that area, and I have, too." Do not discount your own experience. You have power and responsibility over your fate. Whenever you catch yourself thinking you are a helpless victim, immediately refute that irrational thinking.

Coping thoughts:

- "I am not a helpless victim."

- "I have power over my situation to steadily change and improve it."

- "I do not have to be at all times totally in control of my own and others' actions. They are not helpless victims either."

6. Emotional Reasoning

When you are in the thick of your feelings, it is difficult to reason objectively. And you don't have to. Take some time to feel bad and ventilate your feelings, but put a time limit on it. Then, move into the problem solving stage where you do not let your feelings rule your decision making ability. Feelings are good and healthy, but are not always useful in problem solving.

Coping thoughts:

- "I will let myself feel (bad, angry, sad . . .) right now, but I know these feelings will not always give me an accurate picture of my situation."

- "When I calm down and relax a little bit, I assess my (situation, problem, decision) again."

7. Filtering

If you find yourself focusing entirely on negative aspects of your pain, you need to deliberately shift focus. First, place your attention on coping strategies rather than obsessing about the problem itself. Avoid magnifying your problem. Second, focus on the positive aspects of your situation. Avoid the phrase, "I can't stand it."

Coping thoughts:

- "I can get used to and cope with almost anything."

- "I have skills, resources, and friends. Look how much they have supported me and helped me cope already!"

8. Entitlement Fallacy

It will be helpful for you to challenge the notion of your right to a totally pain free existence. You are not *entitled* to anything except taxes and death. No one said that life would be fair. The key is, what do you do *after* you have been struck by trauma, injury, pain? Do you bitterly debate how life has cheated you, or do you accept your pain and sadness and move on to functioning as well and happily as you can? Happy people who survive the traumas of their lives keep on surviving, growing, and improving.

Coping thoughts:

- "My life has not been totally diminished because I have this problem."

- "I can replace my losses with new things to do, and who knows, I may find something I like better!"

Sally's Case

In Sally's case, she picked "my back is going out again" to work on. The related feeling was fear. She identified other thoughts that were related to her fearful feeling, such as "It'll be just as bad as before," "I'll be laid up again for months," "My boss won't like me." After she was finished searching for all thoughts relating to fear and "My back is going out again," Sally reviewed the list of eight negative thinking styles.

She was able to identify her initial thinking as catastrophizing, polarized thinking, and even a few "should" statements thrown in. She realized that she might not actually have to be laid up for months, that she was expecting the worst (catastrophizing). She realized she was telling herself she should be perfect for the boss, otherwise he wouldn't like her (polarized thinking and a should statement). She realized that when she felt fear, she immediately jumped to the conclusion that all her fearful thoughts were absolutely true (emotional reasoning).

Here's how Sally disputed "my back is going out again":

Is there any rational support for this? Yes, some, because my back went out once before. Is there any reason to believe it might not happen? In this particular situation the pain is not severe and there is no evidence that my back will be as bad and "go out" like it did before. I also remember that I had numerous back strains since my initial injury and have managed through each one without it becoming a major problem.

Since the injury, I've been exercising and practicing stress management regularly. I know how to take care of it in the long run, and I know what to do immediately to make sure the pain doesn't get worse (relax, stretch, slow down).

Here's how Sally put it all together in the *ABCD* format:

A Activating event (stressor)	B Belief system (thoughts)	C Consequences (feelings)	D Disputing
Back pain while typing this afternoon.	*Oh no, my back is going out again. It'll be as bad as before. I'll never be able to do this job right. I'll never work again.* *My boss should be better organized so I don't get stuck like this.*	*Fear* *Anxiety* *Anger* *Frustration*	*I'm expecting the worst (catastrophizing). Even though I'm anxious, that doesn't mean I should jump to conclusions (emotional reasoning).* *My boss doesn't always work like I think he should (should statement).* *Don't worry—it'll take time to do my exercises and get through this (supportive).*

Spend at least twenty minutes each day practicing this model for a period of several weeks. Share it with a friend. With practice, it becomes second nature, and you won't even have to write it down—you'll be able to internally identify and dispute your negative thoughts.

Step 3: Analyzing Your Thoughts

You have determined some of the immediate thoughts associated with your pain and have tried several coping tools. Now is the time to dig a little deeper in analyzing your thought patterns and how they relate to your pain situation.

Let's look at Sally again. She is an avid downhill skier, and prepares herself for the winter season by stretching and strengthening her back muscles regularly. With the first couple of runs, her whole body aches with fatigue and she feels that familiar twinge in her back. But she is exhilarated by the crisp air, the white snow, and the excitement of the run. She says to herself, "I'm not going to stop now—how often do I get to ski on such great powder? And anyway, the lift tickets are too expensive to stop now." She knows she'll feel the pleasure of the hot tub at the end of the day to soothe her aching muscles.

A week later Sally wakes up in the morning before work with a stuffy, runny nose and scratchy throat. She doesn't feel particularly bad, but calls in sick anyway because she decides she needs a day off. And besides, she doesn't want to risk infecting her co-workers.

These two pain situations are quite real, but also very different. In the first one, Sally suppresses a lot of pain for the pleasure of skiing. In the second, the pain is not as great, but gets magnified for other reasons. This illustration isn't about Sally's appropriate use of sick leave, but rather to show that you can make important choices about your pain.

This step was saved for last because it may be the most difficult for you to take. It requires a certain degree of honesty from you, and a nondefensive assessment of the choices you make about your pain. Take time to think about the various situations you've had concerning your pain. Honestly ask yourself if there was a time when you knew you needed, for whatever reason, to magnify your pain. Talk this issue over with a trusted friend or family member. Look for any way you might get rewarded by staying focused on your pain. Keep a log of when your pain gets worse and see what activities (or would-be activities) coincide with these fluctuations. Does your pain change how people relate to you? Does it increase your experience of being cared for, of getting support? Does it help you to avoid unpleasant tasks or stressful events? Do not judge yourself or feel guilty for the choices you made. This awareness is simply a learning tool to help you cope. Acknowledging that you may sometimes choose to use your pain in this manner may help you to control it more effectively.

Summary of Reversing Negative Thinking

1. Reversing your negative thinking can be a useful tool for pain reduction because it helps to reduce anxiety, which in turn reduces pain levels.

2. It eliminates compounding of the pain problem.

3. It opens up options for pain management.

4. With practice, it becomes a habit.

5. It can be applied to other problem areas.

6. It can enhance your relationships with others.

7. It makes you feel better.

Stress Inoculation

Fighting negative thinking is not the complete answer for dealing with your emotional pain. If you work hard at confronting distortions, you may reduce the amount of negative thinking that you do by 50, 60, or even 80 percent. But some residual amount will inevitably slip through. Furthermore, some of your negative thinking occurs at a level far below your conscious awareness. You simply can't catch the thoughts, because they are too lightning swift or too buried for you to recognize them. Sometimes the thoughts are in the form of images that seem to rise unbidden (you see yourself in a wheelchair, you imagine a muscle ripping). Sometimes the thoughts have no words—you just *know* that something bad will happen.

You can use stress inoculation (a technique developed by Donald Meichenbaum) when some of your hard-to-catch negative thoughts have precipitated an anxious, angry, or depressive reaction. Stress inoculation helps you to cope with waves of strong, painful emotion; it helps you make it through without being overwhelmed, even when you are faced with overwhelming feelings. Here's how it works.

1. *Self-monitoring.*   You must learn to recognize the early signs of a strong emotional reaction. Catching the wave of fear, anger, or sadness early is a key to successful coping. Treat your first awareness of a painful feeling, particularly one that seems to be gathering steam, as a red flag warning you to initiate the stress inoculation procedure.

2. *Self-instruction.*   The core of stress inoculation is a process of talking yourself through the pain. In practice, this means developing a list of coping statements that will keep you calmer during waves of painful emotion. The coping statements that you will create for yourself will be in the form of short, pithy commands that remind you of adaptive ways to deal with your stressful feelings.

When you're feeling anxious, angry, or sad, the first thing you need to do is to rid your body of excess tension. So your first coping statements should focus on breathing and relaxing the areas of your body that characteristically hold tension. Here are some examples:

- "Breathe deeply now, full relaxing breaths."

- "Breathe deeply and relax the diaphragm."

- "Tension is a sign to cope. Relax now."

- "Is there tension in my shoulders?'

- "I can breathe away that tension. Let go of it."

Now try to write several statements of your own. Make sure you include the specifics of *where* and *how* you feel tension most. Include any relaxing activities that you know you can do in a few minutes. For example:

- "I'll settle down on the couch and read my favorite book for a while."

- "I'll do my nails and forget this baloney."

- "I'll take a hot bath and listen to some Brahms."

The second set of instructional statements you will write will help you to cope with the feeling itself. The emphasis here is on getting through it, riding it out. Here are some examples:

- "Don't let negative thoughts creep in."

- "If I don't feed it with negative thoughts, this feeling will begin to dissipate by the time I get home."

- "This is just a wave of pain that I will get through."

- "I've survived this before. The wave passes in a while."

- "I'll ride it out and I'll be okay."

- "There's an end to it."

- "I'll reserve a half an hour to feel this way, and then carry on."

- "I can distract myself by balancing my checkbook (or doing some task, or calling someone, or jogging, and so on)."

As with relaxation reminders, you should adapt or rewrite any of these to suit yourself. Or use the statements as models to create coping instructions tailored to your unique situation.

Your third set of instructional statements will help you use the skill of *accepting and distancing*. These statements are reminders to pull back from the painful feeling and see it in perspective. You have entered a brief emotional storm, and it will be over in a while. Accept that you'll feel bad for a time, but know also that the wave will pass and the anxiety, anger, or sadness will recede. Here are examples:

- "I'm doing my best to cope, and I'll just have to feel this way for a little while."

- "I can step back and see the wave, I can get through it."

- "I feel the anxiety (or anger, or sadness), but another part of me is watching me go through this from a distance."

- "I can float by the worst of this and not be too touched by the feelings."

- "I can accept these feelings because I'm doing my best."

- "Pull back and see this for what it is—a brief emotional storm that will be over in a while."

3. Talking yourself through. Make a list of the coping statements that you think will be most effective. Keep them with you so they can be used as reminders to cope when you experience stressful feelings. Be your own coach. Talk yourself through the trauma. The goal is to keep a part of yourself separated from the pain, a detached observer.

Remember that emotional pain distorts your sense of reality. Everything seems black. The pain seems eternal. It's hard to imagine ever feeling better. That's why you need the coach, the detached observer to remind you that the wave will pass. Soon enough you begin to relax or get distracted. The emotion begins to burn itself out.

Harry's Case

Harry had been struggling with irritable bowel syndrome for more than five years. When the cramping flared up, he typically slipped into catastrophic thinking: "This is getting worse . . . How will I keep working? . . . Maybe I have cancer . . . I can't enjoy anything feeling like this." With the help of a therapist, Harry began to exert more and more control over his catastrophic thoughts. And he had fewer episodes of anxious rumination about his health. But there were still times when he felt overwhelmed by a sense of dread. The future seemed filled with pain, and he felt incapable of dealing with it.

Harry's therapist suggested stress inoculation to help him cope with these surges of anxiety. Together they made this list of coping statements.

- "Breathe deeply and relax the diaphragm."

- "Let go of tension in the stomach, let it be fat and relaxed."

- "I'll put the headphones on and listen to some music."

- "This is just a wave of pain, it never lasts more than an hour."

- "There's an end to it, I can survive one hour."

- "I can float by the worst of this and not be done in."

- "When I step back, I can see it's a wave and I'll feel better soon."

Harry modified and added to this list as he went along. He found that some coping statements worked better than others. And some didn't work at all. After carrying the list and using the technique for about two weeks, Harry reported that he felt less stress during his anxiety episodes. "It's like I'm detached, I can see the whole process from a distance. I just watch it gradually fade out."

Further Reading

Beck, A. 1989. *Cognitive Therapy and the Emotional Disorders.* Harmondsworth, Middlesex: Penguin.

Benson, H., and E. Stuart. 1992. *The Wellness Book: The Comprehensive Guide to Maintaining Health and Treating Stress-Related Illness.* Secaucus, NJ: Birch Lane Press.

Coleman, D., and J. Green, eds. 1993. *Mind Body Medicine: How to Use Your Mind for Better Health.* Yonkers, NY: Consumer Reports Books.

Davis, M., M. McKay, and E. Eshelman. 1995. *The Relaxation & Stress Reduction Workbook.* 4th ed. Oakland, CA: New Harbinger Publications, Inc.

Holzman, A., and D. Turk. 1986. *Pain Management: A Handbook of Psychological Treatment Approaches.* New York: Pergamon Press.

Lazarus, R., and S. Folkman. 1984. *Stress, Appraisal, and Coping.* New York: Springer Publishing Company, Inc.

McKay, M., M. Davis, and P. Fanning. 1981. *Thoughts and Feelings: The Art of Cognitive Stress Intervention.* Oakland, CA: New Harbinger Publications, Inc.

McKay, M., P. Rogers, and J. McKay. 1989. *When Anger Hurts: Quieting the Storm Within.* Oakland, CA: New Harbinger Publications, Inc.

Schwartz, G., and D. Shapiro, eds. 1976. *Consciousness and Self-Regulation.* Vol 1–4. New York: Plenum Press.

7

Dealing With Others

Assertiveness

As a chronic pain sufferer, you have probably encountered situations that required you to say no to a request to do something that you knew would aggravate your pain. Did you feel guilty when you said no? Did you put yourself down for having the pain in the first place? Did you blame the other person for being rude and trying to embarrass you? Or did you pat yourself on the back for avoiding a potential problem by saying no?

Arthur felt guilty about not doing his share of the car pooling in the mornings. But his back bothered him so much that it was an effort even to get into the car, much less drive around in it. He didn't think that the other parents in the car pool would understand, so he made up excuses about his unreliable car.

When she found herself in a similar situation, Kathleen realized that driving long distances on her job would put her on the disabled list permanently. This realization gave her the confidence to request a meeting with her boss to work out an amicable solution.

Arthur is engaging in passive, avoidant behavior. Kathleen is being assertive. Are the differences obvious to you? If not, perhaps you need to examine your assertive or nonassertive behavior and its interplay with your pain. Learning to deal assertively with all of the situations that your pain disrupts can make a big difference in how well you cope.

People who show relatively little assertive behavior do not believe that they have a right to their feelings, beliefs, or opinions.

Consider these statements:

Do you think that:	*Or do you think that:*
1. You should always take other people's advice seriously, especially doctors and health care professionals who take time out of their busy schedules just for you?	You have a right to disregard the advice of others?
2. You should always respect the views of others, especially if they are in a position of authority?	You have a right to have your own opinions and convictions?
3. It is selfish to put your needs before others' needs?	You have a right to put yourself first sometimes?

4. You shouldn't take up others' valuable time with your problems?

You have a right to ask for help or emotional support?

5. You should always try to be logical, consistent, and in control?

You have a right to make mistakes, change your mind, or decide on a different course of action?

6. You always have the right to say and do exactly what you feel?

You realize that sometimes you can and need to hear the other person out and can initially keep your opinions to yourself?

Statements one through four on the left can lead to *passive behavior.* If you behave passively, you let others push you around, do not stand up for yourself, and do what you are told, regardless of how you feel about it.

Passivity and chronic pain are a deadly combination. If you always do exactly what the doctor tells you to do, even though you've had previous experience to the contrary, then you are throwing away your own hard-won and tested knowledge and replacing it with a feeble dependency on someone else's supposedly greater insight. If your boss demands the same amount of work from you, and you know that it will make your neck pain worse but you do it anyway, then you are behaving passively.

Statements five and six on the left lead to *aggressive behavior.* If you behave aggressively, you tend to blame, threaten, and accuse people without regard for their feelings. Aggressive people are likely to attack when they don't get their way. They are so intent on being "right" that they often don't hear what others are saying.

Aggression and chronic pain are also a dangerous combination. If you are angry because you have chronic pain and then blame your boss for your misfortune, you are likely to behave aggressively and risk your job. If you expect your doctor to cure you and then lash out at the "incompetence" when he or she disappoints you, you are behaving aggressively. You risk alienating a person who may be able to help you.

All of the statements on the right are *assertive statements.* Assertive behavior involves direct statements and actions regarding your feelings, thoughts, and wishes. You stand up for your own rights and take into account the rights and feelings of others. You listen attentively and let other people know that you have heard them. You are open to negotiation and compromise, but not at the expense of your own rights and dignity. You can make direct requests and direct refusals. You can deal effectively with criticism, without becoming hostile or defensive.

Assertive behavior helps you deal effectively with chronic pain. If you feel that you are not getting adequate advice or service from a health care professional, then you have a right to ask questions and make requests, or to ignore that person's advice and look elsewhere. But if passivity or guilt keep you from making choices like these, then you will have a hard time getting to the problem-solving stage of taking care of your own pain situation.

Problems at home are also made easier by assertiveness. Howard believed that he was primarily responsible for doing all the home repair and maintenance on top of a demanding job. The nature of his arthritis pain made this an unrealistic expectation, but he had trouble asking his family for help. Learning new assertive skills enabled him to request a family conference for the purpose of making changes in work distribution. To his surprise, his family was more than willing to help with some of his tasks.

Identifying Your Style

Reflect on events of the past week where you felt that you responded passively or aggressively. Identify one situation where you can remember the interactions as clearly as possible. Then add other recent events.

Event:	*The other person said:*	*You said:*
_____	_____	_____
_____	_____	_____
_____	_____	_____
_____	_____	_____
_____	_____	_____
_____	_____	_____
_____	_____	_____
_____	_____	_____
_____	_____	_____
_____	_____	_____
_____	_____	_____
_____	_____	_____
_____	_____	_____
_____	_____	_____

Can you identify a typical pattern in your responses or interactions? To help in assessing your behavior, refer to the following lists for passive, assertive, and aggressive behavioral clues.

Passive: Moving Away from the Situation

Verbal clues:
Profuse apologizing, rambling, or beating around the bush. Using words or phrases such as "Um . . ." "Well . . ." "You know . . ." "Never mind . . ." "It's not really important . . ." "Don't bother . . ." "Maybe . . ." "I guess . ." "Don't you think . . ."

Nonverbal clues:
Slouched posture; downcast, averted or tearful eyes; nervous gestures; soft, unsteady, weak, whining, hesitant, pleading, or giggly tone of voice.

Assertive: Balancing Power

Verbal clues:
Clear, direct, honest, respectful, empathic (feeling) statements; nonblaming language. Using sentences that start with "I want . . ." "I think . . ." "I feel . . ." "Let us . . ." "How can we resolve this?"

Nonverbal clues:
Listens well to others; stands upright and comfortably; uses a strong, well-modulated voice; maintains good eye contact.

Aggressive: Moving Against

Verbal clues:
Blaming, accusing, or threatening others; using put-downs, sarcasm, evaluative comments, or sexist or racist terms. Using phrases such as "You'd better . . ." "You should . . ." "You must be kidding . . ." "You better watch out if you don't . . ." "That's bad . . ."

Nonverbal clues:
Shows of strength; a raised, snickering, or haughty tone of voice; cold, detached looks; a rigid or rejecting posture; dominating gestures (finger pointing, pounding table, or intruding into another's personal space).

You'll find it helpful to practice your new behavior with a spouse, friend, or counselor who you know will provide you with constructive feedback. Try out the assertive responses and note the results. You should be able to reach a problem-solving stage more quickly than you did when you used your old passive or aggressive responses. When you're ready, try out your new assertive behavior with your doctor or health care professional. Explain to them that you are practicing dealing more assertively with your pain situations.

Here are specific guidelines for turning your old patterns of passive or aggressive behavior into assertive requests.

Behavior	*Description*
Maintain eye contact and position your body squarely toward others.	Look the other person in the eye *most* of the time. Do not stare fixedly. Lean forward and use hand gestures to maintain his or her attention.
Speak firmly and positively, and loudly enough to be heard easily.	Avoid mumbling, whining, speaking shrilly, or yelling. Avoid dropping your voice at end of sentence.
Use clear, concise speech. Ask directly for what you want or say clearly what you *don't* want.	Avoid numerous repetitions and qualifiers such as "maybe" or "I guess." Avoid self-deprecating statements such as "I shouldn't ask, but . . ."
Keep your nonverbal behavior congruent with the content of your statement.	Don't smile placatingly when refusing or disagreeing. Don't wring your hands when

	requesting. Avoid a rigid face when expressing warmth or praise.
Listen.	Repeat the point that the other person made, clarify, or say something that shows you are hearing him or her.
Maintain a posture and attitude of equality.	Avoid apologetic statements or a tone which belittles yourself or your ideas. Avoid accusing statements or a tone of sarcasm or ridicule. Be respectful of yourself and others.
Take the initiative.	Don't let others choose for you. Take the lead with "I have a suggestion . . ." or "In my opinion . . ."

When you have said what you wanted to say, stop talking.

Rick has chronic pain from an old whiplash injury, which can be exacerbated by stress. He knew that certain situations caused his pain condition to flare up, but he had trouble saying no to some of those situations. He remembered one occasion when he had agreed to go to a particularly gruesome horror movie, knowing full well that his shoulder and neck symptoms would get worse. But he felt too embarrassed to say no, and was afraid that his friend wouldn't ask him out again.

When he talked this situation out with his counselor, Rick realized that he could handle the situation assertively without feeling embarrassed. He explained to his friend that he made a point of not going to those kinds of movies because they stressed him out, and instead set up a date to see another movie he'd been looking forward to. His friend readily agreed, and Rick felt pleased that he had learned to take care of himself.

Rita had always been told that the "doctor knows best," and so she dutifully took all of the medication that he prescribed for her jaw pain. When she realized that the Valium she was taking was an addictive tranquilizer and that she was beginning to need more and more of it to control her tension, she asked her doctor to refer her to a pain specialist. When the doctor said that he could make the referral but that all she really needed was to take a different tranquilizer, she politely said no. She explained that she was not the kind of person who functioned well on drugs, and that she needed to work with a doctor and counselor who could help her get off the Valium and rely on drug-free resources.

Harry was in a similar situation. Everytime he had a vascular headache, he would run off to the emergency room at the local hospital and get a shot of Demerol, a highly potent and addictive pain killer. In this case, Harry's family physician urged him to seek out pain clinic treatment. But Harry kept thinking that the headaches would go away and that each trip to the hospital would be the last. For him, it was easier and more convenient to take a powerful shot which instantly eased the pain than to drive to another town for weekly visits to the pain clinic. Harry didn't realize it, but his dependence on the pain shots was growing, and this drastic remedy was doing little to give him any real control over his pain. When his wife urged him to try other options, he would respond with an aggressive retort, such as "You don't know what this feels like." She responded assertively, not because she blamed or judged her husband, but because the way he was handling the pain made her feel anxious and fearful for him. She made it clear that while she could not promise to put herself at his disposal every time he needed to go to the emergency room, she would be glad to arrange her schedule so that she could accompany him to the pain clinic once a week. Her concern and the reasonableness of her offer finally got through to her husband, and he agreed to try out the pain management program.

Assertiveness and Anger

Being angry is a natural by-product of having chronic pain. There is a lot to be angry about. Your health and well-being have been taken from you, and that loss alone is enough to make anyone furious. It can also be aggravating to find that other people don't always understand what you are going through. At times even your family can seem indifferent. Maybe your doctor wants you to see a psychologist for your pain, and you feel angry because you imagine that he thinks your pain is all in your head. On top of being angry, you hurt, and your angry outbursts only make the pain worse.

The problem is not that you're angry. The problem is that you allow the anger to build up inside of you to the point that you have unproductive and damaging outbursts that interfere with coping. Why can't you let your anger out before you explode? What makes you keep it in?

Many people have problems expressing their anger. You may have been given lots of messages as a child that you were supposed to be nice, kind, and sweet, and that angry emotions were not tolerated. One client, who feared expressing her anger, recalled being sent to her room as a little girl after she lashed out at her mother. The message was "don't talk back." So she quickly learned to bottle up her anger in an effort to be a good child and avoid punishment. Years later she realized that the same message had been carried over to other situations in her life, and that her immediate reaction was often to hide her anger rather than learn to deal with it in assertive ways. When she hurt her back lifting groceries out of the trunk of her car, and the painful spasms stayed with her for months at a time, she felt that her only recourse was to keep her anger and frustration inside. If she let it out for even a minute she would be a "bad" person. But the more tightly she held her anger in, the more frequent were her blowups at her family.

With counseling, she realized that her mother's old message about anger was no longer useful. She had the power to exercise other options in her life. She could let her feelings and needs be known in assertive ways that didn't undermine her relationships.

The point here is not to debate *why* you were given the messages you were—not to analyze your mother's personality, or your father's temperament. Your task is to accept the fact that you were given messages, discover how these rules about conflict affect your pain control skills, throw out the unhelpful rules, and replace them with new, and effective strategies for conflict resolution.

Dr. Nelson Hendler, in *How to Cope With Chronic Pain*, says that productive ventilation of anger can be both a therapeutic release of tension and a sign of a healthy attitudinal change. It is unnatural for a person to remain smooth, calm, and unaffected by a chronic pain situation. But expressing your anger doesn't mean that you endlessly rage and "dump" your feelings. Instead of venting your feelings in thermonuclear bursts, you can learn to turn your anger into a motivational tool that will give you a charge of energy and control. Aggressive angry outbursts can have some very negative consequences:

- Outbursts of anger can alienate and isolate you from others. You put people on the defensive by judging, blaming, and accusing them.

- Outbursts can raise, rather than relieve, your anxiety levels.

- Aggressive anger can be an obstacle to problem solving. Afterwards, the problem still remains; now you have your anger *and* your problem.

Assertive handling of anger, which is the basis for effective conflict management, involves the following six steps:

Guidelines for Handling Anger Assertively

1. Do you really feel angry enough to want and need to work on the problem that caused your anger? Take a deep breath and listen to yourself for a minute.

   When Emma had a back spasm, her husband ignored her efforts to discuss how to reorganize the housework. She realized that she was angry and that the issue would not go away—she needed to deal with it. In another instance, Betty's husband had a busy day and forgot to pick up the laundry. Betty thought about her annoyance and let it go; the issue was not important enough to dwell on.

2. Pick an appropriate discussion time. If possible, arrange a time beforehand and describe the situation that you need to discuss. State the problem in a neutral manner.

   While cooking dinner, Emma asked her husband if later on that night they could set aside time to discuss the housework. She knew that he would be more relaxed later than he was right after he got home from work.

3. Avoid blaming, judging, and accusing the other person. Your blame-offensive will only breed a defensive counterattack.

   Emma accused her husband of being a lazy slob and the main reason that the house was always a mess. He responded by telling her that she'd always been a lousy housekeeper and continued to ignore her requests for change.

4. Make "I" statements about how you feel. Say "I'm feeling frustrated" rather than "You and your stupidity make me feel fed up." "I" statements rarely put people on the defensive, since they are statements of your own feelings rather than accusations regarding the other person's behavior. Feelings are not as debatable as behavior.

   Emma: I'm feeling frustrated and a little angry. My back pain makes it impossible for me to do all the things I used to do. Things are piling up around the house. I don't know how long this situation will continue, but the pain seems to be lessening now that I'm doing my exercises regularly.

5. Say what you need. Make your needs clear and specific. Don't say that you want the other person to "be more considerate" (this is too vague in that it does not specify behavior or time frame). Instead ask for help at a specific time or with a specific problem ("Please help me clear the table after dinner").

   Don't command the other person to feel differently ("You should stop being so cold to me"). This kind of statement assumes that you know what the other person is feeling, which can put him or her on the defensive. Rather than debate feelings, ask for different behavior ("Could we talk for a while before putting on the television?").

   Emma: I'd like to work out an agreeable housework solution with you so that in the meantime the dirt doesn't pile up. If you do the vacuuming and laundry, I'll still cook and dust and sort the clothes.

6. Allow people you're talking to time to respond. Practice good listening skills when they respond: look at them when they talk, don't interrupt until they say they are finished, and

acknowledge that you heard what they said (even though you may not agree with what they said). Here's what Emma's husband said and her response:

Husband: I feel frustrated, too. Not only is the housework piling up, but my boss is pressuring me to meet that deadline ahead of time. I've been preoccupied with my job.

Emma (acknowledging his situation): This is a tough time for both of us, since we're both under pressure.

Husband: I guess I'm willing to go along with your plan if we can let things slide a little this week.

By listening to each other, Emma and her husband worked through her anger, which could have erupted into a screaming match and left the dirty house still dirty. Instead, they were able to get to the problem-solving stage and reach an amicable agreement.

At first this process may seem stilted or unnatural to you, but you'll find that it becomes easier and more natural with practice. Talking this way is really a form of mutual respect and courtesy that can extend beyond your relationship with your family to become a valuable communication skill with friends and co-workers as well. But it is especially important to communicate well within the family during critical times of stress to insure that the family continues to work together.

Chronic pain is a stressor that can tear a family apart, or at least put a dent in how well it functions. When one family member is down and unable to work or perform his or her typical housework duties, the family's harmony is upset. Adjusting to a temporary or long-term change requires patience and flexibility on the part of each family member. It is natural that tensions build up and erupt while members adjust. During these times, you and your family must be able to talk to each other. What hope will you have of accommodating the demands that chronic pain can make if you shut each other out in anger and fear?

Remember that anger is a healthy and natural sign of adjusting to change. But how you express your anger is the key. Handling your anger assertively can bring you closer to your loved ones, rather than isolate you from them. Your physical suffering has already set you apart, and the lonely times it brings are hard enough. Anything you do to encourage intimacy will help you to endure the pain.

Resisting Change

Resistance can be defined as all those behaviors in a system that are obstacles to success. Your system includes you, your family, and the agency or institution that you are using for treatment. Overcoming resistance can be a tricky problem, since resistance takes on many forms that can initially confuse and frustrate both you and your health care professional.

Here are some typical resistant behaviors that you may find yourself doing:

- Being chronically late for appointments or not showing up

- Making repeated excuses for not accomplishing assigned tasks

- Expressing continued confusion about the tasks you are to do and your purpose in being at the clinic or treatment center

- Being excessively passive (such as by expecting others to do everything for you)

- Forgetting to take medications on an appropriate schedule

- Blaming everyone else but yourself

Resistant behaviors in your family may include these:

- Blaming all of the family's problems on the pain itself

- Denying any associated problems in the family that result from pain (such as increased stress at home)

- Making statements such as "There's nothing really wrong here" or "If only someone could find a cure, then our lives would be back in order and the way they used to be"

- Being unsupportive of the pain sufferer's attempts to comply with medical or psychological interventions

Part of your family's unsupportiveness may be demonstrated by family members not involving themselves in any way in your healing exercises. Ted's progress in his biofeedback program was slow and unproductive, partly because of family demands that prevented him from finding quiet time at home to practice his relaxation training. When he finally discussed this situation with his family, he learned that his children thought he had to practice because he was "crazy." He had them listen to and try out the tapes, and their resulting understanding helped to increase his success with the exercises significantly. It also provided some quality family time together.

If you read through these behaviors and find yourself getting upset or feeling that the description is an unsympathetic or inaccurate picture of your situation, please realize that *resistance is a natural part of any effort to change.* It is okay for you to experience some resistance. After all, you are being asked to change your habits, attitudes, and behaviors, and who wouldn't feel at least some resistance to such an enormous demand? In their book *Mastering Resistance,* Carol Anderson and Susan Stewart explain that people often seek therapy in response to changes that they do not like or have not adjusted to. If a person must adjust to something new (such as living with chronic pain and its limitations) and is having trouble doing so, it is natural for that person to resist doctors' and others' efforts to change things even more.

Many people perceive that seeking help for pain means that they have to give up all control and independence. Most people also have a natural tendency to resist being influenced, and the implication that they cannot solve their own problems may lead them to resist the interventions of a health care professional. A fear that they might be labeled "crazy" or told that their pain is "all in their head" can encourage feelings of hostility and defensiveness.

Accepting change and adopting new ideas can be scary, especially when you may not have accepted your chronic pain situation in the first place. So it is natural to feel upset, particularly if you feel that you've been passed from doctor to doctor, and perhaps finally referred to a psychologist or psychiatrist. When you do feel yourself becoming angry and resistant, your first step should be to realize and accept that these are natural reactions. You're in a difficult situation, and your anger and resistance are simply an attempt to maintain control over yourself and your environment.

Your second step is to accept the fact that you have a chronic condition and that you'll have to make some necessary adjustments to help you live as fully as possible.

The last step is for you to take responsibility for your recovery. You are in control. You are the *only one* who can control your pain. To take control, you will have to adhere to your exercise regimen faithfully, make your appointments, take your medications properly, change your negative thinking, and so on. You will have to find the time to practice new skills and the strength to carry on, even when a voice inside tells you that it's hopeless and that nothing will work.

Yes, it's natural to resist. You have been disappointed by doctors and tried things that didn't pan out. You are tired of hurting. But be assured that the self-regulation strategies outlined in this book (and practiced in pain centers all over the country) do work. You need to give the process your time and commitment.

For the Health Care Professional: Decreasing Resistant Behaviors

Resistance can be one of the most difficult obstacles for a health care professional to overcome. What looks like anger and hostility when you first meet a patient can actually be a mask for feelings of intimidation, low self-esteem, and resistance to change. How you handle those first few sessions in a pain management program can be critical in determining whether a patient will attempt to work with you or continue on with his or her doctor-shopping odyssey.

In an article in the journal *Professional Psychology,* Dr. Doug DeGood outlines the following steps for a health care professional to take in diffusing the anger and hostility characteristic of resistance.

1. *Attempt to immediately diffuse a patient's fears about the work you will do with him or her.* Directly address the problem by saying, "You may have some concerns about being sent to talk with me." Reassure the patient that chronic physical problems inevitably produce changes in one's life, and that coping with those changes will be the focus of your concern.

2. *If emotional issues are present, avoid premature efforts to "psychologize" the patient's symptoms.* Any psychological interventions are likely to be rejected unless you have taken the time to establish your credibility as a professional who understands the person's medical problems. DeGood emphasizes that good rapport-building with medical patients requires allowing them to relate to you via their physical complaints.

3. *Try to shape adequate beliefs rather than challenge your patients' misconceptions.* Patients often cling to a belief in a specific "cure" or other myth about their physical condition. Particularly important to pain management programs is the quite common belief that a disorder must be less than legitimate if it can be in any way self-regulated. Try to help patients expand their beliefs, rather than challenge them directly. Help patients move away from focusing on a specific corrective procedure toward a broader rehabilitation plan.

4. *Present self-regulation strategies (or other psychological behavioral interventions) in a positive fashion, rather than as last resort options.* Patients will be more likely to comply with a program if they are convinced that it is a treatment of choice rather than a desperation move. When the medical options have been exhausted, doctors all too often communicate their frustration with a patient. Subsequent attempts to introduce self-regulation strategies may be received by the patient with minimal expectations and equal frustration.

5. *Require the patient to make a meaningful commitment to a self-regulation program.* This requires patients to understand that they must choose whether to actively participate. Adherence to home practice schedules, self-monitoring, and physical exercise and activity are sabotaged when patients feel coerced into participation. You may need to suggest that patients wait "until they are more ready," especially if there are drug addiction problems or underlying psychopathology.

6. *Foster realistic expectations by specifying feasible outcome goals.* Encourage patients to take a broader perspective than the expectation of a "quick fix" from a self-regulation program. Help them understand that they can anticipate only gradual improvement, with fluctuations—but that the long-term benefits will outweigh by far the lack of instant gratifications. Explain that the skills they learn will last a lifetime, regardless of their pain condition.

7. *Integrate self-regulation strategies with other medical treatment.* Clarify the value of ongoing medical interventions as part of a patient's recovery process. Do not encourage patients to abandon other efforts, since this may set up the behavioral treatment for potential failure. Conversely, if inappropriate medication use is a problem, help the patient understand that over-reliance on medication will only sabotage the benefits of self-regulation.

8. *Whenever possible, include a spouse or other significant persons in discussion of self-regulation strategies.* Self-regulation programs can be confusing to family members. It is important to enlist their understanding and support early on in order to help reinforce learning. Family dynamics that encourage passivity, helplessness, and other problems cannot be dealt with in one or two sessions, but their presence may signal you to encourage family therapy in conjunction with the self-regulation program.

Further Reading

Anderson, C., and S. Stewart. 1983. *Mastering Resistance: A Practical Guide to Family Therapy.* New York: Guilford Press.

Bower, S. A., and G. H. Bower. 1991. *Asserting Yourself.* Reading, MA: Addison-Wesley.

Butler, P. 1992. *Self-Assertion for Women.* San Francisco: Harper Collins

DeGood, D. 1983. "Reducing medical patients' reluctance to participate in psychological therapies: the initial session." *Professional Psychology: Research and Practice, 14: 570–579.*

McKay, M., M. Davis, and P. Fanning. 1995. *Messages, The Communication Skills Book.* 2nd ed. Oakland, CA: New Harbinger Publications, Inc.

Meichenbaum, D. 1977. *Cognitive Behavior Modification.* New York: Plenum Press.

8

Vocational Rehabilitation and Chronic Pain

Anyone who has tried to work while suffering from chronic pain will tell you how difficult it is to meet the daily requirements of a regular job. Obviously, a physical laborer who regularly lifts and hauls will be critically hampered by chronic pain. But even a sedentary office worker's productivity will be affected. Research shows that people who have suffered a disabling injury on or off the job exhibit evidence of greater absenteeism, decreased productivity, and increased stress due to pressure from management and co-workers to adequately perform their jobs.

In the event of an acute injury, medical advice is straightforward—rest, appropriate medications, and perhaps traction or physical therapy. But when the pain drags on for many months and you feel that you're unable to return to your job, other issues come into play. You may begin to wonder if you will ever again do the type of work that you used to do. Your family relationships may suffer from added financial and emotional burdens. You may feel lethargic and depressed from lack of activity. Should you return to your old job? Should you attempt to do the same amount of work for the same number of hours? What if you work in a warehouse and your doctor recommends that you not lift over twenty pounds? Or what if you have been doing high-pressure work that you know has been causing or aggravating your headache pain? At this point, you find yourself confronted by a complex set of decisions that must be made about your capabilities, limitations, and desire to return to your former place of employment.

This chapter is about decision making concerning your job, career directions, and career attitudes. Through using the vocational rehabilitation structure already set up in your state, plus a step-by-step decision-making process, you will be able to clarify the issues confronting you and make a decision that you can live with.

Kathleen had a very successful experience working out her back problem with her job. She is a personnel supervisor for a large and busy company. The job requires hours of driving from job site to job site across the state. She developed her back problem after thirteen years of service, and it looked as though her ability to do the job, which includes some lifting along with all the driving, would be seriously threatened.

It took Kathleen a while to figure out how she could do her job and cope with back spasms so painful that there were times when she could not stand up. Persistence on her part and a good attitude on the part of her employers paid off in the long run. Her company allowed her to take time off for regular visits to a pain clinic for counseling and biofeedback sessions. She learned stretching and strengthening exercises for her back, which she practiced daily. She learned to relax during the day by mentally rehearsing several relaxation strategies. She patiently negotiated with her company to rearrange some of the workload, and she took care to demonstrate to them her commitment and energy for her work. Now Kathleen is back on the job, and although she has modified her work schedule, she feels that she is producing as much as she did before her injury. She is also extremely pleased that neither she nor her company lost faith in her ability to cope and work it out.

Kathleen's story is representative of the typical injured worker in this country. Most disabled workers want to return to work. Moreover, if they are encouraged and counseled early in their recovery process, their chances of returning to their jobs or at least to a job, are significantly higher. What can you do to promote your return to work?

You already know what to do for your acute pain. You must follow your doctor's orders carefully, take the needed time off from work, get sufficient rest, and take the appropriate medications. You have to allow yourself time to heal.

When you do go back to work, do not try to perform at the same rate of speed that you maintained before your injury. If your employers expect you to resume your usual amount of heavy lifting, talk to your boss and work out a system that will allow you to do as much work as possible, but without pushing yourself to the point of potential reinjury. Carefully follow the rules of good body mechanics (explained in chapter 3). Copy the rules below and post them near your work site or desk. Share them with your boss or co-workers.

- Push, don't pull.

- Get help.

- Keep objects close to your body when lifting; lift with the large muscles in your legs, not with the small muscles in your back.

- Assume a broad base of support when lifting and a proper pelvic tilt—feet flat on the floor and slightly apart; pelvis tucked up with your back rounded.

- Pay attention to your stress levels. Do deep breathing and other relaxation exercises that you enjoy regularly throughout the day. Don't let the muscular tension build up!

Compensation and Chronic Pain

If you are ready to return to work after your injury but have an on-the-job injury that is currently being litigated, you should check with your attorney first to see if your case will be undermined by your return. The word "litigation" means any legal suit brought for worker's compensation, social security disability, negligence, and so on. In other words, you need to ask your lawyer if the desired outcome of your suit will be affected by your ability to return to work.

It is common for people to sue their employer for compensation when an injury happens at work and they are unable to return to their previous job or to any other job that requires the same kind of work. Sam was a laborer in a rural western Virginia rock quarry whose injury left him physically unable to find other work at a comparable salary in his isolated area. The compensation he received from his former company was enough to provide for his family while Sam decided what new career to pursue. He thought through the possibilities of relocating to an area with more employment opportunities. This is how the system is supposed to work.

But sometimes the compensation system serves to reduce motivation to return to work. Sam's compensation checks are almost as much as the salary he received for the hard work of his old full-time job. If he continues to blame his inability to find new work on his old job injury, it's more than likely that he will continue to receive worker's compensation benefits for years. After worker's comp runs out, or a settlement is reached, Sam may go on to apply for social security disability, leaving him in a position where he may never have to work again. At first glance this prospect may sound ideal, but Sam has actually been having a hard time adjusting to his new role as homemaker, rather than breadwinner. He feels awkward and depressed, and his emotions add to his stress, making it even harder for him to begin the slow climb to recovery and better functioning. He's dissatisfied with his current life, but he's also literally being paid not to work. He finds that the pride and meaning he once found in his job are hard to replace, leaving him feeling "useless" or like a "drain on the family." He may also experience fear about trying to return to work, even if his pain subsides, since he has not tested himself in a real work setting. He may be afraid that if he tries to go back to work, he will fail at the job and he will be fired by his company with no benefits at all. Many people like Sam also find that they are angry at the "system" or perhaps at an old employer who now seems only to want to get them "off the payroll." The anger builds, perhaps leading to vindictiveness that is then inappropriately directed at family and friends.

Sam is one of hundreds of thousands of people caught up in this bind. It is easy to blame the system for providing ready cash without accountability. It is also easy to blame the workers themselves for taking advantage of the situation and possibly prolonging their disability. Yet, the compensation system is a highly complex one, and the problems it addresses are equally complicated. Blaming the system will only make it more difficult to solve the real problems of pain and work. How does Sam break out of this downward spiral? How do you assess your own feelings about work?

This is the time to take an honest look at your desire to return to work. No amount of cajoling from your spouse, advice, doctoring, or nursing will get you back to work if you don't want to be there. The following exercise is designed to help you assess the value of work to you and where it falls on your list of priorities.

Clarifying Your Job Values

This exercise will help you assess the value you place on your current (or most recent job) and see it in perspective with other values you hold in life. Write down your answers to the following questions; try not to debate or qualify your responses, but simply record them as they occur to you.

1. What are three things I value about my current (or most recent) job?

    1. _____

    _____

    2. _____

    _____

    3. _____

    _____

2. What are three things about my job I would change? (Not including problems with disability)

    1. _____

       _____

    2. _____

       _____

    3. _____

       _____

3. What job or jobs have I enjoyed in the past? (Include any childhood or high school experiences)

    _____

    _____

    _____

    What did I enjoy most about those jobs?

    _____

    _____

    _____

4. What kind of job or jobs did you want as a child, teenager, or college student or what career did you always think you would end up in?

    _____

    _____

    _____

5. What activities do you enjoy now? List at random, as they occur to you, all of the things that you like to do in your life, including job, family, church, and so on. You don't have to fill in all the blanks; just write until you can't think of anything else. Don't forget to include your hobbies. Then after you're done, rank your list by putting a number beside each item indicating which you value the most, second most, and so on:

    _____   _____

    _____   _____

    _____   _____

_____   _____

_____   _____

6. Take some time to ask yourself these questions:

    Where did you place your current or most recent job on your hierarchy? Did it even make the list? What about past jobs? What does this list tell you about the values you place on the activities in your life? Were there any surprises for you? What does this list tell you about the amount of time you spend doing the things that are most satisfying to you? Are you willing to make changes in your life so that you can do more things that are satisfying to you? If your current or most recent job is highly valued on your list, are you happy to continue giving it top priority in your life?

7. What are the obstacles to returning to work for you? Make a list of reasons why you feel you cannot return to work now:

_____

_____

_____

_____

_____

In this section, many people list problems that can be solved with more education or information. Listing the specific obstacles provides you with a starting point to begin gathering the help or information you need to return. Do you need help with the fear of returning to work? Do you need to plan your return to work in a gradual way? Do you need to have your work specially arranged for your new limitations? Do you need retraining or more education if you can't return to an old job?

You may find it helpful to talk out your reactions to this exercise with a counselor or a friend. Sharing your thoughts will help you begin problem-solving about the next steps to take. Remember, you always have options. Even though you can readily identify obstacles to returning to work, working with a vocational rehabilitation specialist can help you find ways around the obstacles. For example, you do not have to return to the exact same job, or face compensation and unemployment for the rest of your life. If you have decided that you value your present (or most recent) job and you want to stick with it, there are ways of getting help with reducing your fears about returning. Try the problem-solving sequence if you find yourself in this camp. If you wish to change jobs, skip to the next section.

Problem-Solving Sequence

1. First, make sure you have done the preceding exercise.

2. If you are comfortable talking to your boss, go to him or her and explain your desire to return, making it clear that you can continue doing your old job with a few modifications. If you can't work with your boss, then find yourself an advocate. You can do this by either contacting a counselor at your state's vocational rehabilitation agency, or by getting a letter

from your doctor stating that she or he feels that you can resume employment with some minor modifications to the job. Explain to your doctor that you are clear about your decision to stay on your job and that you want to go back.

3. Get help in assessing what you can and can't do on the job. Find a physical therapist, occupational therapist, or rehabilitation/biomedical engineer through your state vocational rehabilitation agency. Invite that person to come to your work site to help you find ways to modify your job to make the work easier and help prevent reinjury. Here are some examples of common work site modifications (also see chapter 13 for other specific suggestions about work simplification and ergonomics):

   • Reassignment to a less strenuous job

   • Getting help with difficult tasks

   • Working longer hours with more frequent breaks

   • Getting a special chair with good lumbar support

   • Changing the height of a work table

   • Rearranging your work space so that you don't have to reach or getting a device for reaching for distant objects

   • Clustering items that you use regularly around your workplace so that you don't have to get up and down repeatedly

   • Finding a suitable cart to help you push or pull items

   • Finding a stool to prop up your foot when standing for long periods

   You may also need to have your doctor write a prescription to be able to see these rehabilitation professionals so that your insurance will cover the cost of their services.

4. Write up a list of changes you would like to make and discuss the list with your boss. Introduce your requests by saying, "I still want to work for you and I feel that I can be a productive worker with a few minor changes in my work environment."

   If you feel that any pending litigation will be an obstacle in solving your work problems, then wait until your suit is settled. Discuss the situation with your attorney.

Bob and Tom

Bob, aged forty-nine, sustained a severe injury to both of his legs while working at a construction job. He underwent extensive surgical reconstruction of both legs that left him with obvious difficulty in mobility and a severe amount of constant, chronic pain.

After several years of recuperation provided for by worker's compensation, he made an important decision. Even though he had learned how to manage his pain, he knew that it was not going to go away. He could sit at home with it, or he could try to resume full-time employment and be in the same constant pain at work. One factor that swayed him was the thought that he would have more distractions from the pain at work than he would at home. He missed using his expertise as well as the companionship of his co-workers.

Bob made a decision to go back, and took the initiative to get himself rehired. He has been working successfully at this former occupation now for over a year, even though his physician had rated him as over 50 percent disabled in his ability to perform his former job. Bob will tell you flatly that he hurts tremendously, all the time, every day. But working does distract him, and for long periods he simply doesn't think about his pain.

Tom is in his thirties and has a back injury from lifting heavy produce in his supermarket job. Tom has been through back surgery and pain control techniques, seen a psychiatrist, taken medication, and made several other futile attempts to control his pain and get back to work. He has gotten good advice on how to cope and adapt, but Tom always finds reasons why the suggestions won't work. He finally agreed to attend a daily support and educational group at a hospital. Tom had to drive an hour and a half to attend the group. When he got there he would become very anxious and spend his time in the group making gestures and complaining loudly about his pain. Then he would drive for an hour and a half to get home. Tom put in almost a full day's work participating in this group, but he couldn't see that the energy he was putting out in this context could be transferred to a real job.

Part of Tom's problem was that he was afraid of being reinjured. However, a larger part of the problem was that he was holding out for a cure, hoping that someone would find an answer to his pain. When Bob's doctor said, "You're always going to have pain," Bob began to view the pain as a new component to his life, one that he had to adjust to. Tom, on the other hand, refused to accept his pain, and so put his life on hold until the day when he would be cured.

The Department of Vocational Rehabilitation

If there is no compensation or litigation involved in your chronic pain situation and you want to get back to work, then here is another option. Apply to the department of vocational rehabilitation in your state. This service is available to all and is not a welfare program. You have already paid for this program out of your taxes. It is designed to help the injured worker resume gainful employment and it provides counselors and administrators for you to talk with about your employment options. Sometimes this service also provides money for you to get retraining in another field.

Note that people who work for the state rehabilitation agency in your area are working for you—not for the insurance company that covers worker's compensation claims, or the insurance that your business uses. If you do happen to meet a rehabilitation counselor who works for your employer's insurance company, keep in mind that this person's primary goal is to get you back to *any* full-time work. Any suggestions that this person makes may not be the best option for you. The state rehabilitation counselor works for a neutral agency, one that is interested in *your* goals, not the company's. She or he will work with you and your doctor to make a realistic assessment of the extent of your disability, your career goals, and your training or educational needs. The goal is to help you decide what choices will work best for you. Also, note that since this is a state and federally funded program, you can get the same service in every state.

What Services Do You Get?

1. Physical capacities evaluation. This is a test of major motor strength—your ability to lift, bend, stoop, and twist—over a period of time. The counselor goes over this test with you, and then works with you and your doctor to determine whether you can find a new line of work that will fit your physical and educational capacities.

2. Developing a rehabilitation program. You and the counselor will work out an individualized written rehabilitation program for you to follow and mark your progress.

3. *Contacting potential employers.* If there is work available within your community, the counselor will assist you in contacting potential employers and help you come up with a strategy for job placement. As the client, you will be responsible for going to the prearranged job interviews and getting your new job. The counselor can accompany you, if needed, to help explain to the potential employer your physical capacities and the employer's potential liability if you should have a reinjury. Your counselor will also explain to the employer that disabled employees who return to the workforce are, as a rule, highly motivated workers. Evidence shows a lower absenteeism rate among previously injured people once they get back to work.

4. *Job retraining.* If the counselor determines that you cannot return to the same type of work you were doing before your injury and that you need retraining, state agencies may provide funds for job retraining in your area. The state purchases vocational training services from private businesses, industry, colleges, and universities.

5. *Counseling.* Your counselor is available to talk over any difficulties you may be encountering in trying to make a job change. He or she understands the difficulties of trying to cope with chronic pain and working and can provide support and suggestions that can help you with this transition.

Other Rehabilitation Resources

In 1984, President Reagan's Committee on Employment of People with Disabilities established the Job Accommodation Network to provide free information and guidance about functional limitations to disabled people who may need some accommodation in the workplace. These accommodations can assist you in returning to work or continuing to work in your present job. If they cannot assist you they will make referrals to appropriate organizations. They can be reached in the U.S. at (800) JAN-7234 and in Canada at (800) JAN-2262.

The Americans with Disabilities Act was passed and signed into law in 1990 to give civil rights protection to individuals with disabilities. It prohibits discrimination in all job practices including hiring, firing, applications, promotions, compensation, training, layoffs, and so on. Employers are required by this law to make accommodations for employee's with known disabilities, within certain limits. The Job Accommodation Network also sponsors a toll-free line for information on your general rights as set forth in the Americans with Disabilities Act at (800) ADA-9675.

The National Institute on Disability and Rehabilitation Research reports that there are many types of rehabilitation programs encouraging return to work. In addition to the federally funded public rehabilitation program, larger companies employ industrial medical teams to treat and counsel disabled workers. Labor unions have adopted more comprehensive stances for worker protection. Some are lobbying for additional rehabilitation assurances and sponsoring Projects With Industry (PWI) programs that encourage disabled workers to return to jobs. Some employers offer company rehabilitation offices, where they counsel injured employees, educate supervisors and other staff (in an effort to eliminate attitudinal barriers), and initiate work site modifications.

Private rehabilitation programs also provide return-to-work service for business and industry. These programs employ a trained rehabilitation counselor to act as a liaison between the disabled person and the community and to involve the worker with a multidisciplinary team of professionals from the community. Many private rehabilitation clinics also offer a program called "Work Hardening." This program operates on the principle of early intervention. The disabled worker is sent to the program soon after appropriate medical treatment. The staff works with the client on a daily basis to increase muscle strength and flexibility, improve body mechanics and proper work habits, increase confidence and self-esteem, and adapt to helpful devices or modified work sites. Consult your yellow pages under "Rehabilitation Services" or "Vocational Services" to find similar programs in your area.

In addition to state vocational rehabilitation agencies, many colleges and universities offer low-cost or no-cost career exploration programs for individuals wishing to change careers. These programs can provide invaluable guidance in choosing an appropriate alternative career path, and you don't necessarily have to be associated with the university in order to use this service. Another point about these services: they are also used by thousands of American workers who decide after twenty to thirty years on the same job that they want to switch careers and embark on an entirely different direction. Instead of considering yourself an injured worker who is unable to resume your former occupation, try seeing yourself as one of the adventurous ones who is setting out to find a more suitable and exciting career. What have you got to lose? What, if not your boredom, sense of isolation, and reduced standard of living?

If you're on worker's comp or social security and would like to go back to some form of work activity, then consider volunteer work. This can also be a useful strategy if you've been out of the workforce long enough to be unsure of your physical capabilities. There are an infinite number of ways to volunteer, and most nonprofit groups have a desperate need for help. You can look into local hospitals, church groups, youth groups, senior citizens groups, the Red Cross, and so on. Remember that most jobs in this country are located through contacts with other people, and not through the classified ads. Volunteer work is rewarding in itself, but it can also lead to a paying job.

A Warning

The use of drugs and alcohol are a major contributor to the lack of motivation and the inability of many injured workers to resume full-time work. Your condition has already placed you in a situation where the potential for drug abuse is extremely high. It has also probably left you alone for many hours during the day while others are at work or school. Many people in this type of situation let their boredom lead them to turn on the television and drink. Drugs and alcohol kill motivation. If you begin to suspect that you may be drinking too much or taking too many drugs then you probably are, and should seek professional guidance and counseling.

Preparing to Return to Work

1. Before returning to work, cut back on medications that make you drowsy or impair your ability to react rapidly. Be sure to consult your doctor about any changes in medication.

2. Be prepared for new employers to ask questions about your injury and their potential liability if you are injured again.

3. In filling out applications, make sure that you state your injury. While withholding information about a previous injury may initially help you obtain employment, if you are injured on your new job and your employer learns of your original injury, be prepared to be fired. Prepare a statement about any limitations or special needs you now have. Being honest about your injury will be beneficial in the long run.

Further Reading

Bolles, R. N. 1996. *What Color is Your Parachute?: A Practical Manual for Job Hunters and Career Changers.* Berkeley, CA: Ten Speed Press.

Bolles, R. N. 1991. *Job Hunting Tips for the So-called Handicapped or People Who Have Disabilities: A Supplement to What Color is Your Parachute?* Berkeley, CA: Ten Speed Press.

Jones, T. 1980. *Employee Assistance Programs in Industry.* Phoenix, AZ: Do It Now Foundation.

Klarreich, S. H. 1990. *Work Without Stress.* New York: Brunner/Mazel Publishers.

O'Hara, V. 1995. *Wellness at Work.* Oakland, CA: New Harbinger Publications, Inc.

Contacts

National Rehabilitation Information Center (800) 346-2742

American Association of Disabled Persons (407) 880-9232

Job Accommodation Network, U.S. (800) JAN-7234, Canada (800) JAN-2262

Americans with Disabilities Act Information (800) ADA-9675

Online ADA Information Can Be Found At:

http://www.public.iastate.edu/~sbilling/ada.html

Online Information for the National Rehabilitation Information Center Is At:

http://www.naric.com/naric/home.html

9

Pain Centers and Support Groups

It is easy to be confused about what to do and where to go for help when you suffer from chronic pain. Your friends will tell you one thing; you'll read about another; and all of it sounds plausible. But chronic pain is a complex subject. So much research still needs to be done to explain the mechanisms behind it and validate the treatments for it, that you are bound to be confused by the variety of information you hear. One thing is certain—if you sustain an injury, your first step should be to go to a medical doctor for a complete checkup. Your doctor should evaluate you to see that your acute or chronic injury does not involve any related problems. For example, your doctor can rule out a tumor as a cause for your headaches. It's preferable to play it safe through a conventional medical check initially, rather than relying on hearsay or one particular treatment. For example, hypnosis and chiropractic treatments for pain relief can be extremely effective but they should always follow a thorough medical workup.

After you have been medically examined and feel satisfied that you and your doctor understand as much as possible about your pain, then you are free to try any number of other treatments. You may choose to try several simultaneously, or you may settle on just one. In any case, you will have made an educated decision about what is right for you.

At this time there are 1,500 to 2,000 pain treatment facilities in the United States. If you live in or near a big city, you probably have several to choose from. The increasing number of places that will treat your pain makes it important for you know what to look for in a pain center. In this chapter we look at the characteristics of a multidisciplinary pain center and discuss the pros and cons of outpatient versus inpatient settings. We also examine another resource that many pain patients use—the support group.

Multidisciplinary Pain Centers

Pain treatment has been a hot topic for years. So many people have chronic pain that specialty groups, private centers, and pain clinics supported by academic institutions have sprung up everywhere. There are a lot of people professing skill at "curing" pain—which means you need to exercise caution in choosing a center that is right for you and your situation.

Medicine traditionally excels at treating symptoms, not necessarily the whole person. Medical personnel are trained and accustomed to "fix" the pain, or at least attempt to find a cure for it. As new research and attitudes about pain evolve, health care professionals have increasingly sought to enlarge this traditional medical approach by examining emotions and the mind/body interaction with pain. Neither approach is adequate solely in and of itself. But most experts agree that the best approach is a combination of the two, a blending of physical and psychological therapies that encompasses the whole person.

Chronic pain specialists suggest the following criteria to evaluate the adequacy of pain centers:

1. A pain center should recognize the complexity of chronic pain; its disruptive effect on your emotional, social, and vocational life; depression and behavioral changes possibly involved; and the questionable usefulness of surgical procedures.

2. The complexity of the problem requires a comprehensive therapeutic program, combining medical and psychosocial methods to deal with potential underlying physiological states. The program should train you to shake off the dependency and passivity that often accompany chronic pain in order to regain control of the pain and your life.

3. The full-time director of the center, usually a physician, should support this comprehensive approach and be certified in one of the specialties involved in diagnosis and treatment of chronic pain.

4. A staff of professionals trained in other forms of treatment included in a comprehensive program should be available full-time. These generally include a clinical psychologist, physical therapist, registered nurse, certified biofeedback therapist, vocational counselor, and nutritionist. Other kinds of practitioners may also be involved such as social workers, occupational therapists, massage therapists, acupuncturists, and chiropractors.

5. The center should be professionally qualified to review your medical records and tests, perform additional tests when appropriate for diagnostic purposes, do physical examinations, and set appropriate goals for treatment.

6. The program should be able to provide the following treatment services:

   • Drug reduction or elimination as well as proper management of narcotics and tranquilizers

   • Physical therapy and exercise

   • Psychosocial therapy through individual and/or group work

   • Exercises with or without biofeedback to teach relaxation and reduce stress

   • Behavior therapy and/or cognitive therapy for patient and family, to coach you out of your pain behavior and cycles of negative thinking

   • Vocational counseling and rehabilitation

   • A research program directed toward improving treatment and measuring its effectiveness

   • An admission policy that requires referral from a physician who should be kept informed of your condition, consulted, and advised about recommended posttreatment care

Some experts elaborate on these criteria by advising that people should avoid any overly optimistic doctor who advocates that one form of treatment or instrument will end a pain problem. They also advise against using a doctor or center that is noncommunicative, prescribes habituating drugs and routinely distributes them to you without question, or immediately advocates surgery or "cutting out" nerves. Dr. Nelson Hendler, a prominent researcher in the field, cautions that a prospective patient should be wary of anyone who makes exaggerated claims of success or prescribes a single type of treatment for all types of pain. He suggests that people seek out centers with academic affiliations, as these centers tend to have greater access to current research.

The Commission on Accreditation of Rehabilitation Facilities (CARF) has been surveying and accrediting chronic pain programs throughout the country. The Commission currently groups centers into those with inpatient services only, outpatient services only, and those with a combination of both. For a free list of approved programs, write to the CARF Report, 2500 North Pantano Road, Tuscon, Arizona 85715 or call (520) 325-1044 ext. 150. You can also purchase their manual on guidelines for program accreditation. The CARF guidelines are still not fully used throughout the country, so it is difficult to judge a program solely by whether it has been approved by CARF. However, you can get a good idea of the industry standards that CARF has established for pain centers to follow. And if you are an employer looking for a good program for your employees, you may find it easier to obtain insurance coverage for an accredited program, although there is no guarantee that this will be the case.

Another organization, the American Academy of Pain Management (AAPM) also accredits pain programs of all types and has begun keeping a national pain databank of the treatment outcomes of the participating centers. You can write AAPM at: AAPM, 13947 Mono Way, Suite A, Sonora, CA 95370 or call (209) 533-9744.

Inpatient and Outpatient Centers

Many inpatient and outpatient pain treatment centers work on the principle of reducing or eliminating negative pain behaviors and replacing them with positive, healthy behaviors. The basic idea is that learned pain behaviors such as excessive groaning, complaining, or lethargy can be unlearned. This does not mean that the underlying basis for your pain is questioned, either from an organic or psychological point of view. The principle simply means that there are other reinforcers in your environment that encourage or discourage you to respond to your pain in different ways.

Families can be unwitting reinforcers of pain behavior. Consider the case of John and his wife Cathy. Cathy learned early to attend to John's every pain complaint with an abundance of sympathy, food, and suggestions that he go to bed. But a time came when John needed to get out of bed and begin a gradual exercise program. At this point, the reinforcer of bed only served to weaken his muscles further and contribute to his immobility and depression. At the pain center, Cathy learned to encourage John to do his exercises and to ignore whatever protests he made.

In some cases, a sufferer may unconsciously be "using" his or her pain to get a "secondary gain" from other family members. If he or she has been feeling neglected, the pain may seem to be the only viable tool to get attention. This was the situation with John and Cathy. Cathy learned at the pain center to pay attention to John's positive activities, such as his carpentry, and shift the focus away from his pain and complaining. John learned that he could get love and support from doing rather than from being in pain.

Both inpatient and outpatient programs can teach you to understand your pain behaviors, and set up contingencies in your environment that reinforce healthy behavior. Here are some typical simple reinforcers:

- Praise and attention for accomplishments

- Rewards for completing exercises (such as treating yourself to a whirlpool bath at the end of the session)

- Attention and support from family members who are encouraged to participate in your activities

- The replacement of negative attention by family members (such as nagging, threatening, or coercing, all of which can actually reinforce pain and disability) with positive forms of attention such as praise

Inpatient programs have a tighter control over all these contingencies because you are required to stay in or near the clinic for anywhere from ten days to three weeks, depending on the design of the program. The inpatient treatment team works with you daily and rigorously to identify and confront negative behavior and help you relearn positive behaviors as solidly as possible. The size of the staff and the amount of time involved can make these programs expensive. Some pain programs only admit patients to the hospital for detoxification, followed by outpatient treatment, which both reduces the overall cost and is generally more convenient for the patient.

In a typical outpatient program similar services are provided, but you do not stay at the clinic itself. After your initial visit, you are scheduled for follow-up visits over a period of from several weeks to a year or more, depending on your needs. Outpatient programs are less expensive and demanding and can ease you into a lifestyle change without disrupting your home or work environment.

The bottom line with whatever type of program you choose, however, is that any program will be useless if you do not transfer the skills you learn to your everyday life. Studies show that the successful cases from both types of programs are people who regularly use their skills. After completing a program, you should ask your doctor for a referral to health care professionals in your area who can provide you with continuing support and reinforcement.

Support Groups

The word support means just that—you get support from a group of people who have experiences similar to your own and can empathize with you. The use of a support group to help people manage a problem is not a new idea. One of the most well-known support groups is Alcoholics Anonymous, which helped to set the stardard for this type of coping tool in modern society.

There are many types of support groups. Some may be largely educational, while others may be purely social and unstructured. Strictly defined, a support group is primarily a gathering of sympathetic people who share coping strategies with each other. One of the main forms of support a group can provide is the feeling that you are wholly accepted, with whatever problems or limitations you may have. And as you feel accepted by others, you feel more accepting of yourself. The following are additional reasons that make support groups an extremely useful tool for coping with chronic pain:

1. You are with others who also suffer from chronic pain and can intuitively understand what you are going through. A common statement, often made in anger and frustration, is "You don't understand my pain because you haven't had chronic pain." That argument is usually dissolved very quickly in a group where all the members share the same experience.

2. Veteran members of the group who have coped with the experience of pain can identify the stages of denial and anger in dealing with a chronic condition and ease newer members through them.

3. A support group gives you a neutral place to express frustration, disappointment, and any other feelings you have about your experience. Sometimes it helps just to be away from your job, home, or hospital to discuss difficulties and gain perspective on your problems.

4. A support group can be psychoeducational; that is, you can learn how others cope. The group can be a place where you experiment with new behavior, such as role-playing assertive situations, handling conflicts, or practicing good listening skills.

Support groups give you a chance to get out and meet new people at little or no cost. They can bridge the gap between terminating therapy or medical counseling and being on your own—there is nothing so lonely as being in a great deal of pain and totally alone. This way you don't have to.

Sometimes pain groups are spontaneously formed when people see a need for such a group in the community. For example, there is a group of approximately eight members who have been meeting twice a month for three years and is completely voluntary and free of charge. David, a participant since the group started, feels that it has helped him immeasurably since he joined. "After I finished working with my therapist and doctor at a pain clinic, I felt an extreme sense of loss, as if I was left out in the cold with no one to support me. I learned about the group and have been going regularly. It's very reassuring to be with people who understand me and encourage me when things get tough."

Experts who run pain-coping groups know that people in pain can feel socially isolated and alienated. Support groups can provide a sense of social support that competes with this sense of alienation. Groups can include all ages, races, educational and social backgrounds, and are not time limited. Members are encouraged to participate in the group for as long as they feel they are benefiting, and can reenter the group at any time. The group leader, a therapist, helps to educate group members about chronic pain and facilitates group cohesion and confrontation. By confronting each other's myths about finding a "perfect cure" for their pain and other unhelpful beliefs, group members learn to accept their chronic pain and begin to integrate it into a new lifestyle and sense of self. The success of these groups proves that members eventually learn to stop talking about how much the pain hurts and start talking about coping.

For free information and help in setting up or locating a chronic pain support group in your area, write to:

American Chronic Pain Association
P.O. Box 850
Rocklin, CA 95677
(916) 632-0922
Fax (916) 632-3280

National Chronic Pain Outreach Association, Inc.
4922 Hampden Lane
Bethesda, MD 20814
(301) 652-4948

You may find an organization or organizations in the following list for other information or support.

Organizations for Specific Pain Conditions

American Lupus Society
260 Maple Court, Suite 123
Ventura, CA 93003
(800) 558-0121

Arthritis Foundation
1314 Spring Street, NW
Atlanta, GA 30309
(800) 283-7800

Back Pain Hotline
Texas Back Institute
6800 W. Parker Road
Plano, TX 75095
(800) 247-2225

Crohn's and Colitis Foundation of America
386 Park Avenue South, 17th Floor
New York, NY 10016-8804
(800) 343-3637

Endometriosis Association
8585 N. 76th Place
Milwaukee, WI 53223
(800) 992-3636

Fibromyalgia Alliance of America
(formerly the Fibromyalgia Association of Central Ohio)
P.O. Box 21988
Columbus, OH 43221-0988
(614) 457-4222

Fibromyalgia Network
P.O. Box 31750
Tucson, AZ 85751-1750
Info Line: (520) 290-5508
Fax: (520) 290-5550
newsgroup: alt.med.fibromyalgia

Interstitial Cystitis Association
P.O. Box 1553
Madison Square Station
New York, NY 10159
(212) 979-6057

Irritable Bowel Self-Help Group
3332 Yonge Street
P.O. Box 94074

Toronto, Ontario
Canada M4N 3R1

The Lupus Foundation of America
4 Research Place, Suite 180
Rockville, MD 20850-3226
(800) 558-0121
(301) 670-9292
Fax: (301) 670-9486

National Headache Foundation
5252 Northwestern Avenue
Chicago, IL 60625
(800) 843-2256
Fax: (312) 907-6278

Reflex Sympathetic Dystrophy Syndrome Association of America
116 Haddon Avenue, Suite D
Haddonfield, NJ 08033
(609) 795-8845

Spondylitis Association of America
P.O. Box 5872
Sherman Oaks, CA 91413
(800) 777-8189
(818) 981-1616

Trigeminal Neuralgia Association
Claire W. Patterson, President
P.O. Box 340
Barengat Light, NJ 08006
(609) 361-1014

TMJ Foundation
P.O. Box 28275
San Diego, CA 92128-0275
(619) 592-9107

Other Organizations

American Association of Disabled Persons
(407) 880-9232

American Diabetes Association
(800) 232-3472

Courage Stroke Network
(800) 553-6321

National AIDS Information Clearinghouse
(800) 458-5231

National Association for Sickle Cell Disease, Inc.
(800) 421-8453

National Spinal Cord Injury Association
(800) 962-9629

National Stroke Association
(800) 787-6537

Organizations For Health Care Professionals

American Pain Society
4700 W. Lake Avenue
Glenview, IL 60025-1485
(708) 375-4715
Fax: (708) 375-4777
E-Mail: aps@dial.cic.net

International Association for the Study of Pain
909 NE 43rd Street, Suite 306
Seattle, WA 98105-6020
(206) 547-6409
Fax: (206) 547-1703
E-Mail: IASP@locke.hs.washington.edu

American Academy of Pain Management
139747 Mono Way, Suite A
Sonora, CA 95370
(209) 533-9744

American Academy of Pain Medicine
4700 W. Lake Avenue
Glenview, IL 60025-1485
(708) 375-4731

Further Reading

Fishbain, D. 1995. "Types of pain treatment facilities and referral selection criteria: A review." *Archive of Family Medicine*, Vol 4.

Holzman, A., and D. Turk, eds. 1986. *Pain Management*. New York: Pergamon Press.

10

Sleep and Chronic Pain

Chronic pain sufferers often have a difficult time getting a good night's rest. In fact, pain and insomnia are among the most prevalent health complaints brought to the attention of health professionals. While up to 30 percent of the general population complains of insomnia, more than half of those suffering from chronic pain conditions describe themselves as "poor sleepers." When both pain and sleep problems occur together, the negative effects on your daytime functioning and nighttime comfort can worsen significantly. You may notice that if you don't get a good night's sleep you'll find your pain more intense and hard-to-manage the next day. Similarly, anxious and stressful events during the day (such as pain) will interfere with your sleep, in turn lowering your pain tolerance. This vicious cycle can intensify your chronic pain problem, resulting in daytime lethargy, depression, and decreased ability to cope with the stress of living with chronic pain. However, you *can* learn to break the vicious cycle by following some commonsense rules for deep, quality sleep.

In this chapter we first examine what is considered to be "normal" sleep, so that you have a framework with which to compare your sleeping patterns. It is also helpful to understand where *circadian rhythms* fit into sleeping habits. Circadian rhythms are your natural, daily fluctuations of wakefulness and sleepiness. The section on *sleep hygiene,* or the habits you keep surrounding your nightly sleep ritual, provides commonsense guidelines to good sleep. Sleep hygiene involves your diet, sleeping environment, and other sleep behaviors. Additional factors that influence healthy sleep are exercise, relaxation techniques, and obsessional thinking. As you read through this chapter, you may find it helpful to jot down some notes to yourself—they could be in the form of a sleep diary or journal—about your sleep. You may find some surprising information and helpful hints you had not considered before.

Stages of Sleep

If you are sleeping between seven and eight hours per night, you will normally go through four or five cycles of sleep. These cycles last about ninety minutes each. Scientists have named these cycles *REM* (Rapid Eye Movement) sleep and *NREM* (Stages 1 to 4 of nonREM) sleep.

For many years scientists have studied the rapid eye movements, muscle jerks and twitches, and vascular, respiratory, and brain wave activity that goes on during REM and the other stages. The research has helped them discern patterns of sleep, diagnose specific disorders, and gain a greater understanding of the effects of illness on sleep.

You normally begin with Stage 1 NREM sleep, where you become drowsy, your thoughts are incoherent, and you may feel like you're floating or falling. Sleep experts generally agree that Stage

2 NREM sleep begins shortly thereafter. You may begin dreaming at this stage and others have more difficulty awakening you. Then, about fifteen to thirty minutes after you've fallen asleep, Stages 3 and 4 start; although they are separate stages, together they are considered to be the deepest stage of sleep, known as Delta Sleep. This lasts about an hour, at which time you revert back to Stage 2 and almost immediately into REM sleep, where it is thought the most dreaming occurs. You move in and out of these stages throughout the night, with the deep sleep stages becoming increasingly shorter and the REM stages growing longer, lasting up to an hour toward the end of sleep. This may explain why so many people recall vivid dreams upon awakening.

Human need for sleep changes with age. Newborn babies sleep about two-thirds of the time, decreasing to about 50 percent, or twelve hours per night, at six months of age. Children continue to sleep about ten to twelve hours per night, leveling off at seven-and-a-half hours per night with teenagers and adults. By age fifty-five, the hours you sleep increase to eight or more again, but the sleep quality is different—it tends to be lighter and more restless, with typically five awakenings per night. Although a natural function of age, this can also be rather annoying, especially when compounded by a pain problem.

Although there is no hard and fast rule about how much sleep you need, it is customary to sleep the prescribed seven or more hours per night. Some people function well on fewer hours. In fact, studies have shown that sleep deprivation—cutting back on the number of hours you sleep—may be one approach to alleviate depression.

Circadian Rhythms and Sleep

In the forties and fifties, research was done to determine human sleeping and waking cycles around the clock; these cycles came to be known as circadian cycles or rhythms. The word "circadian" is Latin for *circa,* or "about," and *dies,* or "day"; it means "about a day." Dr. Nathaniel Kleitman, often referred to as the father of modern sleep research, once stated that sleep is "part of a perpetual cycle and the most powerful organizer of our lives." When you fall out of sync with your body's natural, daily cycle, you feel disorganized.

Your daily rhythms are synchronized with your body's internal and external cues. The primary internal cue is your inner "body clock," which regulates certain physiological functions such as body temperature and hormone levels. A body clock is one way to picture the control of circadian rhythms. Examples of other bodily functions that are regulated to follow cyclic changes are heart rate, blood pressure, endocrine secretions, metabolism, breathing, and moods.

External cues include the amount of sunlight available and the "social clock," or daily activities such as mealtimes. If time is distorted, for example, when you travel across time zones or are forced to lose sleep due to chronic pain, your body's rhythm falls out of sync with its environment. The results can be unsettling: difficulty falling asleep, restless and disturbed sleep, fatigue, disorientation, and even depression.

Your Internal Time Clock

Human circadian rhythm in individuals can vary from twenty-four- to twenty-eight- hour cycles, with a general average around twenty-five hours. This means that if you were left to your own free will, without any external stimuli, such as changes from night to day or alarm clocks, your circadian rhythms would adapt to a roughly twenty-five-hour schedule. During this cycle, your body temperature rises and falls in a predictable pattern, which in turn affects when you feel sleepy and when you are ready to be awake and alert. Since our inherent rhythm is a little longer than the twenty-four-hour day, we instinctively gravitate towards going to bed an hour later than we should and getting up an hour later than we need to each day. This has an impact on our ability to adapt to schedule shifts and time zone changes.

Body temperature fluctuations account for dips and peaks in mental and physical alertness. Temperatures generally are lowest during the latter half of sleep, about 3 A.M. to 5 A.M., when most of us need to be the least alert because we're in the deepest sleep. Temperatures rise in the morning, peaking somewhere between midday and the late afternoon, and begin to fall again as the evening hours approach. However, there is a great deal of individual variation in the precise times that people peak during the day. This may explain why some people are morning people and others are night people. A morning person's temperature tends to peak earlier than a night person's. Dr. Kleitman discovered that alertness follows body temperature—we feel most alert and perform better when body temperature is highest, and vice versa. Of course, external factors can affect these dips and peaks, such as extreme hot or cold climates, hot or cold foods, and vigorous exercise. And, no matter if you're a morning or night person, it seems that everyone is affected by a well-documented phenomenon called "post lunch dip." This occurs in most adults around 2 P.M., and may be a secondary circadian rhythm having nothing to do with the amount of lunch you've eaten.

In our society we are expected to conform to a twenty-four-hour cycle, which is usually not a tremendous problem for most of us. However, you may notice that on the weekends you tend to go to bed later and get up later, so that by Monday morning you are slightly out of sync with your usual Monday rising time. You'll probably notice though that after a day or two you are back on your regular schedule, feeling rested and alert when you awaken.

Some people, however, have serious difficulty adjusting to a twenty-four-hour cycle. Night people, for example, really don't feel alert and ready to take on the world until the late afternoon hours, and reach their peak alertness sometime in the late evening, when the morning people are yawning and getting ready for bed. (You've heard the term *night owl*—a person who enjoys doing serious work or play in the wee hours.) In contrast, morning people feel that their best hours are in the first half of the day; they usually have a low period in the afternoon and then are truly ready for sleep between 9 and 11 P.M. What does this have to do with coping with chronic pain? You will want to know when you are at your peak periods of the day—when you feel strong, confident, and mentally alert. This may be the best time to participate in the stress and pain exercises in this workbook, for example. In contrast, if you know when you are weakest, most vulnerable, you may experience greater susceptibility to your pain, and feel the most hopeless and helpless in learning to manage it. This also may be the best time to do the soothing stress management techniques such as deep breathing and imagery, suggested in this book.

For example, a freelance artist felt that she produced her best work in the evening hours. She developed the habit of watching late night television to relax after an evening's work. However, her spouse's alarm clock went off at the same early hour each morning. To compensate for waking up early, she took restful but lengthy naps in the afternoon. She found it increasingly difficult to go to sleep at a regular hour with her spouse. The artist had a stimulus control problem—her daytime ritual involved a nap and her pre-bed ritual involved late night television. Combined with these cues, she also fell into her natural circadian rhythm by allowing herself to go to sleep later and later. In order to get back on a schedule more like her spouse's, she would need to reset her body's clock.

If you choose a family lifestyle and a career that allow you to work at your own rhythm and pace, sleep-wake schedules may not be an issue. But if you suspect that you have sleep problems due to unsynchronized schedules, you may want to discuss this further with a specialist at a sleep lab. Sometimes known as "chronotherapists," these specialists can carefully examine your sleep-wake schedule and help you find alternative solutions.

Sleep and Your Diet

When you are distracted by pain you often overlook the simplest things that can get in the way of a good night's sleep. The habits you keep at night and during the day can affect your sleep in ways you may not realize. Throughout this chapter, honestly examine your sleep habits to see which ones may need altering. Consider your personal habits such as diet and mealtime habits.

Caffeine

One obvious food substance to avoid is caffeine. You probably know someone who brags about drinking coffee all day, and then sleeping soundly at night. Chances are, their sleep is affected more than they realize. Caffeine is a powerful stimulant (increases the activity of the central nervous system); most people will notice the uncomfortable shakiness and general arousal with even small amounts of caffeine. In large doses, it can cause sweating, heart-racing, numbness, breathing difficulties, and paranoia. Caffeine is a drug and you can develop a tolerance, but it will always act as a stimulant. Ingesting anything with caffeine in it even one hour before bedtime can cause difficulty falling asleep and fitful or light sleep long into the night. You should not drink caffeinated beverages after 4 P.M. or within 6 hours of your bedtime; if you can cut it out entirely, so much the better. Remember to check the labels on colas, teas, and other drinks that may contain more caffeine than you realize. Some medications and foods, such as chocolate, also contain caffeine.

Nicotine

Like caffeine, nicotine is also a powerful stimulant and, as you probably already know, one of the major ingredients in tobacco. Sleep lab studies show that smokers averaging one-and-a-half packs a day take longer to fall asleep than non-smokers. If you suffer from persistent insomnia, you should seriously consider giving up smoking, not only for the potential benefit of improved sleep, but also for other well-known health reasons. If this is simply not an option right now, try to decrease overall smoking as much as possible and don't smoke within two to three hours of your bedtime.

Be aware that abrupt withdrawal of these central nervous system stimulants can have adverse affects. Following the discontinuation of both caffeine and nicotine, some people experience headaches, restlessness, and feelings of panic and anxiety which may indicate that they are experiencing *withdrawal*. The effects of caffeine withdrawal may only last a week. However, nicotine withdrawal can be much more intense. You need to carefully plan to quit smoking by consulting one of the many books available on the subject, or by checking with your health care professional.

Alcohol

The idea that alcohol enhances sleep is a myth. While the initial effects of a hot toddy or nightcap before retiring are indeed relaxing, alcohol taken before bedtime significantly disturbs your ability to maintain sleep, and may lead you to wake up in the early morning hours. Some individuals find that even small amounts of alcohol have a damaging effect on their sleep. If you are drinking heavily before bedtime in order to numb yourself to sleep and in an attempt to avoid obsessional thinking, you'll find that alcohol generally makes matters worse. Researchers have demonstrated that alcohol initially decreases wakefulness, but as it leaves your body, it increases wakefulness in the last half of the night. This means that in the short-term alcohol is sedating, but the long-term effects are actually *stimulating* because of the alcohol's disruption of your natural sleep cycles.

Mealtimes

Proper mealtime scheduling can enhance your daily routine and help reprogram your body to feel sleepy at the right time. Eating at regular times will get you into a routine, which can help signal sleep time. If you eat a heavy meal before bedtime, you may find it difficult to relax enough to go to sleep, since your digestive tract has to work overtime. Space your meals out at regular intervals, and try to eat at least three to four hours before retiring. Rigid weight loss plans can have an understandably negative effect on sleep quality. You may wake up in the middle of the night with hunger pangs. Try to space out your caloric intake throughout the day (four to six small meals versus two to three large ones), so that you are able to consume some calories before bedtime to get you through the night. If you need a snack before bedtime, drink warm milk. Or, try a combination of carbohydrates, such as bread, cereal, or pasta. There is some indication that foods high in carbohydrates lead to sleepiness and foods high in protein lead to alertness, although studies have not yet confirmed this observation.

Dietary Supplements

There is no specific food or drink that has been proven to promote sleep. However, herbal specialists will suggest a diet rich in calcium and magnesium, including such herbal teas as chamomile, valerian, hops, and passionflower (which also come in capsule form). You may consider homeopathic remedies, which are substances derived from minerals and animal products, as well as herbs. Various studies have demonstrated the beneficial effects of L-Tryptophan, an amino acid found in much of the food we consume daily, including meat, dairy products, beans, and leafy green vegetables. Taken in larger amounts, as a dietary supplement, it's possible that L-Tryptophan stimulates the production of serotonin in the brain, causing you to feel sleepy and content. Currently, L-Tryptophan is not available in pill form. The Food and Drug Administration has withheld it, pending further study.

For more in-depth information about nutrition and health, see chapter 11.

The Melatonin Phenomena

Melatonin, an over-the-counter substance sold in health food stores, has been grabbing a significant amount of national attention. It is a naturally occurring or synthesized hormone which is as yet unproved, but thought to significantly enhance sleep. Scientists are assiduously studying the effects of this hormone; in the meantime, people throughout the country are singing its praises.

According to *Science News,* Melatonin was discovered in 1959 and is secreted in larger animals by the pineal gland, located in the center of the brain. Dusk or darkness triggers melatonin production, and sunlight inhibits it. Humans naturally produce varying amounts of melatonin, but the amounts produced may be affected by conditions such as exposure to light, depression, jet lag, and aging. *Science News* reports that, over time, the pineal gland accumulates deposits of calcium that diminish its melatonin production, which may be one reason many older people have trouble getting a good night's sleep. Lauri Aesoph, N.D., a medical writer, reports that scientists now know that the amino acid tryptophan is converted into serotonin in the body, which in turn transforms into melatonin. This may explain why some foods high in tryptophan, such as turkey, bananas, and liver boost melatonin production. This also ties in with circadian rhythms mentioned earlier in this chapter. Your internal time clock signals secretion of various hormones at different times during the day. Melatonin is thought to play a key role as the biological timekeeper of these hormones, controlling periods of sleepiness and wakefulness.

A prominent researcher in the field of melatonin study is Russel Reiter of the University of Texas Health Science Center in San Antonio. A neuroendocrinologist for thirty years, he has been studying the effects of melatonin on aging, enhancing the body's natural immune system, and inhibiting cancerous tumors. While the results of his studies are encouraging, he presents a balanced viewpoint in exclaiming the wonders of this so-called miracle drug, acknowledging the amount of research still needed. Dr. Reiter recommends a milligram or less taken at bedtime, at the same time every night. He explained that thirty to fifty micrograms will give you what approximates the body's natural blood levels of melatonin. When asked if melatonin supplements suppressed the body's natural production over time, he explained that there is no "rebound phenomena" of insomnia if you were to stop taking melatonin. There are also no complications with drug interactions that he knows of, but he cautions that many drugs have not been tested for their interaction with melatonin. He recommends that pregnant and nursing women, children, and those with autoimmune disease and severe mental illness should avoid melatonin.

Michael Murray, N.D., comments in *Health Counselor* that melantonin plays an important role in the induction of sleep. However, although there appears to be no serious side effects at recommended dosages (one-third to 10 mg) for insomnia, conceivably melatonin supplements could disrupt the normal circadian rhythm. He, along with other researchers in the field, advise caution in using melatonin.

Sleep Hygiene

Do you find yourself going over things you have to do the next day while lying in bed? This is a common example of inappropriately using your bed as an "activity center," or a place where wakeful things are going on that are incompatible with sleep. Using the bed or bedroom as the center of your universe is a natural but detrimental way of coping with physical limitations associated with pain-related conditions. Some people organize their entire daily activities around their bedrooms. The problem is that when you engage regularly in these activities in your bedroom, the bedroom environment becomes associated with wakefulness rather than with sleep. Examples of other incompatible nighttime behaviors in the bed or the bedroom include: arguing, lively discussion, eating, reading exciting books, watching television, exercising, cleaning, worrying (see section on obsessional thinking).

An athlete conditions his or her body through regular training, establishing usually positive habits leading to a greater goal. But negative patterns or habits can be learned too. Sleeplessness can be learned or "conditioned" through certain associations that you may develop consciously or unconsciously. Although you may be someone who enjoys the change of pace of a spontaneous late night movie or intimate discussion, be aware that if you repeatedly continue to encourage poor habits, you may be unconsciously encouraging sleeplessness. You can train your body, much like an athlete does, to respond to certain cues and adopt certain habits to help you perform better. This section helps you look at potential associations you may make, and ways for you to eliminate these associations.

Your bedtime ritual can contain powerful associations that cue sleepiness. For example, brushing your teeth, setting the clock, arranging the covers can all signal sleep time. However, if you associate your bed with stimulating activities such as eating, arguing or watching television (activities other than sex), you may find that you have subtly trained yourself to be *wakeful* rather than *sleepy*. For example, a business executive finds herself running through the next day's activities each night before she forces her eyes shut. She begins to dread the bed, because she associates it with a time when she mentally rehearses. Her mental rehearsal only reminds her of unaccomplished tasks, and thus her imperfections. Another scenario: a freelance artist uses the quiet night to write. She takes naps to compensate for lost sleep and she finds that the slant of the late afternoon sun "cues" her naptime. When she's ready to return to a steady job, it will be difficult to reprogram her body to do without the nap.

Dr. Richard Bootzin is a psychologist who says that a primary goal for the insomnia sufferer is to associate the bed solely with sleep and nothing else. Those who have developed negative associations with the bed—who dread it because they see it as a place to toss, turn, and worry—often find that their sleep is better when they travel away from home or even move into a different room. The cues that usually keep them alert, anxious, or tense are absent, and so they sleep peacefully.

In order to avoid developing negative associations with your bed, follow these guidelines as recommended by Dr. Bootzin:

- Go to bed only when you are feeling sleepy.

- Do not use your bed as an activity center. Sexual activity is the only exception.

- If you do not fall asleep in about ten minutes, get out of bed and go into another room. Do a non-arousing activity (no scary or intense books or television) until you feel sleepy; when you feel drowsy, go back to bed.

- If you are still awake after about ten minutes, get up and repeat your non-arousing activity or another one. Do not return to bed until you feel sleepy.

- Repeat as often as necessary until you fall asleep within ten minutes. Your goal is to associate your bed with falling asleep quickly.

- Get up the same time each morning, regardless of how little you slept. This is an important step and one that is not to be overlooked. A consistent wake-up time will help your body begin to develop a regular sleep rhythm.

- Do not nap. Your goal is to establish consistent sleep cues at regular times; napping can disrupt your sleep cues.

- Option: Sleep in a different room or move your bed to a different location in your room or to another room altogether.

Common Obstacles to This Approach

At first it may feel extremely uncomfortable to be getting out of bed throughout the night. You may resist leaving a warm bed, especially on cold winter nights. Or you may resent the loneliness of a dark quiet house. Some people notice extreme fatigue and sluggishness for the first few days of trying this approach. Others have found that they feel even worse than usual when beginning this treatment, which is a common and understandable reaction. But be assured that this process has been used successfully in retraining peoples' attitudes towards their beds and sleep. Although it is wise for you not to expect immediate improvement, some people have found that they are able to sleep better within a week of carefully following this strategy. With diligence, you will find that the sleep you gain in the long run will more than compensate for the sleep lost initially.

Other Guidelines for Success

- Avoid unconsciously "punishing" yourself for not sleeping by forcing yourself to do an unpleasant activity. It will be much harder to get out of bed if you think you have to face laundry or an unbalanced checkbook. Make it easier on yourself by doing the following: Leave a warm bathrobe and flashlight by your bed. This way you can slip out comfortably without disturbing your partner. Avoid eating, but if you must snack, eat a light food containing carbohydrates or dairy products.

- Don't worry about following the ten minute rule to the precise second; an estimate of the ten minute period will do. The point is that if you find yourself lying in bed fully awake after a reasonable amount of time, *get up*. If you feel yourself dropping off to sleep, but you estimate that it's been twenty minutes, stay there. Avoid clock-watching.

- Tell yourself to get up when the alarm clock rings, no matter how restless your night has been. It's important that you adhere to this last step, because you are re-regulating your internal associations and settling your body into a steady rhythm.

- Chart your progress in a bedside sleep journal. Keeping a careful record of your sleep behavior will help you gain perspective of your problem, and you may spot patterns or connections you had not noticed before. You'll also feel a sense of mastery and control as you see yourself making progress.

You will need to be diligent in following all of the above guidelines in order to break the vicious cycle of your negative associations. But pace yourself and do not expect miracles overnight. Allow yourself to gradually comprehend and adopt the principles you find in this chapter. Make use of your sleep diary. Share it with a trusted friend or health care professional. Ask them for support and encouragement. Success can be sweeter when shared with another who supports your accomplishments.

A Word About Naps

Naps may be beneficial for older folks whose sleep patterns are shorter and lighter, and therefore more restless. However, much of napping's benefits depends on the time of day the nap is taken. This relates to your body's circadian rhythm, which varies greatly with each individual. In general, naps should not be used to replace lost and broken sleep. Studies show that napping cannot substitute for a solid night of good sleep. Since the benefits of napping may depend on the time of day the nap is taken, you may find that if you chose to nap, you function best with a brief (ten to twenty minutes) nap in the middle or end of the day. A general rule of thumb is not after 3 P.M. and not to exceed one hour. You might want to experiment with the time of day that a nap is most refreshing for you.

Be aware of using naps to avoid certain tasks or to compensate for feelings of despair and depression. If you have an underlying problem such as depression, naps can often be draining instead of refreshing.

Environmental Factors To Consider

Noise

If you suspect that you are particularly sensitive to noise, take stock of the noise situation in your bedroom. Experts state that sensitivity to noise increases as you age, and women seem more sensitive to noise than men. If you have noisy neighbors or live near an airport or freeway, and moving is not an option, look into soundproofing your bedroom. This can be done by adding insulation or special building materials to the walls. Healthy satisfying sleep is worth the expense. A cheaper alternative is to experiment with various types of "white noise," such as fans, air conditioners, or audiotapes of ocean waves. You may want to try ear plugs.

Get rid of preset hourly watch beepers or chimers if they disturb your sleep even in the slightest amount. While some people can tune out external noise such as a chiming clock, others may find that the hourly gong only reinforces their obsessional characteristics by reminding them of each passing hour. If you find yourself counting each hour that passes and anticipating the next chime, then turn it off.

Light

If you are disturbed or awakened by too much light in your bedroom, check out the types of eye shades, window shades, and light blocking curtains available. If the blackness of the night makes you uneasy, buy a night-light and plug it in where you can see it easily.

Comfort Issues

Don't forget to appraise the quality of your mattress. Is it too firm or too soft? One pain center client complained of annoying hip pain for weeks until she slept on a very firm mattress and it disappeared.

Dr. Peter Hauri, writing for the Upjohn Corporation, explains that when the room temperature rises above seventy-five degrees, people wake up more often, experience more restless sleep, less dreaming sleep, and sleep less deeply. If the room is too cold, however, you're probably unable to fall asleep. Optimum temperatures range somewhere between sixty-five and seventy degrees.

You may want to consult your physician or pain control specialist regarding certain sleeping positions for your particular injury. For example, if you suffer from back pain, you'll want to find a position that takes the pressure off of your spine. A good way to do this is to lie on your back and support your legs behind your knees with a pillow to ensure that your back is not arched. Or you can lie in the fetal position, bringing your knees toward your chest and placing a pillow between your knees.

The size, type, and softness of your pillow can also significantly influence your sleeping comfort if you have chronic pain. Again, consult your health care professional for suggestions.

Another sleep factor may be the presence or absence of a bedpartner. A restless bedmate is likely to disturb your sleep. You may need to adjust sleeping arrangements if other methods are not successful. If you are accustomed to your bedmate, you may find it hard to sleep well without him or her.

Safety

You may find that you are unable to relax or sleep restfully if you feel your building or neighborhood may be unsafe. Part of your sleep plan may need to include taking steps to make your home more "crime proof" by adding an alarm system, extra door locks, or window bars. As a part of your pre-bed ritual, you may want to take a walk around your home, securing the locks and engaging your security systems. You might also want to consider keeping a phone in your bedroom and close to your bed to increase your sense of security. Take whatever steps you need to feel safe.

Exercise

Exercise can be a key to helping you sleep better. Regular exercise has many benefits—mental and emotional as well as physical—but sometimes it's hard to overcome inertia and get yourself started. The good news is that just a little exercise—taking a walk or gardening—can help alleviate depression, raise self-esteem, and promote a sense of well being, all of which can benefit sleep. Studies of the effects of an aerobic exercise regimen show that exercisers tend to have lower blood pressure, less anxiety, decreased muscle tension, and are able to cope with stress better than non-exercisers. Studies also show that even a small amount of regular exercise—stretching, strengthening, and gentle movements—helps people sleep better compared to those who are completely sedentary. This may be because exercise promotes the release of certain chemical substances in your brain (neurotransmitters) that are thought to be connected to feelings of well being and satisfaction. The key word here is *regular,* because sporadic bursts of strenuous exercise may not be helpful—only painful. There is one caveat: Avoid exercise just before bedtime. Moderate or strenuous exercise at night can have an arousing effect, making it difficult for you to relax. Many studies suggest that the best time of day to exercise is in the afternoon or early evening. Leave yourself about three to four hours between exercising and bedtime. See chapter 3 for more in-depth information about exercise.

Relaxation for Sleep

If chronic pain interferes with your sleep, you need to learn and practice relaxation exercises for two simple and compelling reasons: First, the experience of sleeplessness is itself stressful. It reduces your ability to function, to cope, and to feel good—both mentally and physically. If you can't function, you feel useless. If you can't cope, then stressors begin to pile up. Second, you tense your muscles in response to these negative feelings and behaviors. You grit your teeth in anticipation of sleeplessness. This increases your body's overall tension level, which only makes your chronic pain worse, especially if you suffer from musculoskeletal problems resulting in headaches, backaches, and neckaches.

One step towards healthy sleep is to realize that physical tension and mental anxiety lead to less sleep, which in turn, can make you more anxious and tense. It's a vicious circle, but you can break it by learning to manage the tension in your life. You can learn to identify stress in your body and control its interplay with your sleeplessness.

Please refer to chapters 4 and 5 for examples of useful relaxation techniques. It may be helpful for you to make a tape recording of your favorite exercises, or buy a pre-recorded tape, and have it handy near your bed. If you have trouble falling asleep or find that you awaken in the middle of the night and can't get back to sleep, you can use the tape as an additional resource.

Managing Obsessional Thinking

An underlying issue of any illness or physical disorder is the thought processes you bring to the situation. With physical pain, what you think about your pain determines your ability to cope with it. If you think in a negative way that your pain will keep you from ever sleeping better, this self-fulfilling prophecy will very often come to pass. If you find yourself saying such phrases as "I'll never get better," "This shouldn't have happened to me, "or "I'm so embarrassed that I have this problem; I must be less of a person," then you are doing yourself a disservice by predetermining that you will never improve.

This section is about your thought processes and how they affect your ability to cope with sleep and chronic pain. Before you give into the temptation to skip over this section and move onto the next (saying this "doesn't apply to you"), keep an open mind and read on. Avoid the temptation to dismiss your mind's capability of affecting your body (and to blame it all on outside stress or a physical ailment). Your mind is a powerful tool that can be harnessed to help you cope more effectively.

See if you can spot yourself in the following eight general characteristics of insomniacs:

1. **You have a history of general physical arousal,** meaning your body becomes tensed and you react in a typically stressed fashion to excitement, both negative and positive.

2. **You have a specific tendency towards high muscle tension under stress.** You clench your teeth and tighten muscles, which may bring on tension headaches, back pain, fatigue, and general muscular aches.

3. **You have a fear of failure**. The notion of failing at something is totally unacceptable to you.

4. **You suffer from perfectionistic tendencies.** You cannot allow yourself to be less than perfect, which means you "fail" when you don't sleep well.

5. **You are angry.** You carry anger with you to the bedroom. The anger affects not only your sleep, but your work and home relationships.

6. **You tend to catastrophize.** Your fear of failing and perfectionistic standards combine to put you constantly on the defensive. You can't shake the feeling that others are out to bring you down, and so you expect the worst.

7. **You have a fear of letting go.** You cannot let down your guard, for fear that events and people will escape your control. You must remain ever-vigilant.

8. **You obsess.** Because of your tendencies towards all of the above, you constantly focus on problems and issues, trying to solve them by incessant worrying.

Steps You Can Take to Counteract Negative Obsessional Thinking

Step 1: Awareness

Even if negative obsessional thinking now impedes your progress towards better sleep, you can take steps to harness that thinking and change it into something that works for you, rather than against you. Your first step is to become aware of your brand of obsessional thinking.

Generally, people begin to obsess before bedtime. Take some time to jot down your negative obsessional thoughts just before you go to sleep. You may find it handy to keep a small notebook next to your bed to use exclusively to chart your sleep progress. You may find that you have many other types of thoughts that do not fit neatly into the categories provided here. Simply write them down in your own words and become familiar with them. The purpose is to provide yourself a framework within which to work, so that the prospect of controlling negative thinking does not seem overwhelming.

Step 2: Counteract

After you feel that you are more fully aware of your style of obsessional thinking, you can begin to counteract each thought. Negative thinking arrives with such spontaneity and fury that you will need to arm yourself with as much counter-ammunition as possible. The ammunition will take the form of positive or healthier thoughts delivered with equal force and significance.

First, you may need to abruptly halt the negative thoughts by shouting the word "stop." This may scare the wits out of your bedmate in the middle of the night, so just do it in your head. Other techniques can be used to stop the flow of negative thinking; you can, for example, wear a rubber band on your wrist and snap it at the first sign of an unpleasant thought. Fill the void left by the interrupted thought with previously prepared positive thoughts that are more realistic, assertive, and constructive.

Steps to Thought-Stopping

As soon as you notice that you are obsessing negatively, choose a way to abruptly halt the unproductive flow of thinking. Some people find that loudly imagining the word "stop" works the best, while others raise their hand, snap their fingers, or use the rubber band technique described above. As soon as you've said "stop," let your mind empty of every trace of the distressing thought, but allow any neutral or pleasant thoughts to continue. Try to keep your mind blank or on neutral topics for about thirty seconds. If the upsetting thought recurs within thirty seconds, imagine "stop!" again. Keep doing this until you have successfully extinguished the thought several times in a row.

It will also help if you remember to breathe deeply and in a relaxed manner at the conclusion of every stop sequence. The relaxation that deep breathing brings will cue the way for you to more fully accept the positive thoughts you substitute for the negative ones.

The following statements are designed to replace each negative thought. Read them over thoroughly. You may not agree with them at first. This is natural and perfectly acceptable. However, in order for you not to continually lose sleep because you obsess, you will need to find an agreeable replacement, a statement in which you can believe. This list of counteracting statements are just examples. You may find that you get the best results from developing your own healthy rejoinders to the negative thoughts. Blank lines are available under each counteracting statement for you to write in your own.

Examples of Counteracting Statements

1. When you feel yourself tensing up, say to yourself:

   - "I can relax."

   - "My muscles are becoming limp."

   - "I am calmer."

   - "Breathe deeply."

   _____

   _____

2. Fear of failing:

Think out in advance examples of successes. When obsessing on failures at night, shift focus to an example of success and say to yourself, "Sometimes I succeed, sometimes I don't. Time to relax and sleep."

- "I am not a failure."

- "I have succeeded in life before."

- "Just because I can't sleep tonight doesn't mean I'm a failure."

- "I will not suffer tomorrow if I lose sleep tonight."

_____

_____

3. Perfectionism:

- "It's okay to be less than perfect."

- "No one says I have to be perfect."

- "There is no such thing as a perfect person, and if there were, that person would be very boring."

- "Enough kicking myself for one night. Things may look different in the morning."

_____

_____

4. Anger:

- "I will leave my anger outside of the bedroom."

- "All these things making me angry will be waiting for me tomorrow. I can deal with them then."

- "Let go of anger thoughts. Time to relax."

_____

_____

5. Catastrophizing:

- "I do not need to be defensive. These feelings keep me from relaxing."

- "Let it go. I'll face it in the morning."

_____

_____

6. Letting Go:

- "I am learning not to have to control everything."

- "Stay flexible. If it can go wrong, it probably will."
- "Let it go."

_____

_____

7. Obsessing:

- "I will counteract each negative thought with a peaceful, soothing thought."
- "I will not let these thoughts drive me crazy."
- "I will dismiss them one by one, and replace them with thoughts that will make me sleepy."
- "I see my negative thoughts floating like autumn leaves on the surface of a stream, drifting around the bend and out of sight."

_____

_____

Replacing your negative thinking takes time, patience, practice, and commitment, so don't give up if you don't notice immediate improvement in sleep onset and quality. You've spent a lifetime collecting your own unique brand of negative thoughts; allow yourself time to unravel them and develop better habits.

You may find that using visualization to augment your thinking can add power to your positive thoughts. For example, as you repeat the positive thoughts, visualize yourself as a powerful, confident, and relaxed person. See yourself speaking assertively. Imagine yourself cool under pressure. Recreate feelings of pleasure at your success at staying cool, assertive, and confident. If this is not possible, you may want to choose a positive scene or object, one that evokes feelings of peace and calm. Please refer to chapter 5 for more information on visualization.

This technique of replacing negative thoughts can work at any time throughout the night, whenever you notice yourself becoming anxious and full of worries. All you have to do is practice enough, so that it becomes second nature to react positively rather than negatively. A particularly vulnerable time in the night is in the pre-dawn hours—3–5 A.M.—when it's easy to feel overtaken by anxious thoughts. If you awaken frequently during these hours and have difficulty getting back to sleep, prepare yourself before you go to bed each night to administer positive phrases to yourself as soon as necessary.

An Additional Note

As you've seen in this chapter, sometimes sleep problems are not related to complex physical or mental disorders, but are simply the result of poor habits. However, it's a good idea to consult your physician to rule out any possibility of sleep disorders which may need to be evaluated in a sleep center. Certain sleep problems are serious enough to require immediate medical attention and should not be ignored.

Summary

Chronic pain complicates your insomnia problem, as sleep disturbances complicate your experience with pain and illness. But there is a way to regain control and break this cycle. By committing yourself to being patient and persistent in practicing healthy sleep techniques, you should see sleep improvement over time. Psychological research has shown that successful management of insomnia associated with chronic pain requires consistent adherence to this regimen for eight to ten weeks. The self-management approach implies that you take responsibility for implementing the recommended changes and that you take an active role in the treatment process. You may find that your sleep pattern gets worse the first few nights of practice and that you wake up in the morning feeling more exhausted than usual. Do not get discouraged. With time and repeated practice, your sleep pattern will improve. If you faithfully implement the techniques described in this chapter, but continue to experience insomnia due to chronic pain, it is a good idea to consult your physician regarding referral to a sleep clinic and/or a multi-disciplinary pain center. You can benefit from the additional support and reinforcement of other patients, as well as careful guidance from health care professionals in correcting any errors or barriers that interfere with the process of regaining control of your sleep.

Further Reading

The American Medical Association. 1984. *Better Sleep.* New York: Random House.

Anch, A. M., C. P. Browman, M. M. Mitler, J. K Walsh. 1988. *Sleep: A Scientific Perspective.* Englewood Cliffs, New Jersey: Prentice Hall.

Bootzin, R. R., and P. M. Nicest. 1978. "Behavioral treatments for insomnia." *Progress in Behavior Modification.* Vol. 6, edited by M.M Herren et al. New York: Academic Press.

Catalano, E. M. with W. Webb, J. Walsh, and C. Morin. 1990. *Getting To Sleep.* Oakland, CA: New Harbinger Publications, Inc.

Davis, M., M. McKay, and E. Eshelman. 1995. *The Relaxation and Stress Reduction Workbook,* 4th ed. Oakland, CA: New Harbinger Publications, Inc.

Dryer, B., and E. Kaplan 1986. *Inside Insomnia: How To Sleep Better Tonight.* New York: Villard Books.

Hauri, P. 1982. *The Sleep Disorders.* Kalamazoo, MI: Upjohn.

Lamberg, L., and The American Medical Association. 1984. *Straight-talk, No-nonsense Guide to Better Sleep.* New York: Random House.

NIH Technology Assessment Conference. 1995. "Integration of behavioral and relaxation approaches into the treatment of chronic pain and insomnia.: Oct. 16-18, 1995. Natcher Conference Center, Bethesda, MD.

Online Information Can Be Found At:

http://www.cloud9.net/~thorpy/

http://www.sleepnet.com/

11

Nutrition and Chronic Pain

by Catherine Geiser, R.D.

"The doctor of the future will give no medicines, but will interest his patients in the care of the human frame, the diet, and in the causes of disease."

—*Thomas Edison*

A common cliché, "you are what you eat," might not be too far from the truth. Good nutrition is essential for well-being; the food we eat affects how we feel and function. A healthful diet can make a positive difference for someone experiencing chronic pain. Neurotransmitters, chemical messengers in the body, are responsible for transmitting feelings of tiredness, calmness, and alertness. As we learned earlier, they are relayed from one area of the body to another. The neurotransmitters' final destination is in the brain where physical feelings are interpreted into emotional feelings. Feelings are our interpretation of the chemical event. Have you ever noticed feeling sleepy after lunch or find yourself irritable when you are hungry? These feelings may be caused by eating too much or not getting the right balance of food. The food you eat is vital to feeling good. Your body needs the right fuel to work at its optimum; therefore, it is up to you to provide it with a variety of healthy foods.

As you look around, you might think the United States has gone health conscious crazy from the abundance of health food stores and gyms popping up. You will be surprised to discover, however, that the typical American diet is far from what is considered healthy. Americans eat too much salt, refined sugars, caffeine, alcohol, and fat, while virtually neglecting other foods such as vegetables, fruits, complex carbohydrates, and fluids. According to the National Academy of Sciences, 60 percent of Americans' daily energy is derived from sugar and fat. This type of diet is associated with an increased risk of developing chronic diseases, including obesity, heart disease, cancer, degenerative joint disease, high blood pressure, as well aggravating constipation, hypoglycemia, indigestion, headaches, and fatigue. With the hectic pace of today's world, people often resort to fast food. Unfortunately, these foods can contribute to a diet high in fat and sugar, while being low in nutrients. It is an easy habit to adopt when schedules are tight, but there are ways to cook simply and effectively while providing your body with the nutrients it needs and desires.

Eating a healthy diet would be easier if our only motivation to eat was to fuel our body. The reality is not so simple. People eat for a variety of reasons other than physical hunger. Family traditions and culture play a critical role in the way we eat. Many foods remind us of our childhood or are traditionally served at holiday feasts. We eat to celebrate achievements; we eat to comfort ourselves. There are even foods considered to be comfort foods, such as soups and stews that evoke a warm feeling. We eat when we are emotional or fearful and when we want to feel better. It is difficult to disassociate food from these feelings. What you can do is become knowledgeable about the foods you eat. There is a wealth of information regarding nutrition therapies for chronic pain. Be aware that many of these therapies are yet to be supported by scientific research. However, there are dietary changes you can make to improve your health and assist you in managing your pain.

This chapter will help you evaluate your current eating habits and offer ideas on moving towards a more healthful diet. Through making positive changes to your eating habits you will more likely have the strength, both physical and mental, to manage other areas that can make a difference in controlling your pain. A healthy diet can indirectly help you to stick with your exercise routine, practice relaxation techniques, and keep a positive mental attitude.

Components of a Healthful Diet

Before discussing the components of a healthful diet, take inventory of your current eating patterns. Evaluating your current diet will help you be able to identify areas to focus on in changing to a healthier way of life.

Make a list of everything you ate yesterday on the form on the next page. If yesterday was not typical, you may wish to choose a different day. Note the time, amount of food, method of preparation, feelings, and other activities performed while eating. For example:

Time	Foods and Beverages	Amount	Cooking Method	Feelings	Other Activities
8 A.M.	bran cereal lowfat milk coffee creamer biscotti	1 cup 1/2 cup 8 oz 1 tsp 1		lonely	reading paper

It is not uncommon to have sporadic eating habits with busy schedules. Make meal and snack time an event. Often, you might eat more food if you're watching television or doing another activity at the same time as eating. Take time to enjoy the preparation, smell, and taste of your food. Sit down at the table, and savor the food you are eating. Try not to eat on the run; schedule meals and breaks into your day. Taking the time to ensure wholesome eating habits will bring you a step closer to a healthy diet.

After reading this chapter and referring to your Diet Recall Form, you might identify areas in your diet you want to change. Obviously no one day is indicative of how you eat; however, it should give you an idea of your current eating habits. Remember that good nutrition is the first step to building a healthy body and being able to better deal with the stress of chronic pain.

Diet Recall Form

Time	Foods and Beverages	Amount	Cooking Method	Feelings	Other Activities

Dietary Guidelines

The Food Guide Pyramid in figure 11.1 was developed by the U.S. Department of Agriculture to help people eat a healthy diet. The pyramid illustrates that the bulk of your diet should come from breads, grains, fruits, and vegetables. These foods contain primarily carbohydrates as well as many vitamins and minerals, also known as micronutrients. Milk, cheese, meat, fish, poultry, beans, and legumes should make up the rest of your diet. These foods are high in protein, but can also be high in fat; therefore, you need to choose carefully. Finally, added fat, sugar, and alcohol should be used sparingly.

The following Guidelines for a Healthy diet were developed by the U.S. Departments of Agriculture and Health and Human Services to help people achieve a diet resembling the Food Guide Pyramid. Read the following seven guidelines while thinking about how to incorporate them into your own diet.

Figure 11.1

Food Guide Pyramid
A Guide to Daily Food Choices

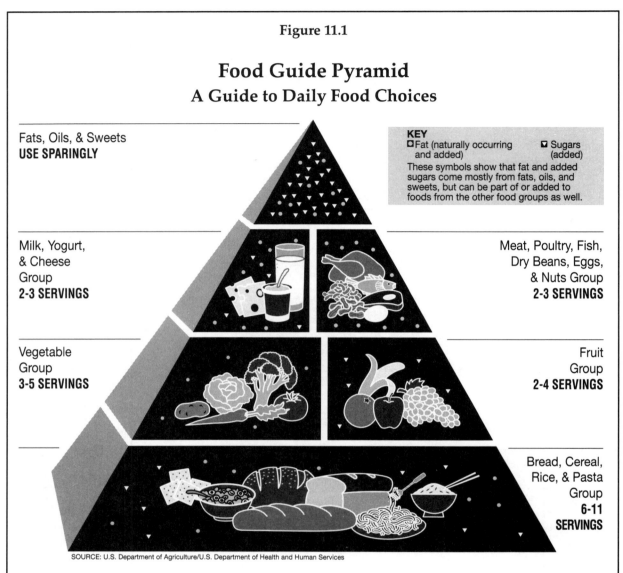

Fats, Oils, & Sweets
USE SPARINGLY

KEY
□ Fat (naturally occurring and added)   ☑ Sugars (added)
These symbols show that fat and added sugars come mostly from fats, oils, and sweets, but can be part of or added to foods from the other food groups as well.

Milk, Yogurt, & Cheese Group
2-3 SERVINGS

Meat, Poultry, Fish, Dry Beans, Eggs, & Nuts Group
2-3 SERVINGS

Vegetable Group
3-5 SERVINGS

Fruit Group
2-4 SERVINGS

Bread, Cereal, Rice, & Pasta Group
6-11 SERVINGS

SOURCE: U.S. Department of Agriculture/U.S. Department of Health and Human Services

The Food Guide Pyramid emphasizes food from the five food groups shown in the three lower sections of the Pyramid.

Each of these food groups provides some, but not all, of the nutrients you need. Foods in one group can't replace those in another. No one food group is more important than another—for good health, you need them all.

Bread, Cereal, Rice & Pasta Group	Vegetable Group	Fruit Group	Milk, Yogurt, & Cheese Group	Meat, Poultry, Fish, Dry Beans, Eggs, & Nuts Group	Fats, Oils, & Sweets
1 slice of bread	1/2 cup of chopped raw or cooked vegetables	1 piece of fruit or melon wedge	1 cup of milk or yogurt	2 to 3 ounces of cooked lean meat , poultry, or fish	LIMIT CALORIES FROM THESE especially if you need to lose weight
1/2 cup of cooked rice or pasta	1 cup of canned fruit	3/4 cup of juice	1 1/2 ounces of natural cheese	Count 1/2 cup of cooked beans, or 1 egg, or 2 tablespoons of peanut butter as 1 ounces of lean meat	
1/2 cup cooked cereal 1 ounce of ready-to-eat cereal	1/4 cup of dried fruit	1/2 cup of canned fruit 1/4 cup of dried fruit	2 ounces of process cheese		

1. Eat a variety of foods

Eating a variety of foods assures you of getting the fifty plus nutrients you need for good health. Figure 11.2 lists fourteen of the major vitamins and minerals along with their functions. Each nutrient is vital for your body to perform well. One food group alone cannot provide all of the nutrients your body needs to function. This means eating at least five servings of fruits and/or

---

Figure 11.2: Main Functions of Major Micronutrients

Vitamins

Bl Thiamin	Helps body cells obtain energy from food. Needed for nervous system function.
B2 Riboflavin	Necessary for the production of energy within cells of the body.
B3 Niacin	Necessary for fat synthesis, tissue respiration, and carbohydrate utilization.
B6 Pyridoxine	Involved in metabolism of protein and fat.
B12 Cobalamine	Required for the synthesis of DNA, maintenance of nerves, and manufacturing and development of red blood cells.
Vitamin C	Required for the formation of collagen that acts to hold cells together. Also important in tissue repair. Plays a critical role in the immune system.
Folic acid	Important in the production of heme, the iron containing substances in red blood cells, the production and division of cells, tissue growth, and enzyme function.
Vitamin A	Promotes healthy skin and needed for night vision.
Vitamin D	Required for calcium absorption and use.
Vitamin E	Antioxidant preventing the oxidation of vitamin A and other fats.
Vitamin K	Assists in blood clotting.

Minerals

Iron	Important in transporting oxygen through the blood and enzymes involved in the oxidation of fat and carbohydrates.
Calcium	Gives structure and strength to bones and teeth. Important in blood clotting, muscle contraction, and relaxation.
Zinc	Component of several enzymes and insulin. Important in wound healing.

vegetables a day, six to eleven servings of breads, grains, or cereals, two or three servings of dairy, two or three servings of meat, fish, poultry, or beans and legumes each day.

There is a common misconception that if a little is good, a lot must be better, especially in the case of vitamin and mineral supplementation. Your body needs only a certain amount of micronutrients. Any excess will be excreted in your urine or stored in your body at potentially hazardous levels. It has been said that Americans have the most expensive urine in the world because of the amount of vitamin and mineral supplements they consume. If you eat a well-balanced diet, excess vitamin and mineral supplementation is not only unnecessary but can have potential side effects. For example, although vitamin A is necessary for healthy skin and night vision, it can lead to liver damage and headaches in excessive amounts. Vitamin C has been found to cause diarrhea in amounts greater than 1000 mg per day in some individuals. Selenium may lead to tissue damage in combination with niacin, which can also cause liver damage. Zinc has been noted to impair immune response in large doses. The Recommended Daily Allowances (RDA) are defined as the level of intake of micronutrients, based on scientific knowledge, that are judged to be adequate to meet the needs of practically all healthy persons. Margins of safety are incorporated into these values to account for variability between individuals. It is recommended that you do not use vitamin supplements in excess of the RDA. Anyone interested in the use of supplements above the RDA should consult with their physician, dietitian, or pharmacist concerning the risks and benefits. This includes mineral supplements and herbal products, which should be used with caution and preferably with medical advice.

The human body is more than 60 percent water by weight. It is important to drink plenty of fluids each day to keep your body well hydrated, and therefore functioning more efficiently. Remember that old rule of thumb: Drink at least eight eight-ounce glasses of water or other fluids per day, except those containing caffeine, such as coffee and colas.

2. Maintain healthy weight

Our bodies function most effectively when they are neither too heavy nor too light. Many studies have shown an increased incidence of sickness associated with persons at both ends of the weight spectrum. Obesity can compound low back pain and increase the pressure and pain on degenerative joints. Furthermore, being overweight can affect your ability to participate in exercise, which is critical for managing chronic pain, in addition to affecting your self-image and mental attitude. Refer to Figure 11.4 to get an idea of your healthy weight. The broad range within each height to weight ratio allows for individual fluctuations in muscle and bone mass.

Achieving and maintaining your healthy weight is based on this simple equation: Energy in (calories from food) = energy out (exercise and activity). There are two ways to alter your weight—change the amount of food you eat or change the amount of energy you use.

If you want to lose weight, you should decrease the amount of calories you consume while increasing the amount of activity you do each day. Only carbohydrates, protein, fat, and alcohol, also known as the macronutrients, provide calories. Carbohydrates and protein both provide four calories per gram, while alcohol provides seven calories per gram and fat provides nine calories per gram. Fat and alcohol are both calorie-dense—you can eat more carbohydrates and protein for the same amount of calories as a smaller portion of fat or alcohol.

Gradual weight loss is better for you than trying to lose weight quickly. Studies have shown that most crash dieters will regain their lost pounds and more. This is known as "yo-yo dieting" and can be a vicious cycle. A healthier approach is to cut down on your portion sizes, and take a walk

Healthy Weights for Men and Women		
Height	*Men*	*Women*
4'10"		91–119 lbs.
4'11"		94–122 lbs.
5'0"		96– 125 lbs.
5'1"		99–128 lbs.
5'2"	112–141 lbs.	102–131 lbs.
5'3"	115–144 lbs.	105–134 lbs.
5'4"	118–148 lbs.	108–138 lbs.
5'5"	121–152 lbs.	111–142 lbs.
5'6"	124–156 lbs.	114–146 lbs.
5'7"	128–161 lbs.	118–150 lbs.
5'8"	132–166 lbs.	122–154 lbs.
5'9"	136–170 lbs.	126–158 lbs.
5'10"	140–174 lbs.	130–163 lbs.
5'11"	144–179 lbs.	134–168 lbs.
6'0"	148–184 lbs.	138–173 lbs.
6'1"	152-189 lbs	
6'2"	156–194 lbs.	
6'3"	160–199 lbs.	
6'4"	164–204 lbs.	

Source: U.S. Department of Health, Education, and Welfare.

each day. Look at the typical portion sizes on the Food Guide Pyramid. Try measuring out a typical serving size to get an idea what it looks like on your plate. Choose foods lower in fat from each group. This approach will encourage gradual weight loss over time.

If weight gain is your goal, increase the amount of calories in your diet and maintain an active lifestyle for muscle and bone strength. Here are some ideas to increase the amount of calories in your diet:

- Frequent small meals—aim for five or six small meals per day

- Choose calorie dense, healthy snacks, such as trail mix, peanut butter and crackers, or granola bars

- Schedule your meals each day, and stick to your plan

- Always have a healthy snack with you

3. Choose a diet low in fat, saturated fat, and cholesterol

A diet high in fat is associated with the development of chronic disease and obesity. High fat meals can actually slow down the flow of blood and delivery of oxygen to your tissues, making you feel tired and sluggish. All fats are made of three types of fatty acids—saturated, polyunsaturated, and monounsaturated.

Saturated fat is solid at room temperature. Sources of saturated fat include meat and dairy products and some vegetable oils such as coconut, palm, and palm kernel. Saturated fat is the main culprit in increasing serum cholesterol levels, even more so than dietary cholesterol. Increased serum cholesterol levels are associated with the development of heart disease.

Polyunsaturated fatty acid (PUFA) sources include corn oil, safflower oil, soybean, cotton-seed, and sesame oils. Diets high in PUFAs lower the "good" cholesterol, or the cholesterol carrier that transports cholesterol to the liver for excretion. A diet high in PUFAs may be associated with certain cancers, such as breast, colon, and prostate.

Monounsaturated fatty acids (MUFA) are the primary fat in olive, canola, and peanut oils as well as avocados. These oils have a neutral effect on serum cholesterol and should be emphasized in your diet.

Cholesterol is a natural fat-like substance found in all cells in the body. It is necessary for the maintenance of cell walls, hormone synthesis, insulation of nerve tissue, vitamin D synthesis, and bile production. Although necessary for our bodies to function well, increased amounts of cholesterol in the blood (greater than 200 mg/dl) is undesirable. Dietary cholesterol is found only in animal foods, such as meat, fish, poultry, and dairy products.

Foods high in cholesterol

- High-fat diary products
- Beef kidney, brain, liver
- Egg yolk
- Poultry skin

Some fat is necessary in the diet but only a very small quantity. Only seven to ten grams of fat per day is likely to provide enough essential fat. A diet providing 30 percent of calories or less from fat is considered desirable. Too much fat, whether primarily monounsaturated, polyunsaturated or saturated, contributes to obesity and should be limited in your diet. Here are some ways to cut down on fat:

- Use less extra fats such as butter, margarine, and cooking oils
- Use low-fat cooking methods, such as baking, braising, broiling, barbecuing, and steaming, when preparing foods
- Learn to read labels to avoid foods with greater than 30 percent of their calories from fat
- Use only two or three eggs per week
- Trim all visible fat from meat
- Take the skin off poultry before eating

- Choose leaner cuts of meat, pork, and lamb.

4. Choose a diet with plenty of vegetables, fruits, and grain products

Vegetables, fruits, and grain products are primarily made up of carbohydrates, and are relatively low in fat but rich in vitamins, minerals, and fiber. Fiber is found in all plant foods and is the part of food that we are unable to break down and digest. Fiber works as "nature's broom," sweeping food through your intestines. It can help prevent constipation, colon cancer, and diverticulosis. Diverticula are small sacks on the inner surface of the large intestine caused by excessive straining and constipation. Fiber provides bulk and can make you feel full on less food.

Food	*Fiber Content (grams)*
1 cup of strawberries	5.0
1 baked potato	5.5
1/2 cup beans, lentils or peas	8.0
1/2 cup of broccoli or carrots	4.0
3 cups popcorn	3.5
1/2 cup brown rice	2.0

5. Use sugar in moderation

Refined and concentrated simple sugars, such as table sugar and honey, contain few nutrients and little or no fiber. Increased amounts of simple sugars can affect our mood. Have you ever noticed how candy might lift your energy level but an hour later you feel sluggish? These peaks and valleys of energy make you feel cranky and tired. A way to avoid these sugar highs and lows is to eat small meals frequently throughout the day to keep your blood sugar at a more constant level. When eating a carbohydrate-rich food such as fruit, eat some protein or a little fat with it, such as cheese. Foods containing protein and fat will slow the absorption of the sugar and help to maintain a stable blood glucose level and prevent those mood swings.

6. Use salt and sodium in moderation

Sodium is a mineral that occurs naturally in some foods. However, it is added to many foods as a preservative or flavoring. You only need 200 - 500 milligrams (mg) of sodium per day. A diet low in sodium can reduce the risk of hypertension and prevent water retention, especially with individuals taking glucocorticoid medications that can aggravate water retention. Some high sodium foods include:

Snack and convenience foods	Smoked and pickled foods
Condiments and seasonings	Cheese
Bottled sauces	Cured and processed meats
Packaged and canned soups	

7. If you drink alcoholic beverages, do so in moderation

Although you might consider alcoholic beverages a way to relax, they are in actuality a depressant and can affect your mood dramatically. Excess alcohol (greater than one to two drinks per day—four ounces of wine, twelve ounces of beer, or one shot of liquor) can have an adverse affect on your mood in addition to providing a dense source of calories contributing to obesity.

Caffeine/nicotine

Caffeine and nicotine deserve attention as potent and addictive drugs with possible negative side effects. In order to help your body perform optimally, you should use these substances only in moderation.

Many people believe that they can't start their day without their cup of coffee to get them moving. However by mid-morning they find themselves not as alert as they would like and resort to yet another cup of coffee, cappuccino, or cola. Each additional cup of caffeine, however, serves less to wake you up and more to make you jittery and irritable. Therefore, limit yourself to one to two cups of caffeinated beverages per day or less. You might experience headaches as you wean yourself off caffeine; they should go away within a few days. In addition to leading to feelings of irritability, caffeine is also a diuretic—it causes you to urinate more frequently, placing you at risk for dehydration.

Smoking is one of the biggest hazards to your health, and one of the most important habits for a healthy body to break. Unfortunately, nicotine is a potent, habit-forming drug that can be very difficult to quit. Smoking causes poor oxygen circulation in your blood (oxygen is necessary for almost every function in your body, from breathing to healing) and greatly increases your risk for heart disease, as well as cancer. If you are having difficulty quitting, talk to your physician or health care practitioner.

Interactions Between Drugs and Nutrients

People who are experiencing chronic pain are often prescribed a variety of medications to help get relief. Some of the most common pain medications have nutritional side effects that can hinder your body's ability to heal itself. Common medications that are prescribed for pain are narcotics (or opiates) and glucocorticoids.

Narcotics that include codeine and morphine can lead to constipation. If you have any problems with constipation, it is vital for you to consume increased fluids and increase the amount of insoluble fiber in your diet. Insoluble fiber is found in whole grains, beans, vegetables, and fruits; it acts by stimulating the gastrointestinal tract and preventing constipation.

Glucocorticoid medications, including Prednisone and Decadron, can cause sodium and water retention and increase vitamin C excretion. With long-term use, glucocorticoids can lead to muscle atrophy, increased appetite, and weight gain. Therefore, eat foods low in sodium, increase your intake of vitamin C-rich foods such as oranges, strawberries, and green peppers, and consume adequate amounts of protein—for example, two or three servings of lean meat, fish, poultry, or legumes and two or three servings of lowfat or nonfat dairy products per day.

Choosing Healthy Foods—Putting Your Knowledge Into Action

Even armed with all of this knowledge, it can be difficult to choose healthy foods in the supermarket. Learn to read food labels. Claims on food packages and advertisements can be confusing and sometimes even misleading. The new Nutrition Facts food label, developed by the U.S. Department of Agriculture, helps consumers make informed food choices. Almost all packaged foods are required to have this label (see figure 11.5). The label provides information on serving size, calories, fat, protein, carbohydrates and the four micronutrients found to be most deficient in American diets—vitamin A, vitamin C, iron, and calcium.

Now It's Your Turn

Take the time to review the information you have learned regarding your diet. Review the Diet Recall Form at the beginning of the chapter, which identifies the areas where you might benefit from a change in your food choices. Then look over the Guidelines for a Healthy Diet and the Food Guide Pyramid. Below, write down three actions you can take right now to start eating a more healthful diet and in turn help your body to perform at its best. Your goals don't have to be drastic. You can't expect, for example, to cut out all of the fat in your diet at once. A more realistic goal might be to have frozen yogurt instead of ice cream for dessert. Empty out the salt shaker and avoid

Figure 11.5

Reading for good eating
Analyzing the new nutrition label

New Title: *Indicates the product carries the new label information established with the 1990 Nutrition Labeling and Education Act.*

Serving Size: *Serving size is now based on the amount most commonly eaten.*

Total Fat: *The amount of fat included in each serving (in grams). It is recommended that your overall diet, not necessarily any one food item, contain no more than 30% of calories from fat on average.*

New Required Nutrients: *Reflect the current public health emphasis. New required nutrients include saturated fat, cholesterol, sodium, dietary fiber, and sugars.*

Daily Values Footnote: *Daily values reflect current nutrition recommendations. The two listings show daily values for both 2,000 and 2,500 calorie diets. For example, the daily value for fat is 65 grams for 2,000 calories and 80 grams for 2,500 calories. Of course, your individual calorie needs may vary. Remember, the percent daily values are based on a 2,000 calorie diet.*

Servings per Container: *Refers to the number of servings included in the package. This package contains 10 frankfurters (hot dogs).*

Calories and Calories from Fat: *Calories measure the energy supplied from food. Calories from fat reflect the number of fat calories the product provides per serving, not the percentage of calories from fat.*

% Daily Value: *The percent daily values help you see how a food fits into a 2,000 calorie reference diet. They tell you if a food contains a little or a lot of a nutrient. This hot dog only has 2% of the daily value for fat, which is low fat. The overall goal is to attain 100% of your daily value throughout the day by eating a variety of foods.*

Calorie Conversion Information: *Reflects the number of calories per gram provided by carbohydrate, fat, and protein. Notice that fat contains more than twice the calories per gram (9 calories) than carbohydrate or protein (4 calories).*

Nutrition Facts
Serving Size One Hot Dog (45 g)
Servings Per Container 10

Amount Per Serving

Calories 45	**Calories from Fat** 15

	% Daily Value*
Total Fat 1.5 g	**2%**
Saturated Fat 1 g	**5%**
Cholesterol 15 mg	**5%**
Sodium 430 mg	**18%**
Total Carbohydrate 2 g	**1%**
Dietary Fiber 0 g	**0%**
Sugars 2 g	
Protein 5 g	

Vitamin A 0%	•	Vitamin C 8%
Calcium 0%	•	Iron 2%

*Percent daily values are based on a 2,000 calorie diet. Your daily values may be higher or lower depending on your calorie needs:

		Calories:	2,000	2,500
Total Fat	Less than		65 g	80 g
Sat Fat	Less than		20 g	25 g
Cholesterol	Less than		300 mg	300 mg
Sodium	Less than		2,400 mg	2,400 mg
Total Carbohydrate			300 g	375 g
Dietary Fiber			25 g	30 g

Calories per gram:
Fat 9 • Carbohydrate 4 • Protein 4

additional salt on foods. Drink more water per day, eventually working your way up to eight glasses. Hang your goals on the refrigerator or another place you know you'll see them and remind yourself of them daily. Good nutrition is a critical piece of the wellness puzzle. A healthy diet is one step you can take on the road to recovery.

1. _____

_____

_____

_____

2. _____

_____

_____

_____

3. _____

_____

_____

_____

Further Reading

Baird, P. 1993. *The Pyramid Cookbook: Pleasures of the Food Guide Pyramid.* New York: Henry Holt and Company, Inc.

Ponichtera, B. 1995. *Quick and Healthy: Volume II.* Dalles, OR: Scaledown.

Somer, E. 1996. *Food & Mood: The Complete Guide to Eating Well and Feeling Your Best.* New York: Henry Holt and Company, Inc.

Information Regarding Food and Nutrition Questions Can Be Obtained From:

American Dietetic Association/National Center for Nutrition and Dietetics Nutrition Hotline at (800) 366-1655

Online Information Can Be Found At:

http://www.usda.gov

http://www.lifelines.com/ntnlnk.html

http://www.eatright.org

12

Medication and Pain Management

By Robert W. Allen, M.D.

As a chronic pain patient, you have probably met with numerous physicians and tried scores of medications. This is an experience shared by many, if not most, chronic pain sufferers. However, many people have little or no understanding of why they are prescribed certain medications, what effects the medications are supposed to have, and what kinds of side effects to anticipate. In fact, many people take for granted that their medications are appropriate for them. They seem to believe that learning more about their medication is too difficult.

It is true that understanding the proper use of medications can be complex. For example, you may take several medications from more than one doctor and no single doctor is keeping track of them all. You may not only have side effects that are difficult to trace to a single pill, but medicines can *interact* with each other, creating new problems.

If you use medication as part of your pain management program, it is important that you understand both the purpose and proper use of those medications. The more you know about your medications, including how they work, their potential side effects, and their limitations in controlling your pain, the more effective they can be. There are no perfect medications and all will have some side effects. You have to constantly weigh the benefits versus the risks of any medication you take. In addition, it is unlikely that any medication will eliminate your chronic pain condition completely. So, the objective for most patients is to find a medication that can *reduce* the level of pain you are experiencing and do so with as few side effects as possible.

In this chapter I will review the causes of pain and identify how specific medications act on the body when used in pain management. As you will see in the text and tables at the end of the chapter, the medications are grouped according to how they work, how they are used by the medical profession, and their side effects. I will refer to each drug by its chemical or generic name first and will include a brand name for the same drug in parentheses.

How Do We Feel Pain?

In order for a part of your body to experience pain, there must be a nerve supply. Let's use a broken ankle as an example. Your bone has a rich nerve supply and so do the tissues (muscles, tendons, and so on) surrounding the ankle. This nerve supply in the ankle is called the *peripheral nervous system*, which includes all the nerves in the arms and legs. When you break your ankle, the nerve endings in the area are activated or *excited*. This excitement of the nerve sends electrical signals through the peripheral nerve to the *spinal cord*. Nerves in the spinal cord receive the information and carry it on to the brain. Once the signal is in the brain, you are able to translate this electrical information into a sensation of pain. The nerves in the spinal cord and brain are referred to as the *central nervous system*.

Using our example, when you break your ankle, you will generally see swelling and inflammation. What is happening underneath is that the tissue around your ankle is injured and leaks various chemicals contained in the tissue cells. These inflammatory chemicals also sensitize pain nerve fibers, which means that they become much more sensitive and painful. Different chemicals within the nerve fibers also allow nerves to communicate with each other, for example, when the peripheral nerves pass signals on to the spinal cord and then up to the brain, through *pain pathways*. Medications will interact with these chemicals, producing pain relief. We'll discuss these various medications later in this chapter. You can find a further description of pain pathways in chapter 2.

If an injury, such as a sprained or fractured ankle, is recent and the peripheral nerve is activated, but not damaged, we refer to this as *acute nociceptive pain*. If the trauma actually injures the nerve itself, we refer to this as *neuropathic pain* (nerve damage). Acute nociceptive pain typically responds to pain medications and heals more effectively than pain resulting from nerve injury. Neuropathic pain typically last much longer and responds less to standard pain medications. This type of injury is what frequently leads to chronic pain. The majority of chronic pain patients have some form of neuropathic injury or nerve damage. Neuropathic pain can occur in either the peripheral nervous system or in the central nervous system (such as with a spinal cord injury or a stroke) or both. In a neuropathic pain injury, the way that pain signals are transmitted up to the brain appears to be different from normal nerve communication. Unfortunately, we do not fully understand why some patients develop only a nociceptive injury that heals, while others suffer nerve damage that does not heal completely.

How Do Medications Work?

Let's review some important points about pain so you can more clearly understand the role of medications, and where they work in the reduction or elimination of pain. When you burn your skin, break a bone, or undergo surgery, the trauma involved activates pain nerve fibers located in these tissues of skin, bone, or ligaments. And, as discussed above, the damage to the tissue results in the release of potent chemicals that causes an inflammatory reaction (swelling, redness) and also makes the pain fibers more sensitive. Pain fibers located in the skin or bone send chemical messages to the spinal cord (the same way electricity enters your house from the power company when you turn on a light switch). This, in turn, activates nerves in the spinal cord that send messages to your brain allowing you to perceive the process as painful. Think of medications then as chemicals designed to interfere with some of this communication and hopefully reduce the amount of "painful" information that reaches the spinal cord or brain. Sometimes the pain nerve fibers are not activated in a normal way but are injured and may result in neuropathic pain, as you learned earlier. The changes and communications that occur when a nerve is actually injured may be different than what is described above and therefore may not respond as nicely to medications.

What About Side Effects?

Side effects are generally defined as any effects that a medication produces other than those it is primarily prescribed for. All medications on the market have side effects. Consult your physician about the potential benefit and possible side effects of taking a medication. You should know what side effects to expect and that some of the negative side effects can be reduced by changing the way the medicines are taken. Be aware that all side effects are not seen as undesirable, and in fact, a medication may be prescribed for you because a particular side effect may be beneficial for you. For example, while an antihistamine is generally used to help you breathe easier, a common side effect is sedation (or sleepiness) and sometimes physicians will recommend them to help you get to sleep. You should always discuss potential side effects with your physician. Also, do your own research by asking your pharmacist or reading books on medications available in your library or bookstore. It is very important for you to have a relationship with your physician where you can freely express your concerns regarding the medications you are taking. Side effects are not always dangerous, but they may be unpleasant (such as a dry mouth or mild nausea). Therefore, you and your doctor have to weigh the balance of benefit (pain reduction) versus intolerable side effects before you decide to avoid or eliminate potentially effective medications.

Here are a few simple points to remember:

- Try to keep an open mind about medications that your doctor recommends

- Learn as much as you can about what to expect after you take them

- Discuss with him or her your concerns or fears

- If you do decide to try a new medicine, establish a plan that you feel comfortable with, such as when and where to call in case of the appearance of unexpected symptoms or side effects.

No doubt your primary doctor, as well as other specialists, will consider multiple types and trials of medications for your chronic pain. Later in this chapter, I will cover the various classifications of medications including why they are used, potential benefits, and possible side effects.

What Is the Most Effective Way to Use Medications?

You will find in this chapter a great deal of information about the medications themselves. You may grow impatient with the amount of information we have provided. You may wish that we could simply say "You have ___ pain, take ___ drug." However, information alone is not enough to use medications effectively, due to your unique situation. Many factors must be considered before you begin taking a medication. Some factors relate to the type of disorder or pain you have, for example an inflammatory condition or pain due to nerve damage. Other important factors to consider relate to you as an individual, such as your weight, age, sex, allergies, and other health problems and psychosocial concerns you may have. We also must look at the medication and take into account the appropriate therapeutic dose, the side effects, and precautions. These are only a few of the concerns your physician weighs before prescribing a medication. One important goal is to achieve the most effective pain management possible, with the least amount of impairment in your ability to function. If you find out from your physician what course of medication is prescribed, you can look it up in this chapter to familiarize yourself with the drug's properties. Take the book into your doctor, point out the part(s) that pertain to you, and discuss with him or her.

Major Classes of Drugs

The major types of pain medications include:

1. Narcotics or Opioids

2. Antidepressants including Tricyclics and SSRIs

3. Aspirin and Acetaminophen (Tylenol) Products

4. Anticonvulsants

5. Non-Steroidal Anti-Inflammatory Drugs or NSAIDs

6. Steroids

7. Local Anesthetics

8. Minor Tranquilizers or Anti-anxiety Drugs

9. Muscle Relaxers

10. Major Tranquilizers or Antipsychotics

Narcotics or Opioids

Narcotics are pain-relieving drugs including opium and other opiate derivatives such as morphine, codeine, and heroin. See table 12.1. They are frequently used in treating acute pain, or pain that is short-lived during the healing process following an injury or surgery. Narcotics are also used to treat pain in cancer or other terminal illnesses. Essentially, narcotics work in two ways: (1) they tend to reduce the amount of pain signal from an activated peripheral nerve that gets to the spinal cord, and (2) they reduce the amount of pain signal that gets to your brain from the spinal cord. Narcotic side effects include nausea, vomiting, constipation, sedation, mental clouding, tolerance (lack of benefit after a period of time), possible addiction, and sometimes death due to an overdose.

The use of narcotics to manage chronic pain is highly debated among health care professionals because of their potential for addiction and misuse. In part, the controversy exists because some studies have shown that narcotics are not effective pain reducers in chronic neuropathic pain, whereas other studies suggest they can be beneficial. While some patients experience good pain reduction from narcotics and are able to return to many normal daily activities, others either find that narcotics do not effectively reduce pain or that they experience intolerable side effects.

We do not yet know how taking narcotics over a long period of time will affect a person's ability to increase their level of activity or functionality. There are no hard and fast rules regarding the use of narcotics for chronic pain and every pain case should be evaluated on an individual basis. A reputable chronic pain clinic will use a thorough, interdisciplinary assessment to help determine whether narcotic use would benefit you. Many factors are examined in this process. A prior history of substance abuse and dependence (such as alcoholism or cocaine abuse) suggests that addiction could be a problem for an individual using a narcotic. Many physicians are also cautious about the use of narcotics with patients who are severely depressed or suicidal.

The controversy about the use of narcotics for chronic pain also exists because of the stigma surrounding the term *addiction*. Addiction is a broad, umbrella term associated with a lot of negative stereotypes. In the past, both physical dependency and addiction were labeled as one problem. New theory has emerged in the field of pain management which suggests that physical dependency and addiction no longer mean the same thing. It is important that you understand this distinction. In the pain management field, addiction is defined as the "compulsive use of a narcotic that results in physical, psychological, or social impairment with continued use, despite the evidence of impairment." In other words, addicted people tend to abuse the drug. In contrast, people who are physically dependent may not demonstrate all the other negative behaviors that an addicted person might, but their bodies have become adapted to the narcotic so that when they no longer have the accustomed amount of narcotic, they experience withdrawal symptoms. Withdrawal symptoms include sweating, nausea, flu-like symptoms, and a craving for more narcotics if the narcotics are stopped abruptly.

Many pain clinics will ask you to complete a *narcotic use contract* if narcotics are prescribed on an ongoing basis. The goal of this contract is to provide you with your physician's expectations regarding the use of the narcotic before potential problems or misunderstandings arise. Because narcotics are closely monitored by physicians, a contract can help you and your physician develop a specific, detailed plan for your treatment. Knowing what is expected of you up front can provide you with a sense of security and trust about your care. Although each clinic's contract will have its own unique features and appearance, most contracts contain the same basic expectations for patients. See the sample narcotic use contract at the end of this chapter.

It is important for any pain patient to learn and use a range of behaviors to manage his or her pain. Narcotics may be an appropriate medication if you are highly motivated and are capable of following a strict regimen prescribed by your doctor, using alternative strategies (like those mentioned throughout this book) in addition to the narcotic to manage pain, and using the reduction you get in pain to increase your activity.

There are correct and incorrect ways to use narcotics if they are indicated for you. First, if you are dealing with chronic pain, then the medications should be taken on a regular schedule, not just when you feel like it. Second, you should take narcotics that have *longer durations* of action. There are two basic types of narcotics: (1) long-acting narcotics which last for an eight- to ten-hour period, and (2) short-acting narcotics which last about four hours. For example, methadone (Dolophine), morphine sulfate continuous (MS Contin), or fentanyl (Duragesic) patches are all long-acting narcotics, while drugs like Vicodin and Percocet are short-acting. Advantages of the longer-acting narcotics include: less time in pain (since you have fewer times when you are coming off the medication just prior to your next dose) and less chance of liver damage since the long-acting narcotics typically do not include Tylenol, which we now know can cause this in higher doses over time.

A word of warning: You should never increase your dose of narcotics without your physician's instructions. Many patients make the mistake of assuming that if a certain dose helps a little bit, then increasing the dose will help more. This may or may not be the case and should be determined by you and your physician as a team. Escalating narcotic medications without your physician's approval is frequently viewed as abuse and a red flag by physicians. Escalating narcotic medication without medical advice can also lead to overdose, impaired judgment, and accidents.

The role of narcotics in the management of chronic pain continues to be investigated by pain specialists. I believe they may play a valuable role in specific situations. However, narcotics are not the final answer to chronic pain problems in most cases. You may initially feel better when you take a narcotic. This does not always mean, however, that this is the best way to treat your pain, because of the many side effects. As you develop tolerance, the benefits you feel may be short lived. It is important for you to discuss this issue thoroughly with your physician before beginning the use of narcotics and to balance the potential increases in activity with the possible negative side effects.

Antidepressants

Antidepressants are frequently used to manage of all types of chronic pain, but they are especially used with nerve injury pain (neuropathic pain). It is probably also the most misunderstood (by patients) of all medications used in chronic pain management. Many patients have an aversion to taking antidepressants because they are convinced that depression is not playing a role in their pain, or they think that when the doctor prescribes an antidepressant, she or he is doing so because the pain must be "all in their head." The following clarifies the role of antidepressants in the treatment of chronic pain to help reduce some of the confusion about these very helpful medications.

Currently, there are two main types of antidepressants frequently used—*tricyclic antidepressants* (Elavil, Pamelor, and Desyrel) and *selective serotonin reuptake inhibitor antidepressants* (Prozac, Zoloft, and Paxil). *Tricyclic antidepressants* (TCAs) are more commonly used in pain management because they are believed to alter the level and release of chemicals (neurotransmitters) in pain nerve fibers. In altering the levels of these chemicals that are released, they also alter the communication of pain signals to the brain, thereby lowering the pain level that you experience. It is difficult to know how much of the medication is required for beneficial effect. Typically the amounts of TCAs used to treat pain are lower than the doses used to treat depression. In fact, in the majority of cases when your doctor chooses to use low-dose antidepressants, he or she is most likely using it for your pain, not for potential, underlying depression.

Of course, as discussed in chapter 6, there are many cases where depression may indeed be present in addition to the pain. In this case, both pain and depression can be treated with this class of medications, allowing patients to see a reduction in their pain level and an improvement in their mood. For tricyclic antidepressants to have an effect on depression, however, they must be given at higher doses than are given for pain control alone. Side effects of TCAs include dry mouth, drowsiness (especially early morning), morning hangover, and dizziness when you first stand from a lying or seated position. Tricyclic antidepressants may also increase constipation if you are already taking narcotics. An important point to remember is that although you may experience intolerable side effects from one particular TCA, you may be able to tolerate another. Don't rule out this class of medication; it can be extremely beneficial in the management of chronic neuropathic pain.

The second main type of antidepressant, *selective serotonin reuptake inhibitors* (SSRIs), appears to be more effective for treating depression than for pain control at this time. SSRIs have been safely used in the treatment of depression for over a decade now and appear to have fewer side effects than TCAs. In fact, certain SSRIs are often selected to treat depression because they also may have the side effect of decreased appetite, which is particularly helpful for someone who has gained weight due to pain and depression.

All antidepressant medications can be harmful if taken with alcohol. Patients should avoid all alcohol if considering any of these medications for pain management. See table 12.2 for the most commonly prescribed antidepressants.

Aspirin and Tylenol

These pain relievers are often forgotten and neglected by chronic pain sufferers because they do not require a prescription. While they do have excellent analgesic (pain-relieving) properties, they also have equally important side effects, which you should take into consideration.

Aspirin

Aspirin is an effective pain medication for certain conditions. It has potent anti-inflammatory action and is effective when inflammatory chemicals are making pain nerve fibers more sensitive in an acute injury. It is most beneficial for acute pain states, but seems generally less effective for most chronic pain conditions. One chronic pain condition that can be effectively managed with aspirin is arthritis. Arthritis is a condition of ongoing inflammation in the joints (see chapter 18). The inflammatory chemicals that are present in the joint serve to sensitize the pain nerve fibers that are present. Medications such as aspirin lower the concentration of these inflammatory chemicals and subsequently reduce pain. The major side effects of aspirin include gastric irritation (including possible ulcers) and increased bleeding tendencies. See table 12.3.

Acetaminophen (Tylenol)

Acetaminophen does not reduce inflammation, but it can reduce both pain and fever. It is effective for some minor pains and is frequently used in combinations with other stronger pain medications. Side effects are relatively low with Tylenol at lower doses, but the medication is broken down in your liver into a chemical product that can injure the liver if excessive doses are taken. Because of the potential for liver damage, most doctors believe the dose of Tylenol should be limited to between 2000 and 4000 mg per day, or no more than eight Tylenol tablets per day. The same applies to medications containing Tylenol, such as Vicodin or Percocet. If used safely, however, Tylenol can be an excellent addition to your pain management regimen. See table 12.4.

Anticonvulsants

This class of medication includes carbamazepine (Tegretol), phenytoin (Dilantin), valproic acid (Depakote), and gabapentin (Neurontin) (see table 12.5). These are all medications used for the control of seizures. A seizure is believed to be precipitated by nerve tissue in the brain that spontaneously "fires" and sends out electrical signal waves. These medications serve to decrease this electrical activity and reduce or prevent seizures. Imagine a frayed electrical wire in your home. When the electrical wire has lost its protective layer of insulation, the electricity no longer travels smoothly down the wire but can exit through the area of wire damage. If you touch it, you will actually be shocked. This may also be the case with a nerve which has been injured in the body and no longer sends nerve transmissions in a normal way, but rather fires spontaneously because its layer of insulation is missing or damaged due to the injury. The anticonvulsants are able to paint a new layer of insulation over the wire that is frayed and potentially reduce the spontaneous firing and pain associated with the injury. Some typical pains that may respond to anticonvulsants are often described as "stabbing, shooting, and jabbing" pains.

Side effects from these medications may be significant, especially when you first start taking them or when you begin taking higher doses. Some typical side effects may include mental clouding, sedation, and problems with balance. A special concern with carbamazapine (Tegretol) may be bone marrow suppression; your doctor will likely order blood tests to determine the levels of the drug in your body to make sure that you don't develop permanent or harmful effects.

Non-Steroidal Anti-Inflammatory Drugs (NSAIDs)

This category includes ibuprofen (Motrin and Advil) and naproxen (Naprosyn). A more complete list can be found in table 12.6. Tissue trauma or injury results in a leak of chemicals called *prostaglandins*. We know that prostaglandins make pain nerve fibers more irritable and can increase the level of pain you experience. NSAIDs, by interfering with the production of prostaglandins, decrease the level of pain you may experience. However, this class of medication has what is called a *ceiling effect.* This means that there is a maximum dose, which, if exceeded results in no additional benefit, and only increases your chances of experiencing side effects. We also have found that patients with similar clinical problems sometimes experience different amounts of relief from the same NSAID. What this means for you is that there are many NSAIDs available for use, and just because you have side effects or inadequate pain relief with one does not mean that you will not obtain benefit with one of the many others. It is important to try several agents, one at a time, before eliminating this class of medications as an option in the management of your chronic pain. Any side effects you experience should be discussed with your physician.

The side effects of NSAIDs occur as a result of reducing the level of prostaglandins. Stomach or intestinal ulcers can occur and symptoms may include stomach pain or burning, loss of appetite, constipation, or diarrhea. More serious gastric problems include perforation of ulcer and gastric bleeding. There may be some medications, such as omeprazole and misoprostol, which reduce the incidence of ulcers. There is also an increased risk of bleeding with NSAIDs, and if you have any history of bleeding problems you should let your physician know. If you have any history of kidney problems you should also inform your physician, because NSAIDs may interfere with kidney function. Keep in mind that some studies suggest that elderly persons are more prone to kidney function problems.

NSAIDs' side effects may sound frightening. However, if your pain has a predominant inflammatory component, these agents may be the best medications available and can be very safe, with proper monitoring by you and your physician.

Steroids

Steroids are one of the best inflammation-reducing drugs available. They are also among the most controversial in both pain management and general medical use. Originally, steroids were given by mouth over long periods of time to help reduce inflammation in certain chronic diseases (such as arthritis). Unfortunately, some patients developed side effects of bone loss, skin and organ break-down, and swelling. Because of these side effects, the use of oral steroids has decreased significantly, although they are still used occasionally in certain difficult to treat inflammatory diseases and in such situations as severe asthma attacks. You should always talk with your physician before taking oral steroids on a long-term basis. Despite their controversial reputation as an oral medication, however, they have gained widespread acceptance when administered at the epidural space.

The *epidural space* is located along the spine in both the upper and lower back where the individual nerves that go to your legs and arms are located. Occasionally, inflammation or swelling around the epidural space may put pressure on nerves and therefore may contribute to your pain. Steroids can be injected into this epidural space, which will reduce inflammation and possibly reduce the level of pain you are experiencing. You must be careful to allow only those physicians who are specially trained in this technique to perform an epidural injection (anesthesiologists are currently the predominant type of physicians performing this technique). Injecting steroids into the epidural space has a distinct advantage over taking oral steroids. Because the medication can be delivered directly to the inflamed site, the doses required may be less than when orally administered. In general, short-term use of oral steroids and steroids administered by epidural injection may be beneficial if inflammation or edema (swelling) is contributing to your pain.

Local Anesthetics

A *local anesthetic* is applied directly to tissues or nerves for the purpose of "numbing" them prior to surgery or dental work (see table 12.7). They work by blocking the electrical activity of nerves and thereby making the tissue "numb." Some local anesthetics, such as lidocaine, are effective in reducing the level of some neuropathic pains that don't seem to respond to the usual pain medications (see chapter 20 for more on neuropathic pain). However, when used to treat neuropathic pain, they are not applied directly to the nerve, but are given through an I.V. (intravenous route). When introduced into the body in this way, the medication is believed to reduce the irritability of painful nerve tissue that contributes to your pain. The effect of administering the local anesthetic by I.V. is only temporary, but if you find that the procedure reduces your pain, you will likely be given oral medication (pills) that acts similarly to the I.V. anesthetic. For example, when a patient with neuropathic pain experiences good pain relief during an I.V. trial of lidocaine, a tablet called Mexiletene is then typically prescribed. The predominant side effects of Mexiletene are nausea and vomiting. I usually recommend that my patients begin taking this medication very slowly and gradually work up to the level that provides the best, but safest, pain relief. Effective dosages vary with each individual. You should discuss this procedure and these types of medications with your physician.

Minor Tranquilizers or Anti-Anxiety Drugs

Minor tranquilizers (also known as *anti-anxiety medications*) are used occasionally in treating pain patients. The most commonly used type of minor tranquilizer are the *benzodiazepines,* which includes diazepam (Valium), clonazepam (Klonopin), alprazolam (Xanax), and lorazepam (Ativan) among others listed in table 12.8. These medications have a demonstrated role in the treatment of certain psychiatric conditions, particularly those involving acute or severe anxiety, and should therefore be managed by a psychiatrist. The role of benzodiazepines in the treatment of chronic pain is unclear. There are many potential problems with the use of benzodiazepines over time, including addiction, sleep interference, and depression. Many physicians prescribe minor tranquilizers for pain patients to help reduce their anxiety, fear or irritability connected to the pain, rather than for pain reduction itself. Chronic pain experts, however, prefer other techniques such as biofeedback, stress management, coping skills training, and individual counseling to help reduce anxiety and panic and to increase a sense of self-control and empowerment. These more natural ways of reducing anxiety are much safer, have fewer side effects, and in many cases, are equally as effective in reducing pain and stress than the chemical alternatives. See chapters 4 and 5 for more information on such techniques.

Muscle Relaxers

Medications commonly used as muscle relaxers include methocarbamol (Robaxin), carisoprodol (Soma), and cyclobenzaprine (Flexeril). See table 12.9 for more on these medications. They were developed primarily to help reduce the tight, spasming sensations that are often present with muscle pain. However, the term "muscle relaxer" is slightly misleading since they do not appear to act directly on muscles to relax them in most cases. Many physicians believe that these medications work by relaxing or sedating the entire central nervous system (which includes the brain and spinal cord), thereby allowing your muscles to relax. Another muscle relaxer, baclofen (Lioresal), is commonly used with severe spasticity (high muscle tension and "jerky" awkward movements) and is very effective. Diazepam (Valium), a benzodiazepine, is frequently used as a muscle relaxer immediately after surgery when muscle spasms may be a problem. As mentioned in the previous section on minor tranquilizers, however, their long-term use is controversial and generally not recommended for chronic pain management.

Major Tranquilizers

Contrary to earlier beliefs, major tranquilizers, including phenothiazinc, have not been demonstrated to be helpful in the management of pain problems. Their side effects may be significant and should therefore be avoided if possible or used only with great caution.

Other Medications

Sometimes, narcotics are combined with other kinds of medications into one tablet, such as "Tylenol with codeine." See tables 12.10 and 12.11 for combination drugs or drugs that have their own unique chemical makeup.

Taking More Than One Medication at a Time

Patients who have chronic pain often find themselves taking multiple medications of several different types. This may happen for a number of reasons. First, you may have different types of pain, requiring different types of pain medications. Or, you may have other health problems that require medications in addition to the medications that you take for pain (such as blood pressure or heart medications). In some cases, you may find yourself taking medications from different doctors who treat you at the same time. This can easily become a serious problem if you have no central or primary doctor who is monitoring these medications, their interactions, and their side effects.

The danger lies in the potential for *overmedication* (taking too much of one type of medicine). For example, this could occur if you have two different doctors prescribing the same *class* of medication, but under separate brand names. Drug interactions represent another potential danger or source of side effects. Occasionally, when two drugs are taken at the same time, they interact with each other and change the way each drug works when taken alone or when taken with drugs that do not interact. Sometimes these two drugs may have *additive effects*, or in other words, they increase the effect the drugs have when working alone. This can be used "therapeutically" (meaning beneficial), by giving you a lower than normal dose of one medication (which will potentially reduce side effects) in combination with another medication that will enhance the effect of the lower dosage. However, interactions can also be detrimental. Drug interactions may cause you to experience problems seemingly unrelated to your pain that could be a result of taking multiple medications with unknown interactive effects.

In some cases, if you are taking multiple medications and have had pain for a long time, it may be difficult for your doctor (or any new specialist) to evaluate your problem adequately. It may therefore be necessary for you to discontinue your pain medications for a period just prior to an evaluation by a physician. However, if you have been on narcotic medications or minor tranquilizers over several months or years, you may have become dependent and you may need the assistance of a physician to *detoxify* from these medications. This process can be handled in a number of ways, from admission to a drug treatment center to a slow tapering off of the medications on an outpatient basis. It is important to not discontinue your medications without discussing it first with your doctor!

One Last Word

Many people in this country have become passive consumers of health care. They have learned to come into a doctor's office, tell him or her their symptoms, and take a prescription with them as they leave. Let me encourage you at this point to become active consumers of your health care. Don't be afraid to talk to your physician. Tell your health care professional about problems or side effects you may be having with your medications immediately, before taking action on your own. When you have questions about your condition or medications, ask your physician. You and your physician must form a partnership, or better yet, make your doctor a part of your entire treatment team if you are working with more than one type of health care provider. Good communication is the key to good health and proper pain control management.

Further Reading

Burger, A. 1995. *Understanding Medications: What the Label Doesn't Tell You.* Washington, DC: American Chemical Society.

Silverman, H. M. 1994. *The Pill Book,* 6th ed. New York: Bantam Books.

Taking Your Medications Safely. 1996. Springhouse, PA: Springhouse Corp., Nurse Advisor Books.

Thueson, D. 1994. *Over-the-Counter-Drugs.* Oakland, CA: New Harbinger Publications, Inc.

Willis, J. 1995. *Using Over-the-Counter Medications Wisely.* Rockville, MD: Dept. Of Health and Human Services, Public Health Service, Food and Drug Administration.

Online Information Can Be Found At:

http://pharminfo.com/

http://www.pharmweb.net/

http://www.wilmington.net/dees/

Multimedia Materials:

The Pill Book: An Illustrated Guide to the Most-Prescribed Drugs in the United States. 1993. Ver. 2.00, CD-ROM, Carlsbad, CA: Compton's New Media.

TABLE 12.1
NARCOTICS

DRUG NAME	TYPICAL DOSE	FREQUENCY	COMMENTS
PROPOXYPHENE (Darvon)	*65 mg*	*Every 4–6 hrs*	*Weak narcotic.*
CODEINE	*30–60 mg*	*Every 4–6 hrs*	*Weak narcotic.*
MORPHINE (Roxanol)	*10–30 mg*	*Every 3–4 hrs*	*Highly variable dose.*
MORPHINE (MS Contin) Controlled Release	*30–100 mg*	*Every 8–12 hrs*	*Long-acting.*
HYDROMORPHONE (Dilaudid)	*2–4 mg*	*Every 3–4 hrs*	*Short-acting.*
LEVORPHENOL (Levo-Dromoran)	*2–4 mg*	*Every 8–12 hrs*	*Long-acting.*
METHADONE (Dolophine)	*5–10 mg*	*Every 8–12 hrs*	*Long-acting.*
FENTANYL PATCH (Duragesic Patch)	*25–100 mcg*	*Every 3 days*	*Applied to the skin.*
LONG-ACTING OXYCODONE (Oxycontin)	*20–40 mg*	*Every 8–12 hours*	*Long-acting. Newly approved by FDA.*
BUTORPHANOL (Stadol Nasal Spray)	*1–2 puffs*	*Every 4–6 hrs*	*Poor choice for chronic pain.*

TABLE 12.2
ANTIDEPRESSANTS

DRUG NAME	TYPICAL DOSE	FREQUENCY	COMMENTS
AMITRIPTYLINE (*Elavil*)	*25–200 mg*	*Every 24 hrs*	*Tricyclic. Well-documented positive effects on pain.*
IMIPRAMINE (*Tofranil*)	*25–200 mg*	*Every 24 hrs*	*Tricyclic.*
NORTRIPTYLINE (*Pamelor*)	*25–200 mg*	*Every 24 hrs*	*Tricyclic.*
DESIPRAMINE (*Norpramin*)	*25–200 mg*	*Every 24 hrs*	*Tricyclic.*
DOXEPIN (*Sinequan*)	*25–200 mg*	*Every 24 hrs*	*Tricyclic.*
TRAZADONE (*Desyrel*)	*25–200 mg*	*Every 24 hrs*	*Good for sleep.*
FLUOXETINE (*Prozac*)	*20–40 mg*	*Every 24 hrs*	*Selective Serotonin Reuptake Inhibitor (SSRI). Anti-obsessional qualities.*
PAROXETINE (*Paxil*)	*20–40 mg*	*Every 24 hrs*	*SSRI. Anti-obsessional qualities.*
SERTRALINE (*Zoloft*)	*50–200 mg*	*Every 24 hrs*	*SSRI Anti-obsessional qualities.*
VENLAFAXINE (*Effexor*)	*75 mg*	*Every 12 hrs*	
NEFAZADONE (*Serzone*)	*150 mg*	*Every 12 hrs*	
FLUVOXAMINE (*Luvox*)	*50–300 mg*	*Every 24 hrs*	

TABLE 12.3
ASPIRIN

DRUG NAME	TYPICAL DOSE	FREQUENCY	COMMENTS
Bufferin	*650 mg*	*Every 4–6 hrs*	*Combined with many other drugs.*

TABLE 12.4
ACETAMINOPHEN

DRUG NAME	TYPICAL DOSE	FREQUENCY	COMMENTS
Tylenol	*325–500 mg*	*Every 4–6 hrs*	*Combined with many other drugs. 4000 mg per day MAXIMUM. Can cause liver damage or death in overdose.*

TABLE 12.5
ANTICONVULSANTS

DRUG NAME	TYPICAL DOSE	FREQUENCY	COMMENTS
CARBAMAZEPINE (Tegretol)	*200–400 mg*	*Every 8 hrs*	*Need regular blood levels checked.*
PHENYTOIN (Dilantin)	*100–200 mg*	*Every 8 hrs*	*Need regular blood levels checked.*
VALPROIC ACID (Depakote)	*250 mg*	*Every 8 hrs*	*Need regular blood levels checked.*
GABAPENTIN (Neurontin)	*300–600 mg*	*Every 8 hrs*	

TABLE 12.6
NON-STEROIDAL ANTI-INFLAMMATORY DRUGS (NSAIDs)

DRUG NAME	TYPICAL DOSE	FREQUENCY	COMMENTS
IBUPROFEN (Motrin, Advil)	200–800 mg	Every 6–8 hrs	
NAPROXEN (Naprosyn)	250–500 mg	Every 8–12 hrs	Less effect on blood pressure.
KETOPROFEN (Orudis)	50–75 mg	Every 8 hrs	
ETODOLAC (Lodine)	200–400 mg	Every 6–8 hrs	
FLURBIPROFEN (Ansaid)	50–100 mg	Every 8 hrs	
FENOPROFEN (Nalfon)	200–600 mg	Every 6–8 hrs	
DIFLUNISAL (Dolobid)	250–500 mg	Every 12 hrs	
TRISALICYLATE (Trilisate)	500–1000 mg	Every 8–12 hrs	Less bleeding tendency.
INDOMETHACIN (Indocin)	25–50 mg	Every 8 hrs	Greater gastric irritation.
SULINDAC (Clinoril)	150–200 mg	Every 12 hrs	
TOLMETIN (Tolectin)	200–400 mg	Every 8 hrs	
KETOROLAC (Toradol)	10–20 mg	Every 6 hrs	
NAMBUMETONE (Relafen)	1000 mg	Every 12–24 hrs	
DICLOFENAC (Voltaren)	50–75 mg	Every 8–12 hrs	
PIROXICAM (Feldene)	10–20 mg	Every 24 hrs	

TABLE 12.7
LOCAL ANESTHETICS

DRUG NAME	TYPICAL DOSE	FREQUENCY	COMMENTS
LIDOCAINE	5 mg/kg I.V.		By physician only.
MEXILETINE (Mexitil)	300 mg	Every 8 hrs	

TABLE 12.8

MINOR TRANQUILIZERS/ANTI-ANXIETY (BENZODIAZEPINES)

DRUG NAME	TYPICAL DOSE	FREQUENCY	COMMENTS
CLORAZEPATE (Tranxene)	3.75–7.5 mg	Every 8 hrs	
FLURAZEPAM (Dalmane)	15–30 mg	At night	
CHLORDIAZEPOXIDE (Librium)	5–10 mg	Every 6–8 hrs	
DIAZEPAM (Valium)	5 mg	Every 8 hrs	Also used as a muscle relaxer.
ALPRAZOLAM (Xanax)	0.5–1 mg	Every 6–8 hrs	
LORAZEPAM (Ativan)	0.5–1 mg	Every 8–12 hrs	
OXAZEPAM (Serax)	10 mg	Every 8 hrs	
BUSPIRONE (Buspar)	5–10 mg	Every 8 hrs	
CLONAZEPAM (Klonopin)	0.5–2.0 mg	Every 12–24 hrs	

TABLE 12.9

MUSCLE RELAXANTS

DRUG NAME	TYPICAL DOSE	FREQUENCY	COMMENTS
CARISOPRODOL (Soma)	350 mg	Every 8 hrs	
METHOCARBAMOL (Robaxin)	500–750 mg	Every 8 hrs	
CYCLOBENZAPRINE (Flexeril)	10 mg	Every 8 hrs	
CHLORZOXAZONE (Parafon-Forte)	250 mg	Every 8 hrs	
ORPHENADRINE (Norflex)	100 mg	Every 12 hrs	
BACLOFEN (Lioresal)	10-20 mg	Every 8 hrs	Frequently used for spasticity.

TABLE 12.10
NARCOTIC COMBINATIONS
(Narcotic in medication is listed first)

DRUG NAME	TYPICAL DOSE	FREQUENCY	COMMENTS
PROPOXYPHENE plus ACETAMINOPHEN (Darvocet)	*1–2 tabs*	*Every 4–6 hrs*	
CODEINE plus ACETAMINOPHEN (TyCo)	*1–2 tabs*	*Every 4–6 hrs*	
HYDROCODONE plus ACETAMINOPHEN (Vicodin)	*1–2 tabs*	*Every 4–6 hrs*	
OXYCODONE plus ASPIRIN (Percodan)	*1–2 tabs*	*Every 4–6 hrs*	
OXYCODONE plus ACETAMINOPHEN (Percocet)	*1–2 tabs*	*Every 4–6 hrs*	

TABLE 12.11
OTHER MEDICATIONS

DRUG NAME	TYPICAL DOSE	FREQUENCY	COMMENTS
BUTABITAL plus ASPIRIN plus CAFFEINE (Fiorinal)	*1–2 tabs*	*Every 6–8 hrs*	
BUTABITAL plus ACETAMINOPHEN plus CAFFEINE (Fiorecet)	*1–2 tabs*	*Every 6–8 hrs*	
TRAMADOL (Ultram)	*50–100 mg*	*Every 6–8 hrs*	

Sample Narcotic Use Contract
Opioid Analgesia Guidelines

Goals of opioid trial/treatment:

●

●   .

Proposed medications: _____

Prescribing MD: _____

Proposed duration of treatment/trial: _____

Anticipated reassessment interval: _____

- Opioid analgesic medications (Methadone, MS Contin, Vicodin, Lor-Tab, Percocet, Percodan, Tylenol with codeine, Fentanyl, etc) are to be prescribed by a single physician.

- If your physician is to begin an opioid trial, a letter will be sent to your primary or referring physician requesting that he/she not continue to prescribe opioids for you. If the opioid trial appears successful, your physician at the P.M.C. will make efforts to transfer prescription writing to your primary M.D. for long-term follow-up.

- Trials of opioid medications will require at least monthly visits for evaluation of analgesic effect, side effects, and for any adjustments of doses that may be necessary.

- *No opioid medications will be refilled over the phone.*

- No lost or stolen prescriptions or medications will be replaced. You are responsible for your own medications, and it is your responsibility to verify that prescriptions are filled correctly and that the medication supply will last until your next scheduled follow-up visit or unless increases are made before the follow-up visit.

- No increases in medication doses should be made without the approval of the prescribing physician. *No prescriptions will be refilled early due to independent increases in medications. These independent increases in medication dosing will not be tolerated.*

- Inquiries regarding opioid medication use should be made during normal business hours i.e., Monday through Friday, 9 A.M. to 4 P.M.

- During medication trials, all patients are expected to comply fully with their individual treatment recommendations. Failure to keep any scheduled appointments will be interpreted as an act of noncompliance, and may result in involuntary medication taper and/or discharge from the center.

** It is understood that emergencies do arise and under special circumstances, exceptions may be made to these policies. Individual cases will be reviewed and modified as necessary.

- In the event that the opioid trial is unsuccessful, care will be provided during the necessary medication taper. Referral to facilities specializing in medication detoxification may be necessary.

CAUTION: OPIOID MEDICATIONS MAY CAUSE DROWSINESS. ALCOHOL SHOULD NOT BE CONSUMED WHILE TAKING THESE MEDICATIONS. USE CARE WHEN OPERATING A CAR OR DANGEROUS MACHINERY. FEDERAL LAW PROHIBITS THE TRANSFER OF THESE DRUGS TO ANY PERSON OTHER THAN THE PATIENT FOR WHOM THEY WERE PRESCRIBED.

I, the undersigned, attest that the above guidelines have been explained to me, and that all of my questions and concerns regarding treatment have been adequately addressed. I agree to comply with the above guidelines. I have received a copy of this document.

Patient signature: _____   Date: _____

Witness signature: _____   Date: _____

Physician signature: _____   Date: _____

13

Back and Neck Pain

The most common of all chronic musculoskeletal pains is back pain. Some studies show that the lower back area, known as the *lumbar region*, accounts for about half of all reported pain, with the neck area accounting for another 20 percent. In terms of time lost at work, an estimated 550 million workdays are lost due to pain with over 60 billion dollars of lost productivity.

While back and neck pain is a problem for all age groups, a surprisingly large number of injuries occur in young people, ages twenty to thirty. This may be because people fresh out of school were probably active throughout their school years, but have graduated and started to work at sedentary jobs. Their muscles lose some of their tone and flexibility and become more injury prone. However, the greatest concentration of injuries occurs in the thirty- to forty-year age range, as people continue to do their normal activities and as the aging process begins to show. Your spine normally deteriorates slowly and almost imperceptibly with age. Before you experience pain in your back and neck due to the aging process, however, most of your muscular pain is due to injury.

This chapter introduces you to principles and practices that will help prevent the muscular sprains and strains that occur before the normal deterioration of aging. You will also learn the basics of back and neck pain and examine the current methods of treatment and prevention.

Who Gets Back Pain?

Back pain and injury is not a problem limited to one specific type or group of people. You can have back problems if you work all day at a manual labor job, or you can have them if you sit all day at a desk. Though it is hard to predict exactly when, where, and who will get an attack of back pain, there are some common factors predisposing you to this problem.

- Poor posture

- Poor body mechanics

- Overweight

- Weak, inflexible muscles

- Stress

Your spine is a complex interweaving of muscles, tendons, ligaments, joints, discs, nerves, and cartilage; no two spines are exactly alike. Obviously, a preventative approach would be ideal by practicing good back habits before you feel pain. However, after the pain has started you need to know which measures to take to regain as much mobility or movement as possible and help prevent further injury.

For the purpose of organizing the vast amount of available information, back and neck pain can be caused by problems in the following categories:

- Infections, such as meningitis

- Inflammation, including arthritis

- Metabolic disorders, like Paget's disease

- Neoplasms, such as cancerous or noncancerous tumors

- Referred pain, or pain that originates in places *other than* your back but you feel it there

- Trauma and mechanical problems, as described below

In this chapter, we will explore pain caused by trauma and mechanical problems. Traumatic back injuries are primarily made up of fractures and include both acute trauma (as in an accident) and cumulative trauma (problems that build over time). Mechanical problems make up the bulk of all lower back and neck disorders, such as muscle sprains, strains, and herniated discs. Because the other categories occur so infrequently and they require other specific types of treatment, they are not discussed here. Back problems caused by arthritis are examined more closely in chapter 18.

Anatomy of the Back and Neck

In his book, *Goodbye Back Ache*, Dr. David Imrie explains that the spinal column is the body's principal scaffolding, providing both strength and stability along with movement and flexibility to your body. The bones in the spinal column are attached to and connect the muscles, tendons, and ligaments that permit the body's movement. The spinal column also houses the spinal cord, the vital nerve cable that links the brain to all other parts of the body.

All of the major areas of the spine are made up of box-shaped building blocks called *vertebrae*. In medical terms, the first of those is the *cervical*, or neck, area, which supports the head and neck and allows them to move right and left. Since these vertebrae only have to support the weight of your head, they are smaller, flatter, and more delicate. The *thoracic*, or chest, area includes the vertebrae that are part of the rib cage's protection of the heart and lungs. These vertebrae are fairly immobile and are larger than the cervical vertebrae, since they have to support the weight of your arms and shoulders. The *lumbar*, or lower back, section contains vertebrae that are larger and heavier than the vertebrae above it. This is because they bear the most weight and allow forward and backward bending motion (see diagram 13.1). The *sacral* vertebrae are actually formed into one very large bone at the base of the spinal cord, which is immobile, and wedged in between the two hip bones. The *coccyx*, below the sacrum, is a series of small vertebrae that, together with the rest of the pelvic bones, supports the powerful buttocks muscles. Each vertebrae is numbered, so your doctor can refer to the exact location of an injury or problem. The areas that we will focus on are the neck and lumbar regions of the spine. The spine's flexibility and mobility in these areas combine with the alignment and pressures upon the vertebrae to contribute to defects and fractures.

A healthy back normally curves in four places: at the cervical region, the thoracic region, the lumbar region, and the sacral region (see diagram 13.1). (The overall shape that these four curves make is sometimes called the "double S" curve.) Poor posture, obesity, and muscle spasm can flatten

Diagram 13.1
The Spinal Column

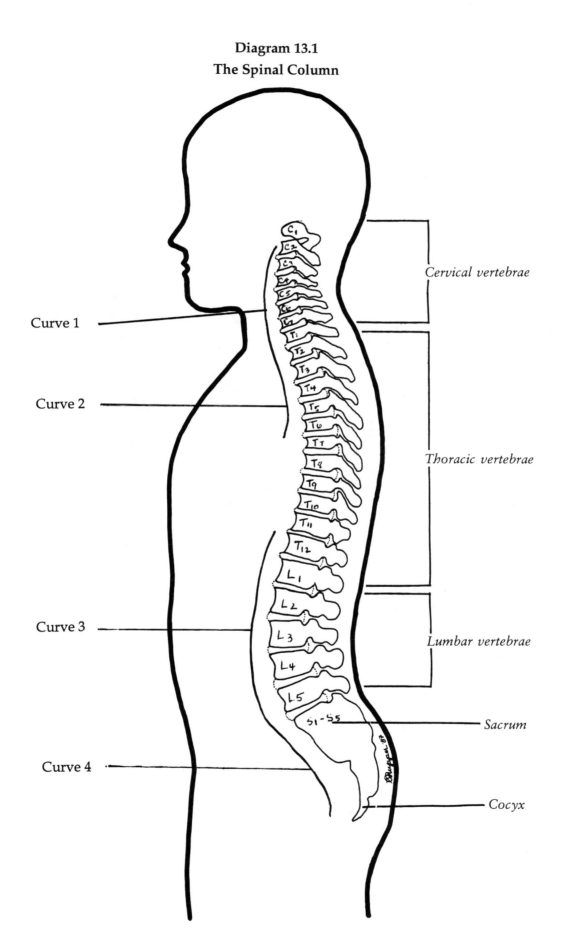

Cervical vertebrae

Thoracic vertebrae

Lumbar vertebrae

Sacrum

Cocyx

Curve 1

Curve 2

Curve 3

Curve 4

Diagram 13.2

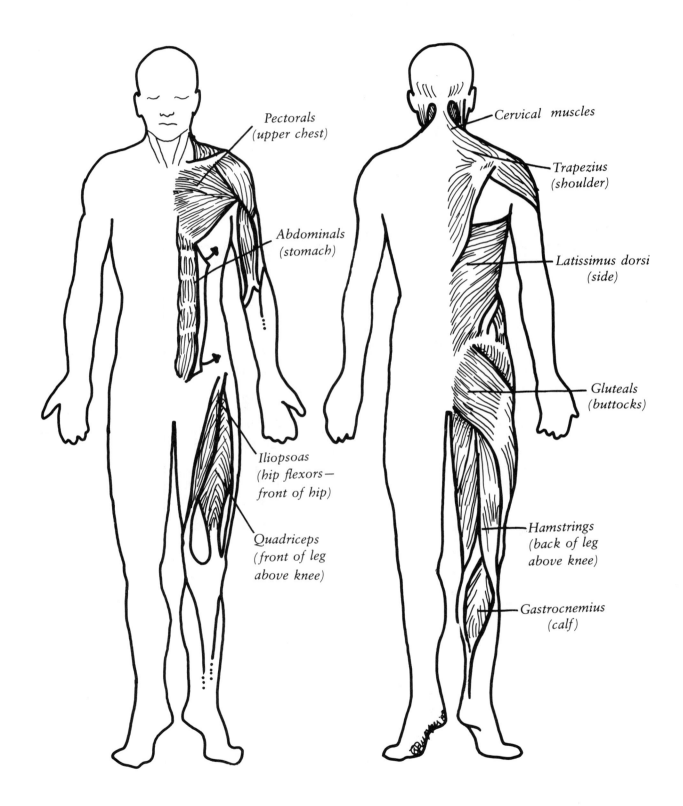

Pectorals
(upper chest)

Abdominals
(stomach)

Iliopsoas
(hip flexors—
front of hip)

Quadriceps
(front of leg
above knee)

Cervical muscles

Trapezius
(shoulder)

Latissimus dorsi
(side)

Gluteals
(buttocks)

Hamstrings
(back of leg
above knee)

Gastrocnemius
(calf)

out or exaggerate most of these curves, causing pain and dysfunction. Curves can also change with muscle disuse or atrophy. Atrophy is a "wasting away" of the muscle due to inadequate nutrition or activity. Exercise, good posture, and proper lifting techniques can strengthen the surrounding muscles and ligaments and restore these curves to a healthy position.

A healthy spine has pressure evenly distributed throughout its curves. This means that all of the muscle groups up and down the spine are working together in a balanced fashion, and no one muscle group is doing more than its share of work. In an unbalanced spine, one or more muscle groups may be taking up the slack for an injured, unconditioned, atrophic, or deficient group, causing the harder-working muscles to fatigue and weaken and be more injury prone. When you compensate for your chronic pain by holding your injured muscles immobile for a long time, you are shifting weight, pressure, and work onto the other muscle groups. You may be standing in a "bent" or otherwise awkward position, causing the muscles to shorten on one side and lengthen on the other. This is why an evenly balanced exercise program is important to restore your body to its pre-injury state.

Diagram 13.2 shows the important major muscle groups to exercise for proper management of back, shoulder, and neck pain.

Vertebrae and Discs

The approximately thirty-three vertebrae that form the spinal column are the building blocks of the spine. They are cube-shaped with bony protrusions that you can feel when you run your fingers up and down your spine (see diagram 13.3). *Ligaments* are tough elastic bands that reinforce the joints and help to hold the vertebrae together. The bony protrusions, called the *spinous processes*, have connecting ligaments that interlock each vertebra and allow for a certain amount of bending and twisting motion. These bony protrusions help to form a canal that houses the spinal cord, which is the vital nerve link to your brain, as mentioned earlier.

Muscles help to hold the spine upright and allow for forward (flexion), backward (extension), and twisting (rotation) movements. You have both deep and surface muscles in your back.

Diagram 13.3

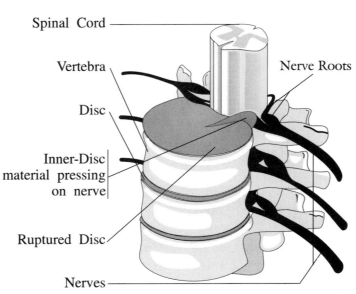

Between each vertebra lies another structure called a *disc*. The disc contains a gelatinous substance called the "nucleus pulposus." This jellylike fluid, together with the bony vertebrae and outer cartilaginous disc, act like a shock absorber in a car. When pressure is applied (such as from lifting), the fluid is compressed; it springs back to its original shape when the pressure is released. Without this spongelike effect of the disc fluid, the vertebrae would grind together and eventually deteriorate.

The disc gel can cause pain by leaking or bulging out and pressing against the nerves located along the spinal column. You may hear this condition referred to as a herniated disc, ruptured disc, slipped disc, bulging disc, prolapsed disc, or a protruding disc. All of these terms mean roughly the same thing—a tear or deterioration of the wall surrounding the disc, which allows some of the fluid to bulge out or rupture and escape. The term "slipped disc" is inaccurate, however, since the disc rarely actually slips out of place. (Sometimes the vertebra can have a crack or defect in it that causes it to slip away from the vertebra below it, but this is a separate condition known as *spondylolisthesis* and is not covered in this book.)

The discs most likely to herniate are those in the cervical and lumbar regions. Sometimes a disc bulges or fluid escapes and it may put pressure on the *nerve roots* (the place where a nerve branches off the spinal cord). Several specific nerve roots converge to form the *sciatic nerve* (a large, thick nerve going out of the pelvis below the sacrum and down both legs). See diagram 13.3. Pressure against the nerve roots causes a type of pain known as *sciatica*. This shooting pain alters the signals sent by the nerves; the pressure of the disc bulge on the nerve tissue leads also to numbness and weakness in your legs. If the disc bulges against the nerve roots in the neck area, you will often feel pain and experience numbness and weakness in your arms. It is important for you to realize however, that not all disc bulges cause pain. One study of people with no symptoms of pain found that almost half had bulging discs upon examination. In fact, ruptured or bulging discs can actually heal on their own with conservative treatment such as physical therapy, medications, and back education. That is why most back surgeons are becoming much more conservative and resorting to surgery only in very clear cases of nerve root compression.

Sometimes bone spurs or scar tissue can also press against the nerve roots, causing decreased movement and sharp pain. Spurs can be thought of like calluses on hands—they may be an attempt on the part of the body or a bone to heal or stabilize itself. Scar tissue may be a result of previous surgery and is often not detected on X rays. Bone spurs can be removed surgically.

It is also possible that a nerve root will be compressed due to a condition known as *scoliosis*. This condition, which can occur in infancy, results in a progressively curved spine, usually in the thoracic or lumbar areas, and has no known cause. This curve may then force the space between the discs to become narrow. A small number of cases occur from habitual poor posture or misalignment of the legs (one leg is shorter than the other).

Diagnostic Tests

Before we discuss treatment of back disorders, let's examine the currently available diagnostic tests, so that when you're sent for a CAT scan or an EMG, you'll know what to expect.

X rays are pictures of the bones of the back and neck taken to rule out diseases, inflammation, abscesses, and other bone disorders. Muscle spasm and soft tissue (muscles, tendons, ligaments) damage such as swelling, both very common causes of back pain, do not show up on X rays. *Myelography* is a special kind of X-ray test where a dye (called *contrast* dye since it helps the fluid and soft tissue stand out in the picture) is injected into the spinal fluid space to assess soft tissue damage around the spinal cord or nerve roots. This test requires you to stay in bed for several hours afterward to prevent headaches. It is sometimes performed before surgical intervention, but has in recent years been used less frequently because of the development of other, superior techniques, such as *magnetic resonance imaging*. *Discography* is a process similar to myelography, where the dye is injected into the disc making it easier to see on X-ray films. A *CAT scan*, or Computerized Axial Tomography (also known as a CT scan), is a type of X-ray scanning procedure that enables your doctor to see more closely and in much greater detail any soft tissue damage. The word "axial" means that the view is shown in layers, much like a sliced loaf of bread. The computerization of this process is what gives the CAT scan its much greater clarity than other types of radiography.

Electromyography (EMG) is a test where a very thin needle-type electrode is inserted into the muscle to electrically measure the nerve and muscle condition and the muscle's ability to contract or relax. This process thereby assesses any damage to the muscle's ability to function. Electrode insertion can cause some discomfort.

Magnetic resonance imaging (MRI) uses an electromagnetic field to stimulate the nuclei (the central parts of a cell) in tissue, which in turn emit radio signals that are transformed into a picture of the problem area. *Thermography* determines "thermal imbalance" in tissue and bone by measuring the amount of heat radiated from the problem areas and translating the heat into electronic signals that form images. Both tests are noninvasive (no piercing of the skin) and without risk and can be especially beneficial as an adjunct to other diagnostic tests.

These tests are generally selected by your physician based on what type of pain you are experiencing and where the pain appears to be located. For example, discography attempts to find problems in a disc while an EMG is performed when problems appear to be in the nerves or muscles. A CAT scan is better for looking at the detail of bones, while an MRI produces a film with more soft tissue details. Thermography is used when a blood flow problem is suspected.

Check with your doctor about the effectiveness and availability of these tests in your area.

Medical Treatments for Back and Neck Pain

Surgery

There are only two situations that usually require immediate surgical intervention for back and neck pain: (1) if there is a mass lesion (a tumor or other disc material) pressing upon the major nerve roots or spinal cord, and (2) if there is spinal cord or nerve root compression from a fracture or other major instability from injury. The following are the most commonly performed surgeries for these conditions:

Laminectomy. The surgeon cuts through the lamina (part of the bony ring surrounding the spinal cord or nerve roots) in order to remove the herniated disc.

Micro laminectomy. Similar to the laminectomy above except the herniated disc is removed by laser, thereby allowing a more precise procedure.

Discectomy. Discectomy for a herniated or ruptured disc is considered following unsuccessful conservative treatment (bed rest, traction, medications) that has gone on from one to four months. A partial laminectomy provides access to the disc, which is then removed. The success rate varies from 40 to 80 percent, based on the patient's specific circumstances. Repeated disc surgeries are significantly less successful, probably due to the buildup of scar tissue around the surgical site.

Spinal fusion. Fusions are sometimes performed for spinal instability, or in order to stabilize the spine following a discectomy. Vertebrae are "welded together" by bone grafts, which are pieces of bone that can be placed between the vertebrae to allow the bone to heal as a single piece. This type of surgery is done if injury or disease has resulted in instability of the spine, or in order to stabilize or straighten the abnormal curves of scoliosis.

Chemonucleolysis. In 1982, the FDA approved the use of Chymopapain, which is a substance injected into the disc space to dissolve the problem disc. Chymopapain is derived from the papaya plant and is related to the active substance in meat tenderizer. One advantage of this process is that it does not require an incision and can be less traumatic to your back than surgery.

Medication

In the acute stages of back or neck pain, when muscles are spasming and mobility is severely hampered, some narcotic medications are extremely useful in helping you to rest and relax. Examples of these are Darvon, Percodan, Vicodin, and others listed in tables 12.1 and 12.10. If the problem hasn't resolved after several weeks however, you will likely develop tolerance to these drugs (they will lose some of their effectiveness), you may feel significant unpleasant side effects (such as constipation), or you may find yourself becoming addicted—all problems that outweigh the benefits. Anti-anxiety medications (or minor tranquilizers) have also been used for people with acute pain, mainly to decrease anxiety associated with the pain and to help them relax. In the long run however, these drugs have been found to have many more negative side effects such as addiction, chronic sleeplessness, and a lowered pain threshold (increased sensitivity). Nonsteroidal Anti-Inflammatory Drugs (NSAIDs) are frequently used for back pain when there is an inflammatory component to the pain, but over time, these can cause serious stomach upset if used frequently. Antidepressants are used quite frequently to treat chronic pain of many types, including backs and necks. Antidepressants are typically prescribed at a much lower dose for pain management than for the actual treatment of depression. These drugs have the advantage of being nonaddictive, and there are now many choices in this drug class that allow for the selection of one that has the most beneficial effect for you with the least side effects. Refer to chapter 12 for more information on appropriate medications for chronic back and neck pain.

Nerve Blocks

Local anesthetic nerve blocks and trigger point injections are used to interrupt the pain-spasm-pain cycle, which can prolong your pain sensation by keeping you tense and anxious. These blocks can help relieve postural stress and allow you to participate in gentle exercise, relaxation techniques, and other rehabilitative treatments. One safe and effective type of nerve block is a *steroid injection* into the *epidural space* surrounding the spinal cord and nerves. Epidural steroid therapy is especially helpful for sciatica, the leg pain secondary to disc disease. Another newer type of block, less common but apparently as safe, is a *facet joint injection*. *Trigger point injections* place a local anesthetic at the actual site of pain in a muscle (a *trigger point* is a tender site in the muscle) or at the referred pain site (see chapter 15 on myofascial pain syndrome) to block the nerve impulses carrying the pain message. All three of these blocks can be extremely useful for at least temporarily alleviating chronic back pain. All are most useful when combined with exercise and other resources from a pain management center. You should not look to nerve blocks for your only treatment for pain, but regard them as part of a comprehensive treatment program.

Other Physical Treatments

Your doctor may prescribe more conservative (less potential for risk) forms of treatment for you, such as *braces*. These are formfitting jackets that look like corsets and help support and immobilize the spine. *Neck braces* hold the chin at a level or slightly lowered position and also support the neck muscles and cervical area. Braces are usually used during the healing phases immediately following an injury or surgery. If they are used continually after this initial phase however, they may lead to muscle atrophy and more pain, especially when the brace is not worn. This is because the brace begins to take over the supportive work of the muscles themselves and your body begins to depend on the brace, instead of the underlying muscles, to hold your head or body up.

Traction is used to straighten and stretch the soft tissue around the facet joints in order to straighten the spine. This may be helpful for pulling the vertebrae slightly apart to allow a herniated disc in the back or neck to heal. Again, this is helpful primarily during the initial healing phases of an injury or surgery, not as a solution for a chronic condition.

TENS (transcutaneous electrical nerve stimulation) devices can perform a useful function by providing an alternate tingling sensation to the pain that blocks the pain signal to the brain. See chapter 2 for a more thorough explanation of TENS units. *Point stimulation*, a newer form of electrical stimulation, may work similarly to acupuncture in providing pain relief. All forms of electrical stimulation can be placed at trigger points or at the site of pain.

Heat can be applied in several different ways. Hot towels or heating pads applied directly to the pain site or hot baths can increase blood flow and soothe tensed and spasming muscles. Moist heat generally penetrates more deeply; several microwavable hot packs are now available, allowing for quicker application and convenience. *Diathermy* stimulates deep muscle heat by means of an electric current applied lightly to the surface of the skin. *Ultrasound* also elevates tissue temperature by penetrating deeply into the muscle with high-frequency sound waves.

Popular heat-generating devices are two hands. *Massage* can be an excellent way to warm and relax a tight muscle by stimulating increased blood flow to the area. But if you or your massage therapist press too firmly on a spasming muscle, the spasm can get worse. Try a hot bath or heating pad first. Any time you feel a sharp pain when using massage, back off. See chapter 2 for more information on massage.

Cold can also be beneficial for back or neck pain, particularly if your condition has been determined to include an inflammatory process. Many people have found that ice seems to "numb" the painful area, providing at least temporary relief. Gel packs are now available that can be frozen or heated, depending on what feels the best to you. Some gel packs are especially made not to freeze solid, but to stay at a consistency like gelatin so that the pack can conform to your back. For some, lightly rubbing the painful area with an ice block until numbness occurs is even more effective than a cold pack because of the more intense stimulation.

Many people with neck or back pain can get some relief, or increase their activity, by paying attention to *posture* and *positioning*. You may fondly remember a parent saying "sit up straight" or "don't slouch" and how you would try to adjust to his or her expectations. When you have a back or neck injury, poor posture may create excess strain (caused by gravity) that keeps your pain at an unbearable level. Several different types of health care professionals can teach you how to stand, sit, and walk in ways that reduce the strain on your spine and thereby reduce pain. Many physical and occupational therapists teach movement classes that may be useful for you, often called "back school," to teach you proper postures and safe ways of moving. For example, men may carry wallets in their back pants pocket, which can cause one side of their buttocks to sit higher than the other, creating tension and pain. Some styles of shoes can also create awkward body postures, leading to back pain. Physical therapists can also suggest cushions or other devices that can help you improve your ability to do daily activities with less pain. Occupational therapists can perform an analysis of your workstations (desk, sink, and so on) to help you design a more *ergonomically correct* system (a system that works best for you as an individual). See pages 186 and 188 for more suggestions on ergonomics.

Sometimes back and neck pain sufferers find relief for acute or chronic pain by using the services of a *chiropractor*, a highly trained health care professional who uses *spinal manipulation* or *adjustment* to correct spinal misalignment caused by disease and injury. A chiropractor works on each specific vertebra, manually moving one segment at a time to bend, twist, or stretch the vertebral joint, helping to reposition it. A newer, and some believe safer, approach by some chiropractors involves the use of a special tool called an *activator*, which "taps" the misaligned vertebra to increase mobility and avoids the traditional manipulation techniques more commonly used. When there is nerve root compression, as with a herniated disc, chiropractors will determine this condition first through a series of diagnostic tests (such as X rays, CAT scans, or straight leg raises) before they attempt to manipulate your spine. If nerve-root compression is present, they may elect other forms of treatment, such as traction tables or other traction devices. A chiropractor may also refer you to a surgeon if you have clear nerve-root compression.

As do physical therapists, osteopaths, and athletic trainers, chiropractors employ a wide variety of treatments to alleviate pain such, as electrical stimulation techniques, acupuncture, or massage. They will work closely with your regular general practitioner to monitor your medication and diet. Chiropractors are also aware of the importance of regular exercise and will often prescribe exercises that enhance back and neck flexibility, strength, and range of motion to supplement regular treatment.

As with other medical treatment, research is still inconclusive regarding the effectiveness of chiropractic treatment. Ask your doctor or friends for a recommendation to a reputable chiropractor in your area. Carefully discuss your back or neck problem with your doctor or chiropractor before you begin any treatment. Manipulation can make some problems worse, such as fracture of a vertebra resulting from the brittle bones of osteoporosis.

What You Can Do

Back Exercises

Consult any two people and you will get two different opinions about what kind of exercise to do for your back. Some say that doing the type of exercise that requires only backward bending (extension) is the best to do; others say bending forward (flexion) is the best. But most experts do seem to agree on one thing: Exercise is critical in rehabilitating your back. As discussed in chapter 3, stretching and strengthening help your muscles to increase their ability to absorb shock and strain and to decrease their tendency to spasm. As your muscles become stronger and more flexible, the chance that you will sustain another injury diminishes. If the stress in your life registers directly in your back, strong and flexible muscles will be better able to withstand potential spasming from tension.

If you have a disc problem, you can still use many of the exercises that are good for back strains or sprains, with the exception of specific exercises that are flagged both here and in chapter 3. Even though a bulging disc poses a special set of problems, the muscles surrounding and supporting the spine are still prone to tension and spasming from the pain and stress of the disc problem. This means you need to keep stretching and strengthening the abdominal and back muscles to protect your vulnerable disc area.

You will need to check with your doctor before beginning any exercise program. A physical therapist, exercise physiologist, or athletic trainer can also provide expert assistance. Your therapist or trainer will look at the normal "S" curves in your back, as well as your posture, walk, flexibility, strength, and endurance before they suggest specific exercises to correct any spinal imbalance. This may mean that you should do a combination of extension and flexion exercises, supplemented by TENS, traction, or whirlpool. The combination of exercise and devices prescribed for you will change as you gain strength and flexibility or as the pain subsides.

A sensible approach to exercise is to start out gradually with passive, gentle stretches and work up to more active exercises. Some experts suggest that you start out on the bed or floor, move up to standing exercises, and finally go on to activities that offer cardiovascular exercise as well as gentle resistance. It is important that you set small, achievable goals for yourself. Many people who find the motivation and energy to begin an exercise program either get frustrated that the progress is not faster and quit, or they work so hard and fast initially that they increase their pain to a point where they *must* stop. While it is likely that you will have some pain following your first attempts at exercise, physical therapists or trainers can help you distinguish between "good pain" (the pain we all feel after exercise because of lactic acid buildup in the muscles) and "bad pain" (the pain that is a result of aggravation of your underlying pain condition). Remember that the best program will be one that slowly increases your strength, conditioning and flexibility over time. The following sets of exercises present a typical program of this kind, but should only be attempted after consulting your physician.

Stretching and Gentle Strengthening

First, increase your flexibility by doing nonweight-bearing exercises. This means that you stretch only those muscles that need it and avoid putting unnecessary and dangerous pressure on your spine. It has become quite common to begin an exercise program for people with back or neck pain using *pool therapy* (gentle exercises in a heated swimming pool), which does help reduce the pull of gravity on your spine. Often, YMCAs and YWCAs offer some type of pool exercise program, and you may also want to consult your local phone book for water programs. If you do not have access to a pool and the expertise of a pool therapist, the following nonweight-bearing exercises can be substituted. Do the following three exercises on your floor or bed for a minimum of fifteen minutes per day for two to three weeks or until pain subsides.

1. *Lower back flattener (posterior pelvic tilt).* This exercise is a gentle strengthener of abdominal and buttocks muscles. Flatten the curve in your lower back by flattening against the floor or bed with your lower abdominal muscles. Hold for at least five seconds. Start with only a few repetitions, but repeat at least three times per day to start.

2. *Hip flexor stretch.* This is a gentle stretch of lower back and hip muscles. Lace your hands under one knee. Pull your leg toward your chest, keeping your lower back on the floor or bed and your other leg slightly bent. Hold for twenty seconds. Repeat three times on each side. DO NOT attempt the advanced flexor stretch in chapter 3 at this point.

3. *Double knee to chest.* This exercise is a more complete stretch of lower back and hip muscles. With your hands laced under your knees, pull both knees to your chest, keeping your lower back flat on the floor or bed. Hold for twenty seconds. Repeat three times.

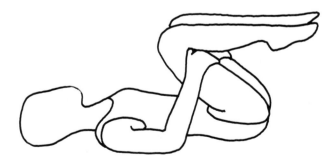

Sitting and Rotation

Now you can progress to more active exercises. Add the three exercises below to the first group of exercises and set aside a minimum of fifteen minutes per day for them for several weeks. Note: Rotation may put added pressure and strain on your back if you have a disc problem. Check with your doctor first to see if these are appropriate exercises for you.

1. *Abdominal curls (curl-ups).* An excellent exercise for stomach strengthening and relieving back strain. Lie down and bend your knees with your feet flat on the floor or bed. While maintaining a pelvic tilt, slowly curl your head, shoulders, and upper back off the floor toward your knees. With your chin tucked, hold this raised position for a count of five. Slowly lower yourself back to the starting position. Repeat five times. When you feel comfortable and stronger doing the curl-up exercise, try the *curl-backs*.

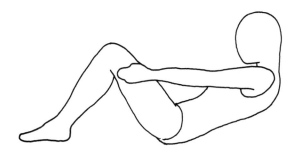

Curl-backs: Start by sitting tilted slightly back, with a C-curve in your spine. Keep your arms folded, your knees bent, and your feet flat on the floor. Lean back one third to one half of the way to the floor or bed, leaning back very carefully and only as far as you feel safe. Pull forward to your original position. Repeat five times. (Caution: When doing curl-backs, do not anchor your feet under a chair or bed. This causes you to use muscles other than your abdominals to lower yourself. Also, be sure to keep your chin tucked and your neck relaxed. Do not throw your head back.)

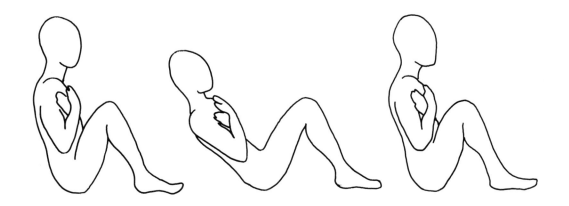

2. *Advanced hip flexor stretch.* This is an excellent lower back stretch and abdominal strengthening exercise. Raise your head and shoulders slightly when doing the hip flexor stretch, tucking your chin to meet your bent knee and tightening your stomach muscles. Hold for five seconds to begin and gradually increase. See picture for hip flexor stretch above.

3. *Lower back stretch and roll.* A good exercise for relieving back strain. (Note: IF YOU HAVE DISC PROBLEMS, CHECK WITH YOUR DOCTOR BEFORE DOING THIS EXERCISE.) With your hands laced under your knees, pull both knees to your chest, keeping your lower back flat on the bed or floor. Hold for twenty seconds. Keep breathing. Now rotate your knees slowly to the right, gently twisting as far as you feel comfortable. Keep your shoulders on the bed or floor. Hold for twenty seconds. Breathe. Slowly roll to the left and hold for twenty seconds. Repeat the sequence three times.

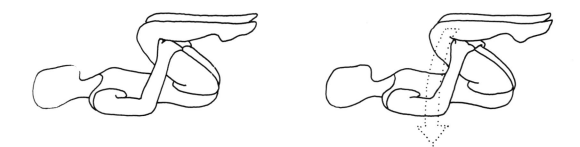

Standing and Extension Exercises

Now you can add two extension exercises and one standing exercise, the side stretch. *Note*: These three exercises may be problematic for people with disc injury or disease, because the backward-bending and side-bending motion narrows the disc space even further and pinches the already protruding disc material, causing more pain. Check with your doctor, therapist, or trainer before attempting these exercises.

1. *Press-ups.* This is a good lower back stretch. (Note: DO NOT DO THIS EXERCISE IF YOU HAVE DISC PROBLEMS. CHECK WITH YOUR DOCTOR FIRST.) Lie on your stomach with your arms bent at the elbow. Press up slowly, keeping your elbows bent. Keep your pelvis and legs relaxed. Repeat ten times. Keep your elbows bent when you first do this exercise. Only after you are comfortable doing press-ups with elbows bent should you attempt the advanced press-ups.

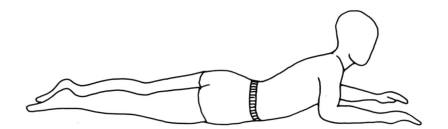

2. *The mad cat.* A good exercise for lower back tension. Kneel on all fours with your back straight. Inhale and round your back, tightening your abdominal and gluteus (bottom) muscles simultaneously. Then, slowly exhale and arch your back, pointing your head and tailbone toward the ceiling. Return to straight back position (don't let your back "sag." Remember to keep your elbows slightly bent and not locked! Repeat three to four times.

3. *Side stretch.* Keeping both knees bent slightly, extend both arms overhead. Grasp your right hand with your left hand and slowly bend to the left, pulling your right arm over your head and feeling the stretch on the side of your body. Hold for twenty seconds. Make sure you don't lock your knees, but keep them soft, and slightly bent. Repeat three times each side.

Cardiovascular Exercises

You can add gentle cardiovascular exercises, such as walking or swimming, once you've become comfortable doing the three groups of exercises previously described. Cardiovascular exercise has been shown to have many overall benefits such as improved stamina, reduction of stress-related hormones, weight control, and improved mood and sleep. Make sure that you spend at least five to ten minutes warming up before you do your activity and cooling down after you finish. Otherwise you may reinjure yourself because your muscles are "cold." You can use the stretches and strengtheners above for this purpose.

Do your exercises regularly at home, once or twice a day as needed for at least fifteen minutes each session. If you feel more pain at the end of a particular set of exercises than you did at the beginning, or if you feel more pain the next day, then you need to stop the exercise and consult your doctor, therapist, or trainer. Remember that you will feel some discomfort as your muscles become stronger and more flexible, but you'll usually be able to tell the difference between pain and the normal discomfort of exercise. You may find that you need to try several different types of exercise before you find a group that suits you. Once you find a group that helps you feel stronger, more flexible, and more pain-free, do those exercises regularly. Your rewards will be great in the long run.

Again, keep in mind that you should be thoroughly examined by your doctor before beginning any exercise program. If possible, get additional guidance from a physical therapist, physiatrist, exercise physiologist, or certified athletic trainer to determine the best exercise for your individual injury, lifestyle, and physical condition.

Neck Exercises

Most neck pain is due to overstretching of the muscles, ligaments, and other soft tissue surrounding the cervical vertebrae. Overstretching and injury may be caused by sudden strain on the neck from jerking or collision when playing sports or from whiplash, when the head is abruptly thrown forward and backward (also known as flexion-extension injury).

If a cervical disc loses its ability to absorb shock and bulges and presses against the spinal nerve, it can cause pain and dysfunction similar to disc problems in the lower back. It can also cause referred pain down the arm, much like sciatica in the leg.

Bad posture is also one of the main culprits for neck pain. If the lower back is allowed to slouch and the head juts forward, the normal cervical curve is flattened, putting a strain on all the muscles supporting the head. If bad posture becomes a habit, as it is when you sleep in a bad position for your neck or slouch when you sit at work, then you are likely to be prone to "cricks" in the neck, or sore, spasming neck and upper shoulder muscles, and muscular headaches by the end of the day.

When sleeping, be sure not to prop your head up on too many pillows, as this will continue to jut your head forward throughout the night. Sleeping on your stomach tends to thrust your head into an overextended backward curve, which strains the delicate vertebral bodies. Sleep in the fetal position, or sleep with a cervical pillow placed in the hollow of your neck. See chapter 10 for more sleeping tips. A lumbar roll is also useful to restore proper posture and protect your neck when sitting or driving. Specially designed chairs (and automobile seats for certain manufacturers) are available that help keep your body supported during long periods of sitting. When used regularly and in combination with exercise, both the cervical pillow and the lumbar roll can help to maintain your spine's normal curve in the lumbar and cervical regions.

The following exercises are stretches and gentle strengtheners for the neck.

1. *Yes-no-maybe.* First stretch your head forward with your chin tucked, then stretch it from side to side, and at last at an angle on each side (the "maybe" position). Hold each stretch for ten seconds and repeat three times.

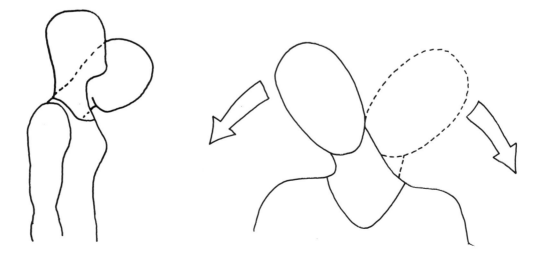

2. *Advanced neck stretches.* These are good for spasming and tightness in the trapezius muscle. While seated, pull your neck forward (as shown, from the top of your head), and then to each side 30 to 35 degrees. Pull your head until you feel a slight stretch in the back of your neck and your upper back. Hold the stretch for twenty to thirty seconds.

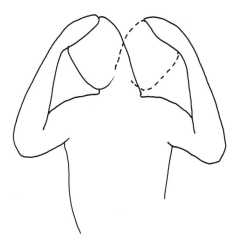

3. *Shoulder shrugs.* Pull both shoulders upward (but do not hunch your neck downward) simultaneously for ten seconds. Do this three times in a row. Gradually increase the time for each shrug.

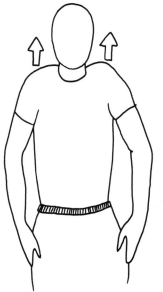

4. *Neck strengthener.* Lie down. Raise your head off the bed or floor and hold for five seconds. Lower your head slowly and press it into the bed or floor for five seconds. Repeat three times.

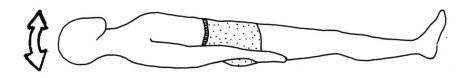

5. *Gentle resistance neck exercise.* Using a towel and giving moderate resistance, roll your head from side to side.

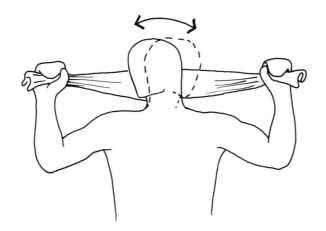

Proper Lifting

Many back injuries result from improper lifting. Lifting the simplest, most harmless-looking object can cause a terrific backache. If your back and stomach muscles are out of condition to begin with, or if you are under a lot of stress and your muscles are tight, then a simple twisting motion such as reaching for the phone or picking up a magazine can throw a weak back into spasm.

Sprains, strains, or tissue tears often occur while lifting or reaching for an object on a shelf that's too high, twisting suddenly, lifting any object that's too far away from you, pulling something heavy, picking up small children, being pregnant, or doing nearly anything when you're feeling tense and anxious.

The principal rule of good body mechanics is to let your powerful leg muscles carry the load. Your quadriceps and hamstrings in your thighs are larger and stronger than your weaker back muscles; let them do the work. Other rules to remember are:

- Maintain a broad base of support by keeping your feet apart for stability.

- Bend your knees; don't bend at the waist.

- Tighten your stomach muscles and buttocks to help support the spine.

- Hold the load close to your body.

- Keep your back upright and avoid twisting.

- Push, don't pull.

- Get help if you need it.

- Sit so that your feet are supported.

- Use a keyboard with your forearms, wrists, and hands straight.

- Sit in a comfortable upright position, looking straight ahead, with relaxed shoulders and gaze slightly down.

- Make sure your lower back is supported by your chair.

Stress Management for Back and Neck

As you probably know, stress can register directly in your back or neck. This is why relaxation and visualization techniques are a perfect component to your regular exercise and medical treatment program. Some relaxation exercises work particularly well with physical exercise. Try doing deep breathing exercises (count to four breathing in and four breathing out) five or six times as part of your daily workout, warm-up, and cool-down. Warm-up breathing will prepare you emotionally and mentally for your exercise, as well as help relax tight muscles. When combined with stretching, cool-down breathing will help you slow down after your workout and keep your muscles limber.

If you are unable to take a break at your desk and your neck or back is aching, stretch it out by doing some of the stretches mentioned above and in chapter 3. Focus on a quick image or word that is relaxing to you, such as the sensation of the sun warming your back or neck, or the words "calm" or "relax." When Margaret is tense, she quickly conjures up the image of herself sitting next to a dark blue sea, wind whipping through her hair. Combine this with deep, slow breathing and she says it works every time. Please refer to chapters 4 and 5 for more ideas about relaxation techniques.

Remember that there are always negative thoughts lurking about, ready to pounce on, and sabotage, your best efforts and intentions. You may say to yourself, "Give up—it's hopeless. I'll never get better." This kind of thinking is self-defeating, and if you indulge in it regularly, you will have a far more difficult time making progress. Refer to chapter 6 for more ideas on controlling your negative thoughts.

Finally, respect your limits. Learn to say no to tasks and activities that you know will aggravate your back or neck pain. Don't be embarrassed about asking for help when you need it. Think about proper lifting techniques before you move something. Avoid twisting and sharp movements. Exercise, but do it in a reasonable, moderate way. If you set small, achievable goals for yourself you're more likely to succeed. Pace yourself when you feel good. And most of all, take care of yourself!

Further Reading

Branch, C. L. 1994. *Low Back Pain.* Kansas City: American Academy of Family Physicians.

Imrie, D. 1984. *Goodbye Back Ache.* New York: Fawcet Book Group.

Kerkaldy-Willis, W., and C. Burton, eds. 1992. *Managing Low Back Pain.* 3rd ed. New York: Churchill Livingstone.

McKenzie, R. 1993. *Treat Your Own Back.* 6th ed. Waikanae, New Zealand: Spinal Publications.

McKenzie, R. 1993. *Treat Your Own Neck.* 2nd ed. Waikanae, New Zealand: Spinal Publications.

Macnab, I. 1994. *Neck Ache and Shoulder Pain.* Baltimore: Williams & Wilkins.

Oliver, J. 1994. *Back-Care: An Illustrated Guide.* Boston: Butterworth-Heineman.

Wei, N. 1995. *Low Back Pain: What You Need to Know and What You Can Do About It.* Frederick, MD.: N. Wei.

Wilson, A. 1994. *Are You Sitting Comfortably?: A Self-Help Guide for Sufferers of Back Pain, Neck Strain, Headaches, RSI, and Other Associated Health Problems.* London: Optima.

Online Information Can Be Found At:

http://weber.u.washington.edu/~crc/IASP.html

http://neurosurgery.mgh.harvard.edu/ncpainoa.htm

http://pc1.mednwh.unimelb.edu.au/pubs.htm

Multimedia Resources:

A Patient's Guide to Low Back Pain. 1993. Version 1.0. (six 3 ½" discs plus guide) Libby, MT: Medical Multimedia.

14

Fibromyalgia

by Dorothy Waddell, M.D.

What is Fibromyalgia?

Fibromyalgia is a painful condition which, by definition, affects many areas of the body. If you have fibromyalgia, specific spots or points on your body are painful when pressed, and yet you may not believe them to be the cause of the pain you feel, or you may be unaware that these points even exist. Other symptoms that are characteristic of fibromyalgia are poor sleep, general stiffness, and a pervasive sense of fatigue.

For a relatively common health problem (about 5–15 percent of patients seen by rheumatologists have it), surprisingly little is known about fibromyalgia. In fact, only in the past ten years have researchers established fibromyalgia as a real entity and not a disease that is "all in your head." Many doctors now in practice never learned of it in medical school or they may have even been told it was a "wastebasket diagnosis"—a term you pull out of the wastebasket and use as a label for patients whose complaints are imaginary. This term is also used for patients whose complaints reflect an emotional response to stress in their lives, which implies that these patients don't have a real problem at all.

However, fibromyalgia is rapidly becoming an accepted diagnosis, with an increasing number of researchers working on this problem around the world. Clues are emerging that suggest possible malfunctions in the nervous system are causing the problem; with that information, researchers are working to identify effective treatments.

A History of Fibromyalgia

A brief look at the history of this problem will give us an idea of how rapidly work on it is now progressing. As recently as 1979, a rheumatologist named Hugh Smythe published the first article in a major medical journal to call attention to the problem. In it, he pointed out that he and his colleagues were seeing patients who could not be labeled as having any of the accepted musculoskeletal disease such as rheumatoid or degenerative arthritis, but who seemed to resemble one another enough to represent a distinct clinical entity. In this and several subsequent papers, he proposed criteria for this entity, which he termed *fibrositis* ("itis" at the end of a word means inflammation, and "fibro" stands for fibrous or muscle tissue). His original criteria included both the presence of tenderness at specific sites and disturbed sleep. The poor sleep was associated with morning fatigue and stiffness, although lab tests to check the function of the liver, kidney, blood cells, and proteins were usually normal. This was in contrast to most other rheumatic diseases (except degenerative arthritis) in which laboratory test results were usually abnormal and could be used in determining the cause of the disease.

Other rheumatologists who were also especially interested in understanding this problem began to come forward. By 1986, these physicians published the results of a meetings held in San Francisco, where the diagnosis was firmly established and given the name *fibromyalgia*. They chose a new name because "fibrositis" came from the initial belief that the condition was a result of inflamed muscles, but researchers had determined that inflammation is *not* present in fibromyalgia. Across the medical profession, however, there was still disagreement as to how to define who was a "fibromyalgia patient." Finally in 1990, a group of researchers published a definition of fibromyalgia that effectively separated fibromyalgia patients from both normal individuals and people with rheumatic conditions. We will now look at the criteria they proposed.

How is Fibromyalgia Diagnosed?

Fibromyalgia is now diagnosed when a person has had the following:

1. Musculoskeletal pain for at least three months that affects many areas of the body. Pain must be both above and below the waist. It must also be on the right and left sides of the body and it must occur along the spine (neck, upper back, or lower back).

2. The pain must have been present for longer than three months.

3. Examination of eighteen specific spots on the body that were named "tender points" (usually places where muscles or their supporting structures attach and not where the pain is) identifies at least eleven of which are painful. Note that these "tender points" are *painful*, not just sensitive, so the term is somewhat misleading. Patients primarily report a generalized muscle pain and fatigue. Note also that people are usually unaware that the tender points exist until they are examined and the exquisitely "sore" spots are touched. See Diagram 14.1.

An earlier definition of fibromyalgia included symptoms of other health problems, which actually occur in fewer than half of patients with fibromyalgia, but which are still much more prevalent than in the general population. These other problems include irritable bowel syndrome (see chapter 19) and tension headaches (see chapter 16). Other complaints include small areas of soft-tissue swelling that feel more prominent to the patient than to an outside observer, painful nodules in the tissue below the skin (subcutaneous), marked redness of the skin when pressed or stroked, and at times a "mottled" (blotchy) or "reticular" (net-like) appearance of the skin, especially of the arms and legs. Note that all these conditions are "functional," that is, they reflect some abnormalities of the body's regulatory functions, for instance, in maintaining normal bowel movements or blood flow in the skin.

Fibromyalgia is not the only condition associated with musculoskeletal pain. Another common cause for aching, burning, or cramping musculoskeletal discomfort is called *myofascial pain*. Unlike the situation in fibromyalgia, the pain may be localized, or may affect only one muscle or

Diagram 14.1
Fibromyalgia Tender Points

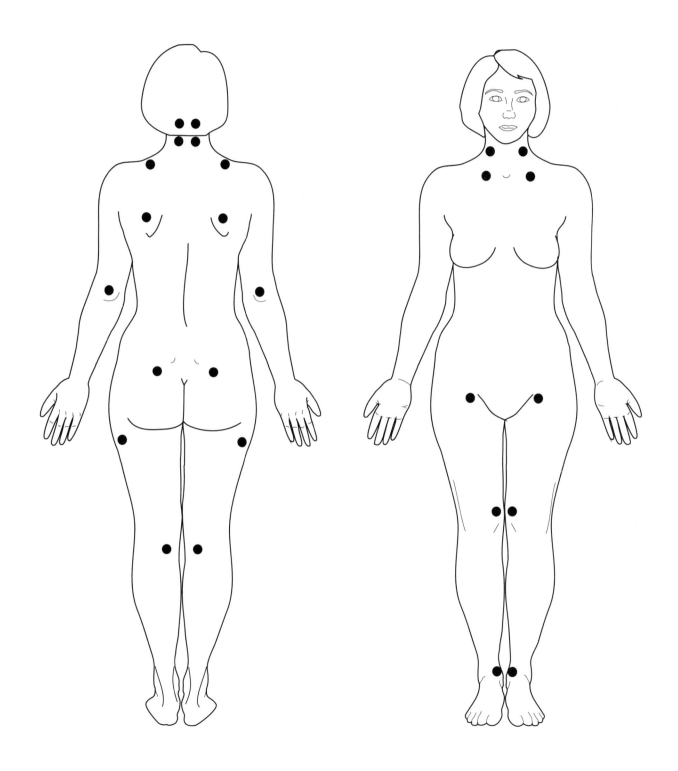

muscle group. Or the pain may be widespread as in fibromyalgia. See chapter 15 for a detailed discussion of myofascial pain.

Who Gets It?

The majority of patients with this problem are women. On average, women make up about 85 percent of fibromyalgia patients in medical centers in the United States. In one study, with data pooled from several medical centers, 93.2 percent of the 1228 fibromyalgia patients were Caucasian, versus 1.7 percent African-American and 4 percent Hispanic. As yet, we do not know the reason why most fibromyalgia patients are Caucasian women, but it may suggest that African-Americans and Hispanics are underrepresented in the general populations served by those clinics.

Fibromyalgia can begin at any age, but usually people are in their thirties when they first notice symptoms. Most studies have been done with patients who are between thirty-five and sixty years old. Although it is thought that fibromyalgia never actually goes away completely, it is most problematic in midlife. No studies have been published that look carefully at fibromylagia in elderly individuals.

What Causes It?

About half of the people with fibromyalgia feel that it began with a specific pain complaint, for example a shoulder or hip pain that seemed to spread to other parts of the body. Another quarter of them give a history of unusually intense life stress, which they feel was a trigger for the musculoskeletal problem. The rest can identify no cause. Smythe writes of a fibromyalgia-prone personality who seems to be in "overdrive." Even after pain develops, this individual pushes ahead, ignoring the physical problem or working through it—perhaps finishing off a ten-hour work day by going to the gym for a workout. Although Dr. Smythe has observed this tendency to "overdo" in the fibromyalgia patients he sees, currently researchers do not agree that the overdoing pattern predisposes you to develop fibromyalgia. In the individuals who give such a history, the problem appears to be one of *dysregulation* (loss of the ability to regulate), in that the body has lost the sense of how to relax and how to recover normal musculoskeletal function.

Another prominent aspect of fibromyalgia is *sleep disturbance*. Sleep lab studies in the 1970s showed that specific phases of sleep, namely Stage 4 (see chapter 10), were interrupted. It was also shown that if normal people, who had no sleep or pain problems, were systematically awakened during the Stage 4 phase of their sleep, they would not only become fatigued but would develop pain similar to that of fibromyalgia patients. A study of a small number of well-conditioned athletes, however, showed that they did not develop the fibromyalgia-like symptoms when they were awakened. This suggests that physical conditioning might help to prevent the development of fibromyalgia.

Recent studies have not confirmed that conditioning can *prevent* fibromyalgia, but studies have confirmed that interrupting a sleeper systematically during Stage 4 and also Stage 3 sleep will result in increased pain sensitivity, headache, and neck pain in half or more of the subjects. Given that these are relatively brief experiments, the effect of many days of being deprived of sleep could be even more profound. If lack of sleep results in pain and pain is a definite cause of poor sleep, the question of what causes what can indeed be complicated.

Some researchers have always thought that *emotional factors* play a significant role in this disease. Others have vehemently denied that they do. The evidence so far is inconclusive. When looking at the role of emotional factors, such as anxiety and depression, in any chronic illness, it is essential to consider whether the emotional problems came before the illness (and therefore may have a role in its cause) or whether they developed as a result of, or after, the illness.

It is difficult, to gauge the emotional health of people before they become ill, except through the distorting lens of hindsight. Therefore studies have tried to compare fibromyalgia patients to others who have similarly painful musculoskeletal conditions (such as rheumatoid arthritis) as well as comparing them to healthy individuals. A number of studies have shown that fibromyalgia patients have more depression and anxiety and focus on bodily symptoms more than healthy individuals and patients with other kinds of painful conditions. However, other studies suggest that a majority of fibromyalgia sufferers do not appear to fall outside the norms for emotional health. In summary, there is no agreement among experts on the role of emotional factors in fibromyalgia about whether they are the *cause* or the *result* of the problem. Regardless, many have observed that stress certainly seems to worsen the symptoms of fibromyalgia and over time, depression may arise as a person feels fatigued and "worn down."

What Can Be Done About It?

Research in this field is very active. As we gain more understanding of the nervous system abnormalities in patients with fibromyalgia, especially in regard to how pain is regulated, it is likely that new treatments will emerge. Some are already being tried at a number of medical centers, both in the United States and in Europe. Current experimental treatments include the use of *growth hormone*, a substance which is of importance not only in the normal development of a child to an adult but also in the regulation of biological processes in the adult. The use of drugs that affect the ability of nerves to carry and pass on messages to other nerves is also being explored. As we learned in chapter 2, the transmission of information from one nerve to the other is carried by neurotransmitters. The nerve responds to the neurotransmitter chemicals at specific locations, or "receptors," on the nerve endings. Drugs that either block or facilitate the nerve impulse transmission may do so only for specific types of nerves. Both pain and moods may be affected in this way. A considerable effort is being made to identify drugs that specifically block pain transmission in fibromyalgia, and some promising results are being reported. See chapter 12 for more information about medications and pain.

At present, fibromyalgia is a disease that is *managed* rather than *cured*. The cornerstones of treatment focus on improving sleep and exercise patterns. Medication can be helpful, but is secondary to lifestyle changes.

Sleep Habits

Getting an adequate amount of quality sleep is absolutely essential and must be recognized as an important treatment goal. Allow ample time in your schedule for this important activity and follow all the commonsense rules for giving your body a chance to rest in a healthy way:

- Limit fluid intake after the evening meal, especially if you are likely to have to get up in the night to urinate.

- Limit or omit beverages containing caffeine (cocoa, tea, and colas, as well as coffee) after the evening meal.

- For some people, drinking a beverage such as warm milk or an herbal tea containing chamomile or valerian root at bedtime can facilitate sleep onset. It is a matter of balancing the capacity of the bladder against the value of these gentle sleep-inducing agents!

- Avoid thinking of topics that are either stimulating or worrisome in the hour before bedtime. If you usually read at bedtime, select topics that are restful. Some people find it helpful to read a boring book.

- Another useful strategy is to listen to the radio. Most people will choose a relaxing music program. Some, however, will say that the talk shows, played softly, provide the diversion that best allows for the onset of sleep.

- See chapter 10 on other strategies for improving sleep.

Medications and Sleep

If you've tried managing your fibromyalgia with effective diet and sleep practices as mentioned above, and you still wake up as tired, or even more tired than you felt when going to bed, then medication may play a helpful role in restoring a normal, restful sleep pattern. Fortunately it is not necessary to use drugs that are potentially addicting. The only drugs that have been clearly demonstrated to be helpful with fibromyalgia are from a family of antidepressants called *tricyclics*. See chapter 12 for more information on these medications.

A small dose (much less than is prescribed by doctors for the treatment of depression) of an antidepressant can be very helpful. People who use antidepressants report that sleep is longer and more restful. The medications are safe for the vast majority of fibromyalgia patients. (The only potential hazard is for the rare individual in whom the nerves that control the heartbeat mechanism are abnormal. For that reason, a person who has some risk factors for heart disease may be asked to have an electrocardiogram before beginning the drug.) Side effects such as dry mouth and daytime drowsiness are annoying for some people but usually subside after one or two weeks.

Exercise

Exercise is the other key component of a fibromyalgia treatment program. It is essential to do it, but equally essential not to do it too aggressively or to increase the duration and intensity of the exercise too rapidly. Both cardiovascular and strengthening exercises are recommended. A number of researchers around the world are working to identify the structure of an exercise program that will prove to be the most effective for people with fibromyalgia. Always check with your doctor to find the right type of exercise program for yourself. The final answers will probably not be forthcoming for a number of years, but the preliminary findings are of considerable interest.

Several research groups have reported that overall pain decreases and quality of life improves in those who exercise. For example, in Portland, Oregon, twelve fibromyalgia patients who performed cycling exercises three times a week for fifteen to twenty minutes, had decreased muscle pain and improved overall functioning. In Finland, patients were given individualized exercise programs that were designed to either increase strength or physical endurance (cardiovascular conditioning).

In both groups, overall pain intensity decreased, but in those who did endurance training, the number of tender points decreased as well. In Norway, individuals were randomly assigned to receive either stress management training (a nonexercise program) or aerobic exercise. Those in the exercise program had decreased pain, fewer tender points, and increased work capacity. Those who received stress management training only had decreased pain and depression as well as decreased tender points, but work capacity was unchanged. Four years later, the individuals who continued to show improvement in terms of decreased pain and fatigue and increased work capacity were those who were exercising regularly. Those who no longer exercised regularly had lost all gains they had made during the study. The message is that exercise can be of great benefit, but only as long as you exercise regularly. You may need to start your aerobic exercise program very slowly, but most therapists recommend working up to twenty minutes of sustained aerobic exercise, three times per week. See chapter 3 for more specific guidelines.

The person who suffers from fibromyalgia can learn to live with it and to create a full and satisfying life despite the limitations it creates. Here are some important points to remember:

- Be consistent with your exercises, stress management, and sleep hygiene.

- Develop practice patterns you can sustain for life. For example, be realistic in your exercise goals; find something you *enjoy* doing so you will keep doing it.

- Don't overdo but don't underdo either. Being inactive over time leads to fatigue and muscle atrophy even in people without pain.

Notice that the "treatment" for fibromyalgia is a prescription for health that virtually anyone would do well to follow: get enough sleep, exercise on a regular basis, take care of your emotional needs and don't push yourself too hard.

Further Reading

Backstrom, G. 1995. *When Muscle Pain Won't Go Away: The Relief Handbook for Fibromyalgia and Chronic Muscle Pain*. Rev. ed. Dallas: Taylor Publishing Co.

Ediger, B. 1994. *Coping With Fibromyalgia*. Toronto: LRH Publications.

Fibromyalgia. 1993. Chesterfield: Arthritis and Rheumatism Council for Research.

Gibson, B. A. 1994. *Fibromyalgia: Exploring the Possibilities*. Clearwater, FL: Gemini Press.

Pellegrino, M. J. 1993. *Fibromyalgia: Managing the Pain*. Columbus, OH: Anadem Publishing,

Starlanyl, D. J., and M. E. Copeland. 1996. *Fibromyalgia and Chronic Myofascial Pain Syndrome: A Survival Manual*. Oakland, CA. New Harbinger Publications, Inc.

Information Regarding Support and Education Can Be Obtained From:

Fibromyalgia Network
P.O. Box 31750
Tucson, AZ 85751-1750
info line: (520) 290-5508
fax: (520) 290-5550
internet: alt.med.fibromyalgia

Fibromyalgia Alliance of America
P. O. Box 21988
Columbus, OH 43221-0988
(614) 457-4222

Online Information Can Be Found At:

http://www.alpha.net/dci/fibro.html

http://Prairie.Lakes.com/~roseleaf/

http://www.w2.com/fibinfo.html

15

Myofascial Pain

by Dorothy Waddell, M.D.

Musculoskeletal pain is one of the most common reasons that people give for seeking help from a medical doctor. In one general medical practice in Los Angeles, 31 percent of consecutive new patients came primarily for musculoskeletal complaints. In most of them a diagnosis of "myofascial pain" was made. Likewise, myofascial dysfunction was the cause of pain in 85 percent of the people who entered a chronic pain program in New York. In Baltimore it was 74 percent. Chiropractic and osteopathic medicine came into existence largely to address painful musculoskeletal problems that did not improve when conventional medical treatments were applied. The same can be said of acupuncture and of the many forms of hands-on body treatments that are practiced throughout the world. Many eastern therapies focus on myofascial pain and include treatments of specific muscle "points" on the body, all types of massage, movement or patterning therapies, and others.

What Do We Mean When We Say "Myofascial Problems" or "Myofascial-Dysfunction"?

"Myo" stands for the muscles, "fascial" for the tissues that wrap around the muscles to add strength and to facilitate attachment to the bones. Injury to these structures can happen for many reasons. Myofascial pain may be the result of a relatively trivial problem, such as a "pulled hamstring" when you do prolonged exercise without stretching and warming up first. Or it may occur as one manifestation of a serious medical problem that can persist for months or years if not effectively treated, affecting virtually every aspect of life. The term "myofascial" may seem at first to be a complicated way of describing very simple problems. However it replaces many other terms that were used in the past and have been a source of confusion. Words such as "myositis," "fibrositis," and "fibromyositis" suggested that the painful tissues were inflamed or infected, since "itis" means inflamed when it occurs at the end of a word. This was misleading since we know that inflammation and infection do not account for the problem we are now calling "myofascial dysfunction." These two words tell us what tissues are affected and they tell us that their function is not normal. In this chapter, we'll look at what myofascial pain is and then at what it is not.

So What Exactly Is Myofascial Pain?

When a muscle is subjected to injury or is overstressed, several changes occur in it.

1. The muscle becomes stiff so that movements are restricted, and it may even feel weak, as though it is unable to handle a load or perform activities that would normally be very easy. In the case of your hand, normal activities such as lifting, clenching, or holding a pencil would become difficult. In fact, we can't measure strength loss in the muscle, but it definitely *feels as if* it is weaker.

2. The muscle becomes painful either at the onset of the injury or pain may develop only after some time has passed. Just what physiological processes mark this border between "pain/no pain" is not well understood, but clues to the presence of a problem may be present long before pain occurs. These clues include the *loss of normal mobility* and the appearance of *muscle trigger points*, as will be described below. After the pain develops, it has several interesting characteristics. First, the pain following an injury is in the same place for people with and without myofascial pain problems. If the injury is a minor one, the painful area may be small. But if it is more serious, the painful area will be larger, more intense, and it will spread in a characteristic way. This enlarging pattern of pain may remain directly over the injury, but more often it spreads beyond the injured muscle, sometimes quite a long way. Less often, it can form a pattern in which the pain actually seems to skip some muscles in between the injured area and other muscles where the pain is felt. This means that you may feel pain in a muscle that has no apparent injury, and all the muscles around the sore spot feel normal. It may require some detective work on your and your physician's part to find the actual site of injury when this pattern occurs. Luckily the pain patterns are similar in most people, so an experienced professional will usually be able to find the problem muscle or muscles in a matter of minutes.

3. The muscle develops trigger points, which are small areas on the muscle that are very painful when touched. These points are found by exploring the muscle with the tip of your finger and by pressing firmly. If you are on a trigger point, it will hurt. Also, pressure over the point may trigger pain that spreads far beyond the place being pressed. These tender spots are therefore called "trigger points." The points in any specific muscle are located in the same place in all of us, so that if three people, for instance, have injured the same muscle, such as a pulled hamstring, the trigger points will be in the same place in all three people. The pain caused by pressure will be in similar locations for all three as well.

In summary, these three qualities, (1) stiffness that leads to loss of movement, (2) specific patterns of pain, and (3) trigger points, characterize the condition known as "myofascial pain." A fourth characteristic, which does not occur in everyone, is a feeling that the muscle is weak, even though there is no objective loss of muscle power. This often concerns people who feel that their muscles are not functioning normally; however, loss of strength cannot be confirmed by testing.

What Does Myofascial Pain Feel Like?

People use diverse words to describe myofascial pain. Sometimes they report an aching quality; other times they describe it as a deep burning sensation or a feeling of muscle tightness and spasm. If the muscle crosses a nerve or if a large nerve passes through the muscle, the pain may have a more "electric" quality, following the path of the affected nerve. There may also be other abnormal sensations or numbness even though there is no objective loss of power. This may cause concern in people who feel that their muscles are not functioning normally. It is not a sign that damage to the muscles has occurred; the feeling of weakness will go away when the myofascial problem has been effectively treated.

Are There Other Pains in the Muscles That Are Not Due to Myofascial Pain?

Having said what myofascial dysfunction *is*, it will be useful to talk about what it *is not*. Other conditions that may cause musculoskeletal pain include:

Inflammatory conditions (such as tendonitis and bursitis): When inflammation occurs, doctors name it for the tissue that is affected and add the suffix "itis" to indicate that inflammation is present. For example, inflammation can occur in a muscle's tendon or in the thin, silky smooth and moist sac called a *bursa,* which cushions the tendon or other structure in a joint and prevents irritation due to rubbing when the joint is moved. When a tendon or a bursa is subjected to too much wear and tear, the tissue becomes swollen, red, and sticky. This is because cells and fluid move into the tissues and specific chemicals are released in order to help the body recover from the injury. We call this "tendonitis" or "bursitis" because either the tendon or bursa is inflamed. If you have this, you probably feel pain and find it difficult to move normally because your body is healing and repairing itself. As we have seen, pain and limitation of motion occur also in the case of myofascial pain, but they represent a different process entirely—a process that has important implications for treatment.

Normal "aches and pains": You will not find these familiar words in the index of any medical textbook. But you are probably well aware of their annoying discomforts. Aches and pains develop when you don't move enough or don't move at all for a long period of time. Doctors can easily distinguish them from myofascial pain because these types of aches and pains disappear if we simply stretch and move around, especially if you move enough so that aerobic metabolism can occur (for example, by walking briskly for twenty minutes or more). Consider how your body feels after a cross country ride in a car or a very long airplane flight. Not only are you uncomfortable, but you may find that in some places your body actually feels painful. That is because bodies were meant to move periodically. Relaxation of a cramped, tired or tight muscle is important, because if we sit around for long periods of time without moving, spontaneous muscle contractions begin to occur. Health researchers demonstrate this by monitoring the electrical activity in those muscles. At first, when people consciously try to relax a muscle, the electrical activity that signals the normal contraction of muscle fibers nearly disappears. However, if people are forced to sit for a prolonged period and continue to try to relax without any movement, electrical "spikes" reappear. Muscle fibers begin to spontaneously and randomly fire, but not in the typical coordinated patterns of movement. This kind of muscle discomfort is easily relieved with stretching, and does not lead to severe or chronic disability, as it usually does with myofascial pain.

Where Are Some of the Most Common Locations of Myofascial Pain in the Body?

Note: In the examples given below, pain originating in myofascial structures may be only one aspect of the problem. Joints, discs, or other soft tissues may be abnormal and also play a role in producing the symptoms. However, without understanding the role played by the muscles, treatment may be unsuccessful.

Neck

The back of the neck is covered with several thin layers of muscles. Injury may occur from something as dramatic as a car accident or as common and apparently trivial as sitting for several hours doing desk work. Trigger areas in the midneck can cause headaches of either a "tension" or a "vascular" type. However, the location of the headache may hide its connection to a muscle problem in the back of the neck, as the pain may be felt behind the eyes, on the crown of the head or, more vaguely, just "somewhere inside" the skull. If you are experiencing such headaches, search for the trigger points by exploring the back of your neck, from the midline to the bulging bony prominence behind your ear. Sometimes the points are at the base of the skull, just as the bone curves under them. If you actually have a headache at the time of your search, the connection usually becomes obvious as you press the point and feel your headache pain increase. Inducing the pain in this way is not at all dangerous. In fact, it is a good way to demonstrate the source of the headache and begin to treat it (for example, in the case of frontal pain which is often confused with sinusitis).

Whereas a little pressure causes pain, if you continue to press, or to have someone else apply pressure while you relax as much as possible, it is often possible to gain some relief or even to abort the pain. Using finger pressure in this way is a treatment in many Asian cultures and goes under names such as shiatsu, jin shin do, or acupressure. Identifying the muscles that are the source of the headache is also an essential step in finding out what you are doing or have done in the past (activities, postures, old injuries) that may have caused the muscle dysfunction. In turn, understanding the cause(s) of the pain is usually the first step to preventing its recurrence.

Shoulder

Myofascial problems in the shoulder can occur suddenly, as when a tennis player or swimmer overreaches a stroke. Or they may come on slowly, causing a deep aching pain that is bearable at first, but becomes more incapacitating as time goes on. Women over forty are especially susceptible to the latter scenario for reasons that are not yet understood. The muscles that are most often affected cover the shoulder blade—top (supraspinatus), bottom (infraspinatus), and inner surface (subscapularis)—as well as form a cuff over the shoulder itself. The pain can be misleading, in that it radiates from the muscle along one side of the arm, down as far as the hand "as if" it originated from a nerve. However, it does not have the sharp, lancinating, or electric qualities that nerve pain can produce. By pressing firmly on the muscles that cover the scapula, your fingers will usually turn up one or several trigger points. Because of the trigger point location, people who have this problem often complain of severe discomfort if they sleep on their side. In fact, sleep loss can be a severe problem and adds to the troubles people experience with shoulder dysfunction. When mobility is lost in the shoulder even everyday activities, such as combing your hair or pulling your wallet out of your pocket, may be impossible to perform. Because several other structures (for example, inflamed biceps, supraspinatus tendons, or structures within the shoulder joint itself) may be causing shoulder pain, it is advisable to have a medical evaluation if the symptoms do not easily resolve with a self-managed treatment regimen.

Lower Back

Myofascial dysfunction may be the major cause of lower back pain or it may be only one of several factors that are causing discomfort (see chapter 12, "Back and Neck Pain"). Treatments for myofascial dysfunction are noninvasive and present little risk, so it benefits you and your doctor to identify and eliminate the myofascial component of the problem if it is a significant one. The large muscles that run along the length of the spine and that cover the buttocks are obvious candidates for the cause of myofascial back pain. Less obvious are small, very short muscles that join the individual segments of the vertebral column and may cause specific pain and loss of mobility. In contrast to larger muscles, the shortness of the these muscles make it more difficult for you to stretch them out to gain some relief.

Three large muscles, the *ileopsoas,* the *piriformis,* and the *quadratus lumborum,* all run deep to the *paraspinous muscles* and form the back wall of the abdomen. The ileopsoas muscle causes pain that is felt deep in the lumbar spine but which also may appear in the groin. The muscle itself is difficult to find, lying deep in the abdomen and virtually hidden under the muscles of the anterior thigh, making self-examination difficult. The pain caused by all three of these deep muscles can be completely incapacitating. Diagnosis is made more difficult by the fact that many physicians are not taught about the sort of back problems these muscles can cause, and so they tend not to look for abnormalities in them. Specialists who are likely to know about this group of muscles include physiatrists and osteopaths. Consultation with one of these specialists could be helpful if you find that your back pain is not improving with your exercise program and other strategies, and yet you have been told that all the studies show no real cause of your problem. Other medical specialists who are likely to be helpful if your back problem is a myofascial one, are physical therapists who specialize in "soft tissue problems" or "manual medicine," or chiropractors.

Temporomandibular Joint

This joint, often called the *TMJ,* is in action much of the day, whenever you speak as well as when you chew food. In fact, muscles around the joints may be active even when you are "at rest." Even thinking alone, without speaking out loud, can trigger activity in these muscles, unless you consciously relax them. The tension in the jaw muscles may continue throughout the night, either as clenching or as "bruxing," a word for grinding the teeth. Many people don't know that they clench and grind all through the night, but their sleeping partners have no illusions on that point. (If you don't know whether you are among the legions of those who brux, ask your bedmate.) Pain may be felt in the jaw or in the ear, or may spread up the side of the head where it can cause headaches. In fact, this "jaw" problem may fool both the sufferer and the physicians by masquerading primarily as a headache problem. You can find some of the common trigger areas on yourself if they are present by pressing firmly with your index finger right in front of your ear and sliding your finger forward, over the hinge of the jaw, or by pressing over your temple where there is often a slight indentation in the bone. You can also reach up along the underside of the jawbone where two muscles (the medial pterygoid and digastric) may harbor trigger points. If you feel you may have a TMJ problem, check first with your primary care doctor and your dentist, who may prescribe a splint to wear at night. If necessary, either of these practitioners may refer you to specialists, such as neurologists or oral surgeons who specialize in this kind of problem.

As the tension in these muscles may reflect life tensions, the perspective gained from a psychological evaluation may be helpful. Many psychologists and biofeedback therapists are trained to teach relaxation of the jaw muscles. Learning the relaxation skills may be the cornerstone of treatment for many who have a muscle tension TMJ problem. See chapter 17 for more on temporomandibular problems.

How Do You Treat Myofascial Pain?

The primary goal of treatment is to restore the normal movement of the muscle and its supporting tissues. In order to do that, the tenderness and sensitivity of the trigger points is eliminated or reduced. Two things are accomplished by this: the pain is alleviated and it becomes much easier to mobilize the muscle, allowing you more freedom to pursue your normal activities.

Things You Can Do For Yourself

Stretching

Stretching is the basis of any treatment for myofascial dysfunction and for the muscle pain problems we have been describing. Although it is a skill we are born with, as anyone who has observed a newborn baby work its way into a delicious head-to-toe stretch knows, it's a skill many of us have forgotten by the time we have grown up. We often learn, in a hectic world, that in order to get anything done, we must try very, very hard. Thus, for example, a person who is trying to stretch out his or her calf muscles before running, will tense the muscles and force them into a stretch. When muscle is forcibly lengthened it will do what it has been programmed to do, namely contract, making an already tight muscle tighter. To stretch effectively, you need to combine focused relaxation with gentle easing into greater muscle length and flexibility. Hatha Yoga is an ancient practice that accomplishes the goal of increasing overall muscle flexibility as well as inducing relaxation while using poetic imagery. It is best learned with an instructor, although some of the public television station yoga programs are excellent. Several good books have been written about stretching from the Western perspective (see Further Reading list at the end of this chapter).

Topical Agents

"Deep heat" salves and ointments, also known as *counterirritants*, are among the oldest healing remedies known to humans. They have been used in ancient cultures throughout the world. But now the reasons for their effectiveness have been validated by modern pain researchers. Although other tools are available for treating pain, few are as safe and easy to use. Your choices range from Ben-Gay and Vick's Vapo-Rub to the more exotic eastern Tiger Balm. Some stronger prescription creams (like Zostrix) are now available as well. All can be effective. If you have access to stores selling Chinese medicinal products, similar agents have been imbedded on cloth or plastic and can be applied to any area of the body like a Band-Aid. Called "plasters," they extend the effectiveness of these remedies and are especially valued at night when musculoskeletal pain can be especially troublesome.

Heat

Heat softens, soothes, and comforts. It is especially important to be sure that your muscles are warm before stretching. Special devices to assist in this can be expensive and complex. If you have a serious problem you may want to invest in a *hydrocolator*, which is a thick pad that can be heated in a microwave oven and holds the heat for hours. However, simpler, less expensive remedies are also available that may work just as well for you. A hot water bottle or a towel soaked in very hot water can function effectively. Wrapping either in another dry towel or flannel blanket will help the heat or warmth last much longer.

Cold

Cold decreases the intensity of pain and will limit swelling that occurs in response to irritation of the tissues, either from an injury or from medical treatments such as physical therapy or injection. Many cold gel packs are for sale in drug stores or medical supply stores. They are cooled in the refrigerator or freezer and then used until they become warm again. Usually stored in the refrigerator, they are cold enough to be effective and remain soft, but they warm up more quickly than a plain frozen block of ice does. Ice is an effective analgesic or pain killer if applied for at least ten minutes.

Rubbing or massaging the area with ice seems to be more effective than just applying the ice and holding it there. Since vigorous physical therapy treatments may cause an "injury response" or swelling in the area treated, many physical therapists advise icing the area right after the treatment and then again at home.

"Should I use heat or cold?" is a common question and a very tricky one to answer. The medical world seems to be divided into two camps: one would have you pack every sore place in ice. The other would have you heated up and avoiding ice. Depending on the circumstances, either heat or ice may feel just right or may be unpleasant. It's a good rule to let your body guide you. If it eases your pain, makes you feel more relaxed and lets you move or exercise more easily, you've probably made the right choice.

The above remedies have proven themselves over the years as simple and effective. Used or performed properly, they are inexpensive, safe, and can be good adjuncts to other medical treatments.

Things that the Doctor Can Do for You

Treatments for myofascial pain include medications, injections, and a variety of physical techniques, most of which are covered in other sections of this book.

Medications

Drugs that can be helpful are muscle relaxants (like Flexeril), analgesics, especially the NSAIDs (like Advil), and acetaminophen (Tylenol). Over-the-counter medications can often be as helpful as prescription medications. So many treatments are available for this problem that narcotic analgesics are only rarely needed. See chapter 12 for more specific information about medications.

Injections

If trigger points persist despite appropriate exercise and experimentation with the above suggestions, a *trigger point injection* may be helpful. This is a simple procedure that involves the injection of small amounts of local anesthetic, such as lidocaine (see chapter 12), into the center of the trigger point. Such injections should always be followed by application of heat and then by stretching exercises, either in the medical office or a nearby physical therapy clinic.

Physical Techniques

Sometimes the muscles seem to resist all efforts to relax and release. In those situations, the problem may lie within the joints controlled by those muscles. Some medical practitioners (including osteopaths and chiropractors) have been trained to loosen the joints by *manipulation* (skillful movement of the joints with their hands). Once the joints are moving normally, the muscles will relax much more easily.

Other health professionals who have received special training in treating myofascial problems include physical therapists, body workers (or other "hands-on" therapists), acupuncturists, movement patterners (Feldenkrais method is one example and a prototype of this type of therapy), and a host of others. You select them in the same way that you choose your doctor or dentist, namely on the basis of credentials that document their training in the skills you are seeking and from friends or professionals whose word you trust and who can verify the effectiveness of the work. Before you seek the help of nonphysicians for your problem, it is wise to have a medical evaluation in order to be sure that it is not masking a more serious underlying diagnosis.

A Final Word

Whatever approaches you use to manage your pain, whether on your own or with the help of professionals, the most important step you will take is to identify the factors that have led to your problem in the first place. These may be physical, such as typing for hours at a time or lifting heavy boxes many times during a move, or postural, such as lying in an awkward position to read or watch television from your bed. Or they may involve stressors that are nonphysical like having heated arguments with your partner or tensing up whenever your supervisor at work comes around. Identifying and reducing stress is as important here as with the other types of pain in this book.

If you are having trouble determining sources of your pain and stress, you should consider consulting with health care professionals who are trained to work with pain, including physicians, psychologists, physical therapists and others. All of the triggering factors you identify can become perpetuating factors of your pain and may undo the effects of treatment if they persist. Only by correcting these underlying causes will you be able to achieve the resolution of your painful muscle problem.

Further Reading

Anderson, B. 1980. *Stretching*. Bolinas, CA: Shelter Publications. (Can be ordered by writing: Shelter Publications, P.O. Box 279, Bolinas, CA 94924).

Blakey, W. P. 1994. *Stretching Without Pain*. Sechelt, B.C.: Twin Eagles Educational & Healing Institute.

Lycholat, T. 1995. *The Complete Book of Stretching*. Ramsbury, Marlborough, England: Crowood.

Pulley, M. 1990. *Solving the Pain Puzzle: Myofascial Pain Dysfunction*. 3rd ed. Dallas: MyoData.

Travell, J. G., and D. G. Simons. 1992. *Myofascial Pain and Dysfunction: The Trigger Point Manual*. Vols 1 & 2. Baltimore: Williams & Wilkins.

Videotapes

Anderson, B. 1987. *Stretching—the Video*. Palmer Lake, CO: Stretching, Inc., (One 60 min. VHS videotape can be ordered by writing: Stretching, Inc., P.O. Box 767, Palmer Lake, CO 80133).

16

Headaches

Douglas E. DeGood, Ph.D.

There is ample evidence that headache is a pain condition highly responsive to the types of self-regulation techniques described in this book. This should not come as a surprise to you, since headache is the one chronic pain condition that most of us link with everyday emotional tension or stress. You may also already know that headaches are a most peculiar type of pain disorder in that they are usually benign—that is, not symptomatic of serious lasting tissue damage. This benign status makes it much easier for doctors to casually dismiss headache complaints than it is for the headache sufferer to dismiss the headache discomfort.

If most headaches are in fact not associated with lasting tissue damage, can it be concluded that headaches are "imaginary" psychological events without any actual physical basis? The answer is clearly no. In fact, real physical events are involved in all headaches. If you experience serious recurrent benign headaches it is likely that you have a biological tendency toward some chemical or neurological disturbance of brain structures. This tendency seldom has a single "cause," but is a result of stress stemming from a variety of physical, psychological, and environmental factors. Stress, however it is defined, does not magically transform itself into a headache. On the contrary, there is a considerable degree of bodily involvement in the transformation process. In some individuals, stress affects nerves, muscles, and blood vessels of the head, neck, and upper torso in such a way that these structures give rise to the pain of the headache. Certainly most of you have noticed the discomfort that can occur in head, neck, and shoulder muscles with stress, fatigue, and overexertion. More recently we have come to recognize the important role posture and physical conditioning of these muscles play in creating vulnerability to headaches.

There are also a few noteworthy exceptions to the general benign status of headaches. Headaches can be secondary to traumatic head injury or they may accompany a number of illnesses, some of which can be serious. Headaches are also one of the most common symptoms of tissue damage from tumors, strokes, or, more rarely, intercranial infections. Anyone who develops headaches for the first time or experiences a new pattern of headache symptoms should be medically evaluated prior to beginning any treatment plan.

Physical Mechanisms of Tension and Vascular Headaches

Tension Headaches

It is estimated that nearly 50 percent of the population suffer at least occasionally from tension headaches. In fact, tension headaches may be the most prevalent pain disorder of our contemporary age, possibly a symptom of the stress of modern life.

You may be confused by the multiple meanings of the word "tension." Sometimes the word may imply the emotional arousal caused by the major and minor hassles of daily life. Other times the term is used specifically to refer to the mechanical contraction of muscles in the region of the head and neck that result in a tension headache. While both meanings are appropriate, in this chapter we will primarily use the second definition. Thus, for our purposes, the terms "tension" and "muscular contraction" headache are used synonymously.

The pain in tension headaches usually includes most of these characteristics:

- Gradual in onset, often beginning in the upper neck (occipital area) and working forward

- Highly variable in intensity and duration from one headache episode to another

- Experienced as a bandlike tightness, heaviness, or pressure around the head

- Constant, rather than throbbing

- Bilateral (affecting both sides of the head)

- Often becomes worse over the course of the day, especially on busy, stress-filled days

Excessive tension, and sometimes spasms, of the powerful muscles controlling the jaw, often play a major role in chronic tension headaches. While this jaw tension may be emotional in origin, it can also be due to poor tooth alignment or other dental problems. (See chapter 17 on TMJ.)

The pain of the tension headache may come from several sources in addition to the jaw. First of all, tight muscles in the shoulders, neck, and head can become fatigued and irritated. Just imagine how painful your hand would become if you clenched your fist hour after hour. Tightness of the muscles in the head and neck region can have a similar effect. Second, blood flow to tight muscles can be pinched off, causing the muscles to eventually become *ischemic* (that is, suffer from inadequate blood supply), adding to the pain. Third, tensed muscles can put pressure on nerves and blood vessels, pinching them between the skull and the surrounding bands of muscle fibers, causing a secondary source of pain sensation. This secondary pain can feel like a burning, throbbing neuralgic irritation, combined with the characteristic dull ache of the tension headache. In rare cases, the tension headache may trigger the even more severe pain of a vascular headache.

Migraine (and Other Vascular) Headaches

A migraine headache is the best known of the vascular headaches—those headaches that arise from changes in blood vessels in the face, head, and neck. These blood vessels are sometimes unnaturally narrowed (vasoconstriction), usually followed by a rebound period of unnatural widening (vasodilation).

Vascular headaches are less common than tension headaches, affecting approximately 20 percent of adults. Two-thirds of these adults are female, a fact that suggests a possible hormonal link.

Most vascular headaches are one-sided, most commonly associated with a particular blood vessel in the temple or above or behind one of the eyes. It is a pain that cannot be easily ignored. You often become very light sensitive when one of these headaches strikes and the pain can be so intense that it overwhelms your ability to attend to and concentrate on even routine activities. The chronic migraine sufferer will almost always eventually seek medical assistance.

The classic migraine is the outcome of a complex process involving the neurological and neurochemical regulation of blood vessels in the head and neck. What triggers off this process of constriction and dilation in the first place is not entirely clear. It is thought that brain-regulating hormones originating in the hypothalamus may alter the level of circulating catecholamines such as serotonin and norepinepherine, which in turn affect blood flow. Circulating serotonin levels are known to be high in the brain just before a migraine, but low during the headache itself. Emotional stress or excitement may trigger this entire process, although emotional stress need not be the exclusive precipitant. Hormonal changes, temperature changes, food, drink, and drug reactions are also common triggers.

Whatever the trigger, the somatic process appears to begin with vasoconstriction, causing localized ischemia (obstruction of blood supply) in the brain. This in turn appears to be responsible for the *prodromal warning aura* (changes in vision, tingling or weakness of the limbs, dizziness, or faintness), which can warn of an impending migraine attack. The vasoconstriction then stimulates the production of counter-regulatory neurochemicals intended to maintain adequate blood flow and thus proper nutrition in the cells of your brain. When this corrective effort is too vigorous and overshoots the normal target level, it produces a "rebound" vasodilation. This excessive dilation and the subsequent swelling of certain blood vessels, which corresponds to the throbbing painful stage of the migraine, is thought to irritate nerve endings in the walls of the overstretched blood vessels.

The pain in migraine headaches usually includes the following characteristics:

- Preceded by prodromal warning signs or aura

- Unilateral (on one side of the head), often focused in one temple or above or behind one of the eyes

- Often accompanied by nausea and vomiting, a so-called "sick" headache

- Can sometimes by prevented with vasoconstricting drugs

- Headache pattern is often found in close relatives, suggesting an inherited predisposition

Actually, only about 15 percent of headaches fit the above described classic pattern of *migraine with aura*. More frequent are vascular headaches that lack a distinctive prodromal aura and may also not be distinctively unilateral in nature. This more common pattern, formerly referred to as a "common" migraine, is now simply called *migraine without aura*. Its symptoms can be similar to classic migraine in all ways with the exception of the lack of an aura.

Still another vascular headache pattern is the so-called *cluster headache*. These are intense vascular headaches that are usually brief in duration (often about twenty minutes). They have been given the name "cluster" because they may occur with great frequency over a period of several days or weeks, and then disappear for several months before again returning. Although brief in duration, these headaches may produce the most severe pain of all benign chronic headache syndromes.

We now recognize that many chronic headache sufferers experience symptoms of both tension and vascular headaches. This pattern, called a *mixed headache*, has symptoms characteristic of either headache type. The two types of symptoms may occur simultaneously or sequentially, although usually the muscle tension will be noticeable at first. It will typically be the more intense vascular symptoms that will prompt the patient to see a doctor.

Both tension and vascular symptoms may also follow a head or neck injury leading to a *posttraumatic headache.* While such symptoms are common for a day or two after a head injury, the pain usually resolves in a week or two. However, in some cases, even with a minor injury and no other signs of cortical damage, headaches may become persistent, possibly due to long term dysfunction of muscles.

Finally, *sinus headaches* are often confused with migraines. The sinuses are air pockets within the bones of the nose, cheeks, and forehead. Mucous secreted in the linings of these air pockets normally drains through the nose. Oversecretion, blockage, or infection can increase sinus pressure and cause pain across the cheeks and forehead. Sinus headaches often respond to treatment with decongestant and mild analgesic medication. Severe headaches in the region of the sinuses, in the absence of sinus congestion, may actually be vascular headaches involving blood vessels in or near the sinuses.

Stressors, Stress Reactions, and Personality Factors in Headaches

Stressors are those people, things, or events that cause us to experience stress in our lives, while *stress* is our physical and emotional reaction to stressors. Stressors that bring on headaches may vary from mundane hassles of completing your daily schedule to deeply distressing personal losses and disappointments. Often feelings of stress are accompanied by negative emotions such as anxiety, depression, or anger. However, for some individuals, stress symptoms can also stem from positive feelings or excitement.

It was thought for many years that there was a "headache personality" type. People who were headache prone were allegedly tense and driven, had difficulty expressing their anger, and set very high standards for themselves and others. However, researchers have never been able to support the existence of such a headache personality.

Certainly the goal of stress management training for headaches is not to change your basic personality, but rather to give you some new strategies for handling your characteristic thoughts, feelings, and actions in response to stressors. Certainly how you respond to stressors may play a role in your susceptibility to headaches. Some people have developed effective cognitive and physical coping skills that serve to reduce or limit the negative emotional impact of stressors. Good coping skills greatly reduce the likelihood that a particular stress will become chronic, and it is the chronic, seemingly unsolvable problems that are most likely to result in serious pain.

We must also remember, as stated in the opening of this chapter, that headaches are an outcome of complex interactions of mind, body, and environment. At least equal in importance to differences in coping skills are individual physiological differences in the body's response to any positive or negative increase in stress. The natural physical response is an increase in muscle activation along with an increased production of certain neurochemicals. These neuroactive substances stimulate the nervous system, resulting in widespread changes, such as an increase in heart rate, blood pressure, respiration rate, sweat gland activity, and dilation of bronchial air space. Blood vessels near the skin surface and the gut are also constricted, with corresponding increases in blood flowing to the brain and large muscles. This is part of an evolutionary-based survival mechanism, the so-called "fight-or-flight" response, preparing your body for protective action in the face of possible threat or danger.

However, the exact strength and form of this biological fight-or-flight reaction varies considerably from person to person. Even more important than your immediate reaction to stress is your return to normal or long-term adjustment following your initial reaction. Some people display a pronounced cranial blood vessel reaction that could lead to migraines, while others display a more generalized vasoconstriction throughout the body that could place them at risk for developing hypertension. Muscular reactions for one person may occur predominantly in muscles of the jaw, while for another in the neck, and for still another in the back. Thus, the same stressor may lead to a tension headache for one person, a migraine for another, or lower back pain for still another.

The only definite conclusion we can draw concerning the origin of headaches in individuals is that it is usually impossible to sort out the exact contributions of objective stressors, personality coping skills, and purely physiological predispositions. A tendency to have headaches certainly does not constitute proof that an individual has inadequate personality skills for coping with the stress of living. In fact, many chronic headache patients are highly successful individuals. Many are energetic achievers and leaders with considerable attributes. Whether or not their personality traits are any different from those who are not prone to headaches is not really that important. What is important is that if you have the particular response pattern that leads to headaches, then you do need to be concerned about your ability to reduce your stress reactions—certainly more so than someone who has not inherited or acquired this particular response pattern. Self-regulation skills training benefits everyone, regardless of personality type. If you automatically dismiss these suggested strategies, saying "This doesn't apply to me because I'm not that type of over-achiever," then you will miss out on the positive effects that relaxation training can have.

Drug Treatment

The first line of treatment for chronic headaches is usually medication. Aspirin and other mild analgesics can be quite effective in controlling tension headaches. A wide range of medications has been used with vascular headaches, including drugs that directly affect vasodilation and the autonomic and central nervous system neurochemistry. Opioid (narcotic) analgesics or powerful tranquilizers may be used temporarily in the midst of an acute attack, particularly if the headaches occur only occasionally.

If you begin to have several headaches a week, you might take more medication to manage the pain. However, problems with tolerance and addiction to medication can develop, where continually increasing amounts of drug intake does little to control the pain. In time, such medications, especially opioids and tranquilizers, may reduce the body's production of endorphins and enkephalins—the body's natural, self-produced neurochemical pain reducers. Ultimately, a reciprocal relationship between headaches and medication may emerge, wherein the medication may temporarily relieve pain but at the same time set the stage for more pain. The headache reaction may become conditioned to the level of medication in the bloodstream, so that every time the level of medication in the blood drops, the headache returns with ever-increasing vigor.

Rationale and Directions for the Use of Self-Regulation Techniques

The emphasis placed on the shortcomings of medication is not to imply that medications have no role in headache management, but rather to alert the chronic headache sufferer that there are lesser known but safer and equally effective, alternatives to medication. In fact, a recently convened independent panel established by the National Institutes of Health, has concluded from available data that cognitive-behavioral self-regulation therapies are effective treatments for pain, especially headaches. Multiple studies have indicated that 50 to 70 percent of patients benefit from these strategies, a figure similar to the response to medication, but without the associated risk of side effects.

Self-Regulation Strategies

- Deep Breathing

- Progressive Muscle Relaxation

- Autogenics

- Imagery

- Biofeedback

- Self-hypnosis

These self-regulation strategies are all intended to promote general cognitive and physiological relaxation. Refer to chapters 4 and 5 for explanations of each technique. Most people find that intentionally making themselves feel more relaxed is like turning down the "pain volume." Common reports are that "the pain is still there, but it no longer grabs me and sets my nerves on edge."

From a cognitive-behavior perspective it is important that you think of your relaxation training as a *coping skill* rather than a *treatment*. This skill can be used whenever pain or feelings of tension become disruptive. It can also help you reduce the fear of pain, and allow you to attempt activities that you may have previously avoided. Finally, if you can achieve a relaxed mind/body state, learning sensory alteration (for example, direct self-suppression of pain via hypnotic analgesia) becomes easier. However, such pain suppression is an unpredictable individual skill that some patients learn readily with dramatic results, while others, despite considerable effort, will have less favorable benefits. Fortunately, nearly everyone can reduce their pain by learning to feel more relaxed, even if they find it difficult to develop a more profound pain suppression skill.

Tension Headaches

The rationale for using self-regulation strategies to treat headache is quite simple. Using such skills, you can learn to prevent or reduce the tightness of muscles of the head, neck, and upper torso. It follows that in so doing you can prevent, or at least reduce, the pain emanating from these structures.

It will help you to view using the necessary self-regulation skills for dealing with tension headaches as a three-part process. First, you must be able to self-monitor, that is, develop sensitivity to early signs of increases in muscle tension, or any other early sign of discomfort in the head, neck, and shoulders. Second, you use specific self-regulation exercises to counter this muscle tension. Third, you generalize this skill to situations outside the relaxation training setting. When you are able to put all these skills together, you can respond to early warning signs of increase muscle tension with a relaxation response, and do so even while engaged in other activities.

Vascular Headaches

The rationale for using relaxation training to counter migraine or other vascular headaches is more complex than for tension headaches. In fact, using relaxation as a counter-headache response may contradict the intuitive experience of many migraine sufferers. Migraine patients often report the surprising experience of noting the onset of a headache during times of low stress—while sleeping, on weekends, or while on vacation. If you are a task-oriented individual who faces frequent deadlines, these headaches may occur only after you have completed your tasks and expect to enjoy some recovery time.

The key to understanding this ironic migraine pattern lies in the "rebound" nature of these headaches. The physiological events that accompany a time of stress do not directly cause head pain, but instead set the stage for the headache. This preheadache stress phase is associated with the increased release of a number of stress neurohormones that may stimulate sympathetic activation leading to vasoconstriction of sensitive blood vessels. This vasoconstriction, in turn, can produce localized ischemia in the brain of susceptible individuals, leading to the prodromal aura of a forthcoming headache. The ischemic activity will also stimulate counter-regulatory neurohormonal activity in an effort to increase blood flow to the constricted arteries. Once the stress is over and you have the opportunity to relax, this counter-regulatory effort may be so powerful that it overshoots the mark, causing the opposite vascular response, namely, overdilation. Unfortunately, along with the swelling of the overdilated artery comes the ironic "relaxation" headache.

Given this set of circumstances, the goal of self-regulation training is to learn to stabilize these vascular extremes by controlling the initial stress-related vasoconstrictive response. As with tension headaches, you must learn to recognize the early cognitive and physiological signs of stress, and then attempt to "relax away" the muscle tension and characteristic autonomic nervous system activation that can set the stage for your eventual rebound headache. Thus, self-monitoring and using relaxation as a coping response is critical before the second, more painful stage of the headache begins. Once the painful overdilation phase has been reached, it may be too late for you to intervene with a self-control strategy. For some individuals, muscle tension of the back and neck itself may irritate nerves and blood vessels and be a trigger for vascular spasticity initiating a migraine. In such cases, the tightness of the back and neck can also serve as an alerting mechanism that it is time to try to relax away the muscle tension and hopefully prevent the onset of the headache.

Nonaura Migraine

The self-regulation and intervention strategy for tension headaches and migraines with aura is quite similar for nonaura migraines. Since the migraine without aura may develop full-strength very rapidly or already be present upon waking from sleep, catching it early and countering with a relaxation response, however, can be most difficult. For individuals facing this predicament, the best thing to do is attempt to self-monitor subjective tension levels throughout the day, especially on busy or stress-filled days, or for that matter in any situation that has led to a headache in the past. Attempt to take an occasional relaxation break. In this manner you may be able to reduce the upswing of stress-related neurochemicals that may later trigger, with little warning, a sudden rebound headache.

Posttraumatic Headaches

One of the more significant changes in therapeutic technique since the first edition of this workbook is the increased integration of EMG (electromyography) biofeedback techniques with physical or exercise therapies. This is important for all types of headaches, but especially the posttraumatic headaches that are common following whiplash-type injuries of the muscles, tendons, and ligaments of the neck. Pain is also common at the locations where these neck structures are attached to base of the skull and to the bones of the spine and shoulders. Chronic discomfort following such an injury may result in disuse and deconditioning, which may lead to a loss of flexibility and strength. Deconditioning in turn makes the muscles more vulnerable to spasm and fatigue-produced aching headache. Thus, a vicious cycle is established linking pain, inactivity, and spasm to even more pain. Fortunately, general relaxation training and hypnotic analgesia may speed the effects of therapeutic exercises and counteract this cycle. Furthermore, muscle (EMG) biofeedback during movement can foster efficient and posturally correct use of painful muscles and joints.

Choosing an Appropriate Self-Regulation Strategy

Having read the list of self-regulation strategies, and having read the chapter on relaxation techniques, you may be wondering how to select a strategy that's right for you. Everyone is different, and everyone learns in quite different ways; ultimately, you will have to experiment to see which approach or combination of approaches gives you the best results. Here are some ideas that may help:

If you have chronically tight muscles in your head or neck and feel that you need help learning to relax, biofeedback may be appropriate. The EMG machine, hooked up to the forehead, neck, and upper shoulder muscles, directly registers the muscle tension in this very sensitive area. With the help of the feedback monitor, you can learn to relax these and related muscle groups that contribute to tension, nerve irritation, and vasoconstriction. Equally important, the feedback may help you identify more anatomically sound postures, make movement more efficient, and speed the transition from muscle tension to relaxation. Exercises to increase flexibility and strength of these muscles may also be a crucial part of this procedure.

If you prefer to learn to relax on your own, rather than working with a therapist, start with deep breathing exercises and progress to a simple technique like progressive muscle relaxation. When you feel comfortable with these, move on to one of the more comprehensive techniques, like self-hypnosis or autogenics. Stick with one of them until you have achieved a reasonable level of confidence. To make relaxation more profound, borrow from some of the mental imagery techniques. If you have used self-hypnosis or autogenics faithfully for several months with no improvement, try another technique. Often a person will respond well to one technique and not to another. Eventually, you may put together a hybrid strategy that really becomes your own technique.

Part of successfully acquiring relaxation skills involves developing what has been referred to as a relaxation "response image," that is, the subjective experience you feel as your muscles relax, your heart rate and blood pressure drop, your hands feel warmer, and your mind feels clearer. Once you recognize that internal feeling, it will become easier for you to reproduce it quickly in a wide variety of circumstances. At that point you truly will have developed an effective stress and pain management coping skill.

Well-established patterns of muscular and neurohormonal responses to stress develop and become habitual over many years. Don't expect to alter such headache-producing patterns easily or rapidly. It may take weeks or even months before you notice significant changes in your headaches even after you have acquired the fundamental relaxation skills. An early positive sign can be any change in the pattern of the headache suggesting that you are doing something that is beginning to disrupt well-entrenched bodily responses. Your warning signs may be somewhat different, or the headache itself may occur at a different time of the day. Since positive improvement may be gradual, it is important for you to keep careful records of the intensity, frequency, and duration of your headaches.

It's easy to feel discouraged in the midst of a painful attack unless you hold fast to the belief that in spite of the current pain, tomorrow will be a better day. If the overall frequency of your headaches this month is less than last month, and if your headache diary reveals that the average intensity of your headaches has been gradually declining for several months, rest assured that you're doing something right. If you continue to practice the relaxation exercises daily, you can continue to expect your headache pattern to improve long after your formal self-regulation training has been completed. Even when headaches are not primarily stress-related, the ability to relax at will is useful. No matter what the cause of your headache, you will most likely find the pain more tolerable when both body and mind are as relaxed as possible.

Further Reading

Bakal, D. A. 1982. *The Psychobiology of Chronic Headache.* New York: Springer Publishing Company.

Dalessio, D. J. 1994. "Diagnosing the Severe Headache." *Neurology,* 44 (5 Supple 3): S6–12.

Rapoport, A. M., and F. D. Sheftell. 1991. *Headache Relief.* New York: Simon and Schuster.

Rapoport, A. M., and F. D. Sheftell. 1995. *Headache Relief for Women: How You Can Manage and Prevent Pain.* Boston: Little, Brown & Co.

Schwartz, M. S. 1995. *Biofeedback: A Practitioner's Guide.* 2nd ed. New York: Guilford Publications.

Other Information Can Be Obtained by Calling:

The National Headache Foundation
429 W. St. James Place, 2nd Floor
Chicago, IL 60614
(800) 843-2256

17

Temporomandibular Disorders

by Richard Gevirtz, Ph.D.

One of the most commonly reported sources of discomfort is pain emanating from the jaw, head, and neck. When this pain involves the movement or position of the jaw bone (mandible), it is often referred to as *temporomandibular joint dysfunction* (TMJ). In recent years, this single label has been widely used to describe several probably distinct problems and disorders. Other names that you may hear for these problems include:

- Myofascial pain dysfunction (MPD), which does not refer to the face (as in facial), but to the *fascia*, which is the tissue that surrounds many muscles (see chapter 15 for an in-depth discussion of myofascial pain).

- Cranial mandibular pain syndrome

- Mandibular dysfunction or, more rarely, "Costen's Syndrome"

At present, few experts agree which of these labels are best suited to describe particular groups of symptoms. But as a general rule, many health professionals are now using two diagnostic categories, based on whether actual damage to the temporomandibular joint seems to have occurred. When this damage is present, the diagnosis of TMJ syndrome is often given. TMJ syndrome also includes the symptom of sharp pain localized to the area in front of the ear. When no obvious joint damage is present, the condition may be diagnosed as MPD. Other characteristic symptoms of MPD include unilateral (one-sided) general pain and pain in a larger area of the head, including the temples, neck, and upper back.

Note that even this apparently logical division into two disorders is somewhat arbitrary. Many cases demonstrate symptoms from both categories. Cases of both TMJ syndrome and MPD are also often mistaken for muscle contraction and migraine headaches—and many cases of muscle contraction headaches do have a TMJ component. To simplify matters, in this chapter all of these syndromes are referred to as temporomandibular (TM) disorders.

TM disorders are thought to be fairly common. Many researchers have reported joint clicking and popping in 40 to 60 percent of the population. Some 5 to 10 percent of this group usually report having face pain. Although women constitute 60 to 80 percent of clinic patients, the incidence in men is probably higher than these figures indicate.

The severity of the disorder varies. Patients report symptoms ranging from mildly annoying jaw sounds to severe crippling pain and limited jaw function. At its most severe, a TM disorder can be physically and psychologically devastating.

This chapter will provide those of you who suffer with TM disorders with an overview of key issues in diagnosing your problem and of the range of treatments available to you. Special emphasis is given to the roles you can play in managing or eliminating your pain.

Diagnosis

The symptom that brings most patients in for treatment is pain. A proper diagnosis should be made by a qualified health care professional (someone with experience and training in TM disorders). In order to make a reasonable diagnosis and suggest a treatment plan, your health care professional will need some specific information that you can gather before your first visit. Here are some questions to consider:

Diagnostic Self-Evaluation

1. Do you feel a dull ache or a sharp pain or both?

2. Can you point a finger to the spot where it hurts or would you need to use your whole hand to cover the area?

3. Is the pain one-sided or two-sided?

4. Does it hurt in the morning when you wake up?

5. Is the pain affected by eating, chewing, yawning, or talking?

6. Does the pain begin at a mild level in the morning and get worse as the day goes on? Or vice versa?

7. Does the pain feel better or worse on weekends and vacations?

8. Which muscles around your face and neck are tender to the touch?

9. If someone rubs your shoulders, does it feel good or does it hurt?

10. Do you experience sharp shoulder pain?

11. Do you clench your jaw often or grind your teeth at night?

12. Have you experienced any dizziness?

13. Ask someone to hold your arm and catch it after letting go. Does your arm fall limply or do you have to force it down?

14. Does stress make the pain worse?

15. Do you have frequent headaches?

Dental Evaluation

In addition to investigating these pain symptoms, your dentist can examine you to look for clicking and popping of the TM joint, how far you can open your mouth, whether your jaw moves sideways when opening or closing, whether your bite (occlusion) is proper, and whether there is any sign of wear on your back teeth. Excessive wear of teeth or scalloping of the tongue may indicate excessive teeth grinding (called bruxing) or clenching.

Although a large proportion of the population reports some signs of TM disorders, many people live their entire lives with few symptoms and experience no serious problems. If your pain is more than occasionally annoying, or if you have to change your eating habits to accommodate it, treatment may be necessary.

Causes of TM Disorders

Although specific causes of TM disorders are unknown, most recent research has pointed to a combination of factors rather than a single cause. Sometimes the problem can be caused by a trauma, such as a car accident, a blow to the jaw, or a fall, or it may result from dental procedures. If you experience a sharp pain in the jaw area following such an event, contact your dentist or an oral surgeon immediately. You may have damaged the disc (meniscus) that enables your jaw to move freely.

In most cases, however, trauma cannot be blamed for the problem, and identifying the cause and its treatment becomes a frustrating, painful, and costly experience for the patient. Three general causal theories are currently being considered:

1. malocclusion (poor bite)

2. muscular disturbance

3. psychological disturbance

Malocclusion

For many years, it was believed that a poor bite, or malocclusion, was responsible for most TM pain. It was reasoned that pressure from misaligned chewing surfaces caused soft tissues around the jaw to compress, resulting in pain and loss of blood supply. Most research does not support this theory. Occlusion contributes to TM disorders, but probably in concert with other factors.

Muscular Disturbance

Muscular disturbances have also been implicated in TM disorders. Most of the pain that people experience seems to be muscular in origin. This pain may originate directly from the stressed muscle or may be "referred," or shifted, to another locale. In addition, the pain may be centered in certain specific spots called "trigger points," which are small tender nodules in muscle that are sore to the touch and refer (or send) pain in predictable patterns. The muscles most often involved in TM disorders are the jaw muscle (masseter), the muscles that help control jaw movement (pterygoids), and the muscles of the front of the temples (anterior temporalis), the upper shoulder (trapezius), the front of neck (sternocleidomastoid), and other neck muscles.

While evidence is strong for muscular involvement in TM disorders, it is increasingly recognized that the disturbance should be labeled "neuromuscular," since both the nervous system and the muscles work together as a system in creating the problem. Recent findings suggest the problem is focused specifically in trigger points within the muscles mentioned above that are activated by muscular overload or psychological stress. They seem to be stimulated by the body's emergency nervous system (the sympathetic branch of the autonomic nervous system). This could be the link between stress and pain.

Psychological Disturbance

Little evidence exists to support the view that TM patients can simply be labeled hysterical or neurotic. Instead, health care professionals now recognize that a strong "psychophysiological"

Diagram 17.1

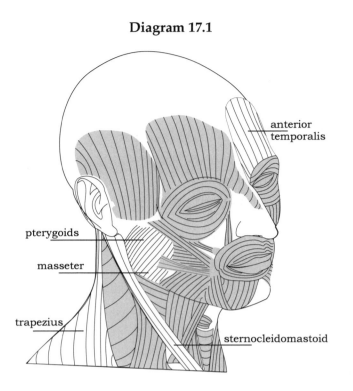

anterior
temporalis

pterygoids

masseter

trapezius

sternocleidomastoid

component is involved in TM disorders. This means that psychological factors such as daily stress create a chronic pattern of muscular disturbance (trigger point activation) and dysfunctional oral habits in some individuals. Thus, a combination of psychological factors (stress, anger, depression) and physiological factors (trigger point activity, muscular bracing, clenching, bruxing, tongue thrusting) join together to cause TM disorders.

The System View

It is vital to use an interdisciplinary perspective when dealing with TM disturbance. Many patients go from practitioner to practitioner looking for help and are given plausible explanations at each stage. A variety of problems may be correctly diagnosed, ranging from poor bite, abnormal jaw movement and function, and oral habits to poor posture, psychological considerations, and functional patterns. But it is only when all the factors are viewed as a system that successful treatment is likely to occur. TM problems clearly represent a variety of disorders, not a single dysfunction. You will need to do your best to keep an open mind in working with your health care professional to diagnose and treat your specific problem.

Treatments

The lengthy catalog of reportedly successful treatments of TM disorders includes (but is not limited to) these approaches:

Structural Change Therapies

1. Occlusal splints (plastic appliances that change your bite)

2. Mock occlusal splints (plastic appliances that make you aware of your tongue position, teeth, and jaw)

3. Orthodontic work

4. Full mouth reconstruction

5. Equilibration (building up and grinding down uneven biting surfaces)

Surgical or Direct Medical Intervention

1. Joint injections (steroids are injected into joint capsule)

2. Corticosteroids (anti-inflammatory medication)

3. TM joint surgery (arthroscopic and open procedures)

Direct Muscular Intervention

1. Muscular exercises

2. Electrical stimulation (muscles are gently stimulated with electrical current)

3. Physical therapy

4. Muscle relaxants

5. Immobilization

6. Trigger point therapy

Pharmacological Agents

1. Tranquilizers

2. Muscle relaxants

3. Aspirin

4. Antidepressant drugs

5. Membrane stabilizers (neuropathic pain)

6. Placebo drugs (almost any credible treatment has some short-term effect)

Psychological and Behavioral Treatments

1. Biofeedback (daytime and nighttime)

2. Relaxation and imagery techniques

3. Counseling

4. Cognitive restructuring and stress inoculation training

5. Group psychotherapy

In addition to these treatments, which are based on at least some scientific evidence, approaches from virtually every health care modality, for example, massage therapy or acupuncture, have been reported as successful.

How can you make an informed decision about the treatment that will be best for you with so vast an array of interventions available? The most important factor that you can use is the type of evidence available in support of the treatment.

The weakest basis for a decision is a simple case-study testimonial (John Doe testifies to his successful treatment with grapefruit seeds). Systematic case studies are better, but limited. The ideal way to determine the best treatment approach is through controlled studies where the treatment group is compared to a credible placebo or control group. The presence of a control group is crucial, since TM disorders have been shown to improve temporarily with placebos alone, and patients often go through cycles of spontaneous remission.

The most carefully evaluated of the treatments listed above have been the occlusal splints, surgery for disc disease, and biofeedback procedures. All have been shown to be effective to some degree after a fairly long follow-up. Many problems still remain in the experimental arena and further study is required.

Structural Change Therapies

Most TM disorder patients have been treated with one of the structural therapies listed. Several theorists have well-developed explanations for these treatments based on jaw imbalance. But however reasonable these theories may sound, they are not scientifically established and a great deal of controversy still remains. It does appear that conservative interventions, such as the fitting of a flat-plane occlusal splint, do alleviate pain and improve function. Based on these results, the Presidential Conference on the Examination, Diagnosis, and Management of Temporomandibular Disorders recommends initial treatment with *reversible* conservative procedures. This means that before you submit to any procedure which is not reversible (can't be brought back to the way it was), you should seek a second opinion—preferably from a dentist or surgeon with special training in TM disorders.

Surgical or Direct Medical Intervention

Most experts agree that surgery should be a last resort. Surgeons have made great progress in pioneering new techniques that make surgery less invasive and more effective; but in most instances you should be able to obtain relief without surgical intervention.

In many patients, X-ray techniques will indicate damage to the meniscus, the disc that cushions and guides the jaw. However, even these cases will often respond to nonsurgical treatment. Furthermore, surgery doesn't always work and can make things worse.

If surgery is recommended, you should get a second opinion. Look for an oral surgeon who collaborates with other health professionals and will try many conservative treatments before resorting to surgery.

Injections into the joint are used for both diagnostic purposes and as a treatment. They can sometimes bring immediate and dramatic relief; but be cautious and do not permit this procedure to be repeated too often. The injection can harm the disc and create new problems.

If you are dealing with medical personnel who have a broad perspective on TM disorders, you will be adequately informed and cautioned. If you are not being "educated" as well as "treated," go elsewhere.

Direct Muscular Intervention

Among physical therapists, a subspecialty has developed that deals specifically with TM disorders. These practitioners use a variety of methods to relax the painful musculature, including ultrasound, TENS (transcutaneous electrical nerve stimulation), sprays, diathermy (stimulation of deep muscle heat by means of an electrical current), massage, postural instructions, advice on oral habits, muscular exercises, and other techniques. Although little data exists on the effectiveness of these procedures, most people familiar with them think that they help, and they rarely do any harm. It is important that the therapist address the disorder as a neuromuscular problem, and not merely apply procedures for loosening up tight muscles. When seeking a physical therapist, look for a practitioner that has training and experience in myofascial therapy techniques such as "spray and stretch," passive stretching techniques, and so on.

Pharmacological Agents

Appropriate medication can be useful in treating TM disorders in the short run, such as nonnarcotic analgesics (aspirin, ibuprofen, and so on), anti-inflammatory agents, anti-anxiety drugs (minor tranquilizers), membrane stabilizers, and sometimes antidepressant drugs. These medications have been shown to produce positive short-term effects, but unfortunately they do not provide a good long-term solution (see chapter 12 for more information about these types of medication). Tricyclic antidepressants can stop night grinding and clenching for some individuals.

Psychological and Behavioral Treatments

The fact that so many diverse treatments have been shown to be at least partially successful in the treatment of TM disorders lends support to the proposition that something other than physical or structural changes are responsible. All successful therapies seem to have one factor in common: the patient's attention is directed towards the jaw and mouth. In addition, most involve supportive relationships with helping professionals.

There is good evidence that behavioral treatments are successful. Biofeedback is the most researched technique of these approaches. Other forms of behavioral treatment, such as cognitive therapy, have also produced positive research results.

Why Psychological or Behavioral Treatment of TM Disorders?

If we exclude those TM disorders that involve clear trauma, arthritic conditions, growth disorders, or other clear disease processes, a unique pattern emerges. In the remaining disorders, there is an interaction between both the structure of the face (or jaw) and oral habits. Oral habits can certainly compound and make the pain you experience from actual TM joint damage worse.

In addition to moving the jaw, supporting the head (which weighs over nine pounds), turning the head, and moving the eyes, lips and tongue, the muscles of your face, neck, and head also have an automatic "bracing" response. When a person feels threatened, they automatically prepare a "fight-or-flight" response to the threat. This response is characterized by tightened neck and shoulder muscles, a clenched jaw, and drawn facial muscles. This tightening is primarily a result of trigger point activation and may also involve actual muscle contraction due to tension.

Psychological stress is the underlying process that fuels this complex bracing system. When an individual with certain jaw characteristics experiences chronic stress, an overload on the craniomandibular system is created. This overload can develop in several ways. Excessive daytime jaw clenching can combine with nighttime teeth grinding to produce it. Clenching or bracing, or bad oral habits such as excessive gum chewing, tongue thrusting, frowning, forced smiling, or jaw thrusting can also contribute to an overload. Highly tensed muscles in the shoulders, neck or forehead are another part of this assault on the craniomandibular system. Many studies in both laboratory and natural situations have demonstrated that psychological stress leads to hyperactivity in the jaw muscles of people with TM disorders.

When enough of this hyperactivity is created, symptoms appear. These may include muscular pain, jaw pain, or both. Sometimes the pain will be far-reaching, covering any area of the head or neck. In some cases the tension of the jaw muscles will create a ringing in the ears or dizziness. Teeth can show wear from nighttime grinding and become sore. Gums can be affected (periodontal disease). Patients may hear clicking and popping noises in their jaws. This noise is due either to the effect of the discs being deranged in some way or to inhibited jaw movement caused by tight, shortened muscles that no longer allow the jaw to move through its pathway freely.

In all these cases, stress (broadly defined) represents the underlying fuel for the disorders. This probably explains why many studies have found TM disorder patients to be more anxious and to have a more difficult time managing life's stresses. Any factor that prolongs the stress will eventually make symptoms worse. Finally, remember that once the pain has begun, the pain represents a major stressor in and of itself.

Psychological and Behavioral Treatment

Be sure that you understand the reasons for your specific symptoms before proceeding with treatment. Go back over the symptoms you listed in the diagnostic section and make sure that you have a clear understanding of what is happening to you. If you are not sure of the source of your symptoms, get help from a professional who will take a comprehensive, rather than narrow, perspective.

Behavioral treatments are aimed at breaking the cycle of chronic bracing, clenching, and teeth grinding. This cycle of pain is broken with a number of tools, including biofeedback, cognitive approaches, stress inoculation, and other techniques.

Biofeedback

Biofeedback refers to a variety of techniques that allow you to see outward signals of how your body systems function and learn ways of changing your behaviors so that you reduce the effects of stress on your body. There are several body systems that are easily measured and that reflect the effects of stress or tension, but *muscle tension* is the main target in work with TM disorders.

A primary technique for measuring muscle tension is called *electromyographic (EMG) biofeedback*. When the brain instructs groups of muscle fibers to contract (or stop contracting), tiny amounts of electrical activity are produced. With modern electronic systems, this electromyographic activity can be detected and displayed to the patient. EMG levels are reported in millionths of a volt, called microvolts (μV). When the person becomes aware of this activity, he or she can learn, with training, to change it, if it is in excess of normal levels. Thus, EMG biofeedback can be used to retrain chronically tight muscles to relax.

For TM disorders, the jaw, neck, or upper shoulder muscles are used for feedback. An EMG assessment can determine what, if any, dysfunctional muscle activity might be involved. By getting readings from all muscles in the head and neck area, an experienced practitioner can get a more complete picture of the dynamics and complexities of the problem. Following this assessment, patients are usually trained to let all of their head and neck muscles relax. This muscle relaxation procedure enables patients to eliminate or minimize pain. EMG biofeedback training typically takes five to fifteen sessions to be effective.

Biofeedback is also used to aid in general relaxation training. This may be especially important in eliminating nighttime bruxing and grinding. Along with the EMG feedback training, patients also learn to produce a calm, quiet state.

As you may remember from chapter 4, the sympathetic nervous system (SNS) is the emergency or "fight-or-flight" system for the body. When the more complex outer shell of the brain perceives any sort of danger or threat, it sends signals to more primitive brain areas to prepare the body for the coming emergency. Using both the adrenal glands (set in motion by the pituitary) and the SNS, the body then becomes an efficient machine for fight or flight.

In this process, heart rate or blood pressure increases. Blood is shunted from the skin surface to the muscles (producing cooler hands and feet). Sweat glands begin to work (especially on the palms of the hands), and muscle trigger points begin to automatically spring to attention. These and other reactions get the organism ready for the threat. When the threat is a physical one, the body recovers normally after the physical effort is made. But when the threat is embedded in thought patterns or more chronic stressors , this emergency system can stay on too long. Such a chronic stress reaction can produce TM disorders. In order to adjust the functioning of the SNS and to combat this chronic stress, biofeedback-assisted relaxation training is used. In this instance, sensors from your hands *feed back* information about sweat gland activity. For most people, a relaxation state will be accompanied by less sweat gland activity in the palms of their hands. This is called an *electrodermal response* (EDR). Information about the temperature of your hands can be measured by a thermistor, a kind of thermometer. As you become relaxed, blood flows to your skin and to your hands, which then get warmer. Other body functions like heart rate can be measured in similar ways.

The goal of all of these procedures is to insure that you relax your body for a short period of time each day. Such relaxation interrupts the chronic stress or emergency reaction and enables your body to return to a more natural level of functioning. Although there is not clear agreement on how much time is required for this daily relaxation, most clinicians recommend at least one period of thirteen to eighteen minutes each day. Initially, you may wish to practice more than once a day until you learn to relax completely. As with any new skill, practice improves performance.

It seems important to produce the relaxation in the middle of the most stressful time of day. If we imagine that an individual's typical day looks like the graph in figure 17.2, we might anticipate that problems will occur. As you can see, tension levels are relatively low in the mornings for this person, then they quickly rise and stay at moderately high levels throughout the day until the evening, when stress levels decline again. Stress levels for this individual appear chronically elevated. The goal of biofeedback-assisted relaxation training is to produce a pattern such as that shown in figure 17.3. Here, by interrupting the chronic reaction to prolonged stress, physical recovery is possible. In this process, the chain of stress leading to pain, leading to additional stress is broken.

What would happen if you constantly tightened up and then relaxed your arm muscle for an entire day? Some stiffness might well occur, but once the muscle was developed, you could probably keep on doing this same activity all your life with no serious consequence. But, suppose you tightened your arm muscle and kept it tight for four or five hours, never letting up. Most probably, you would then have a chronically sore arm. In TM disorders, this kind of chronic pain develops in muscles that have been continuously tensed in the face, head, and neck.

Biofeedback-assisted relaxation training is designed to interrupt this pattern. For most people, a simple change of direction in the level of tension once or twice a day produces powerful positive change. Such daytime relaxation training also seems to relieve nighttime bruxing and jaw clenching for many people. Scientific evidence for this result is somewhat sketchy, but the available research does bear out positive clinical observations.

When choosing a health care practitioner for biofeedback treatment, look for appropriate credentials. One safeguard is to choose *certified* practitioners. An independent certifying agency, The Biofeedback Certification Institute of America, is an internationally recognized source of credentialed practitioners. You can obtain a list of certified professionals in your area by writing or calling:

The Biofeedback Certification Institute of America
10200 West 44th Avenue, #304
Wheat Ridge, Colorado 80033
please send a stamped, self-addressed envelope
(303) 420-2902

In addition, the practitioners you select should have special training or experience in treating TM disorders.

Cognitive Influences on TM Disorders

Another set of treatment approaches that has some scientific backing are cognitive therapy interventions. As we have seen, most chronic bracing and clenching is thought to be related to stress in some way. It is also now recognized that most stresses are heavily influenced by personal appraisal or perception. In other words, how you perceive or think about a particular source of stress in your life has a great deal to do with the impact that stress will have on your body. Many practitioners use special techniques to reduce such cognitive or thought-based sources of stress. In addition, some evidence points specifically to anticipated stress as a trigger for nighttime bruxing and clenching. Dr. Deborah Hopper had her patients with bruxing or clenching problems keep track of their prebedtime worries or concerns each night for an extended period of time. They also wore a device to measure nighttime jaw muscle activity. Anticipated stress or ruminations were better predictors of the nighttime activity than same day stress. In other words, worries were more related to bruxing or clenching than activities of the day.

Let us apply the principles present in chapter 6 to the specific problem of TM pain. If appraisal and perception are the key triggers for chronic stress, then learning to see things differently and process emotions differently may eliminate a major source of the TM disorder.

Negative Thinking

Not only does negative thinking lower the pain threshold (make pain noticeable sooner), but it also may have a direct effect on the facial, head, and neck muscles that perpetuate TM problems.

Joan was quite wrapped up in her own pain and misery and complained about it constantly. When hooked up to EMG feedback, she had difficulty getting her forehead or jaw muscles below 5 microvolts. After some time, I asked her to take a break and chatted with her about her young children. I asked to see pictures. She dug out some snapshots and proudly watched my smile as I admired her beautiful kids. At that moment, I pointed out to her that her muscle levels were 1.5 microvolts, far lower than she had been able to achieve with biofeedback alone.

Joan's response demonstrates the direct role of negative thinking in TM disorders. Since the face and head are intimately involved in emotional expression, it is important to pay attention to the thought and feeling components of pain in those areas.

Figure 17.2
Conceptualization of Chronic Stress

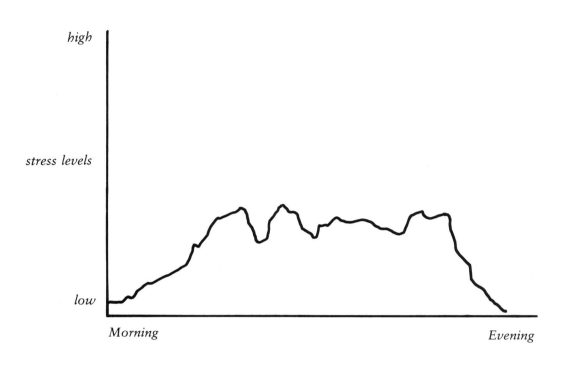

Figure 17.3
Using a Relaxation Period to Break Up Chronic Stress

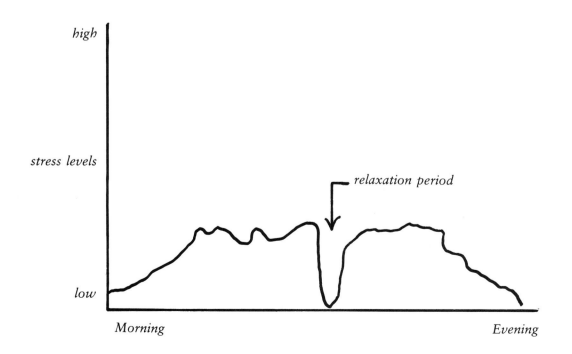

Stress Inoculation

In addition to following the suggestions given for dealing with negative thinking in chapter 6, you also need to learn skills for coping with negative feelings and thoughts that do slip through.

Joyce is an efficient, perfectionistic, and motivated administrator in a large organization. After a dental procedure, she developed a great deal of pain in her jaw, temples, and upper neck. A combination of biofeedback, splint therapy, and physical therapy worked well for her, but she still had some pain. As she worked on countering her negative thinking, she found that she couldn't seem to shake a problem that occurred at work.

Joyce had been assigned a secretary named Grace who was neither competent nor motivated to become so. Joyce had tried to get a replacement, but the bureaucracy of her organization made this change impossible. In effect, Joyce was constantly bombarded by a need to "grin and bear it." She was clenching her jaw and "bearing it" a great deal of the time.

Joyce applied the stress inoculation skills described in chapter 6. She recognized that the situation was an unavoidable stressor. She saw that she needed to become more "stoic" in thinking about her work. Maybe it was unfair or inefficient, but life was full of injustice and waste. Her job was to *get over it* as fast as she could. She charted her "Grace" attacks each day. These lasted for hours at first, but gradually she reduced their length to a few minutes. Simultaneously, she reduced her jaw clenching to an acceptable level and consequently got rid of almost all of her pain.

Psychological techniques are a key to reducing your sources of chronic stress. Review chapter 6 again, and if you need help implementing these principles, consult a cognitively oriented psychologist, psychiatrist, counselor, or social worker.

Other Psychological Approaches

The earlier sections of this chapter should have made it clear by now that anything that helps reduce chronic stress will help many TM disorder sufferers. Although little research evidence is available to prove it, many people are probably also helped by a variety of counseling, therapy, or skills training approaches. Some promising treatments include grief therapy, Gestalt techniques, assertion training (see chapter 7), self-hypnosis or autogenics training (see chapter 5), or traditional psychotherapies.

Lifestyle Changes

Oral Habits

Almost all dental authorities recommend taking the workload off the jaw joint by eliminating gum chewing or other repetitive habits (including pipe smoking). Moving towards softer foods and smaller bites is also recommended.

Some people are tongue thrusters; that is, they push their tongues against their teeth repeatedly. Just becoming aware of this habit can sometimes lead to change. Some people can also stop clenching their jaw just by paying more attention to that behavior.

Oral Health

It is especially important for TM sufferers to maintain good oral hygiene. Key habits here are brushing and flossing teeth regularly.

General Lifestyle

A lifestyle that promotes good general health will also help with stress management. This in turn will alleviate or eliminate TM problems. Regular aerobic exercise and cutting down on dietary fats, sugars, and salt, as part of an overall, balanced diet are often recommended. Some people report that giving up caffeine helps. Cigarettes are another source of trouble. The nicotine in cigarettes is a stimulant that actually creates more stress. In addition, smokers generally have significantly poorer oral health than nonsmokers.

Sleep Patterns

You may find it helpful to regulate your sleep patterns to make sure that you get adequate amounts of sleep. Setting a regular schedule for bedtime and awakening each day is usually helpful in adjusting sleep patterns. While this advice may sound simplistic, note that such regulated patterns can aid in relieving your TM pain. See chapter 10 for more on sleep.

Some Final Words About TM Pain

TM disorders can be potentially serious and are usually quite complex. Make every effort to inform yourself about your problem by insisting on both education and treatment from your health care professional. If you feel like you are being patronized or babied, find another caregiver.

Try to seek out professionals with an interdisciplinary perspective. These are usually dentists who also work with a team of specially trained psychologists, physical therapists, oral surgeons, prosthedontists, orthodontists, ear, nose, and throat specialists, and neurologists. Such a team will have a comprehensive perspective for your specific problem. Avoid anyone who claims to have a fast and easy cure. It may do more harm than good.

You may find that one of the behavioral approaches is effective in treating your TM disorder. Biofeedback and cognitive therapies are two treatments that have been positively evaluated in controlled studies.

Finally, by taking an active role in your treatment and not labeling yourself as helpless, neurotic, hypochondriacal, or hysterical, you can greatly improve your chances of getting better and staying better. Taking charge of your body, with the assistance of appropriate health care professionals, will enable you to understand and manage or eliminate your TM problem most effectively.

Further Reading

Gelb, H. 1980. *Killing Pain Without Prescription.* New York: Harper and Row.

Lasking, P., W. Greenfield, E. Gale, J. Rugh, P. Neff, C. Alling, and W. Ayer, eds. 1983. *The President's Conference on Examination, Diagnosis and Management of Temporomandibular Disorders.* Chicago: American Dental Association.

Taddey, J. 1990. *TMJ the Self-Help Program.* La Jolla, Ca. Surrey Park Press, (800) 833-8865

Information Regarding Support and Education for People with TM Disorders Is Available Through:

TMJ Foundation
P.O. Box 28275

San Diego, CA 92128-0275
Fax: (619) 592-9107

Online Information Can Be Found At:

http://itsa.ucsf.edu/~map/omfs.html

http://www.rad.washington.edu/Anatomy/TMJ/TMJISMAP.html

18

Arthritis

by Stephen T. Wegener, Ph.D.

Approximately one person out of seven will develop some form of arthritis, often called rheumatic disease. Pain is the primary reason that people seek treatment for their arthritis. Rheumatic diseases can be extremely unpredictable, flaring up without warning or remaining a constant, nagging pain. Due to the chronic nature of arthritis, people often become discouraged, feel helpless, and do not seek proper medical care or use effective self-management strategies. All arthritis can be helped if not cured. The first step in developing self-help skills is to learn about your arthritis.

The word *arthritis* means "inflammation of the joint," referring to the disease's common characteristics of redness, heat, swelling, and pain in or around a joint. There are over 100 different conditions covered by the term "arthritis" and most involve some form of inflammation.

Although these diseases have many things in common, each has its own pattern of symptoms and treatments. Here are the two most common types:

- *Osteoarthritis* (OA, also known as *degenerative joint disease*, or DJD) is the most common form of arthritis. It involves the breakdown of the cartilage around the bone or development of bone spurs and can lead to pain and limited function. The joints usually affected are the knees, hips, fingers, and back. OA can result from trauma or injury to a joint. Individuals who are overweight are at greater risk.

- *Rheumatoid arthritis* (RA) involves inflammation that is so severe it can lead to joint deformity, limitations in function, and a decreased quality of life. Persons with RA often feel as though they have the flu—they are tired and aching, but also have swelling and pain in one or more joints for several weeks. Often many joints are affected simultaneously. RA is generally considered to be a systemic (or whole-body) illness.

Other types of arthritis that you may hear about or have experience with are systemic lupus erythematosus (SLE), ankylosing spondilytis, bursitis, and gout. These types of rheumatic disease share several important characteristics with OA and RA. Most of these rheumatic diseases are chronic; that is, they often last a long time or recur frequently throughout life. Most forms have no cure, but can be eased by your health care team and by your own efforts. You should be skeptical of people or products who offer a quick fix.

The warning signs of arthritis are:

Figure 18.1

- Swelling in one or more joints

- Early morning stiffness

- Recurring pain or tenderness in any joint

- Inability to move a joint normally

- Unexplained weight loss, fever, or weakness combined with joint pain

- Symptoms like these persisting for more than two weeks

If you have two or more of these signs, you should see a doctor for a diagnosis and to receive proper treatment. It is particularly important for you to know what kind of arthritis you have in order to receive proper treatment and plan your self-management program.

Identifying which joints are painful or stiff will help you to communicate with your health care team and plan your self-help program. Use figure 18.1 to mark the joints that are problematic for you.

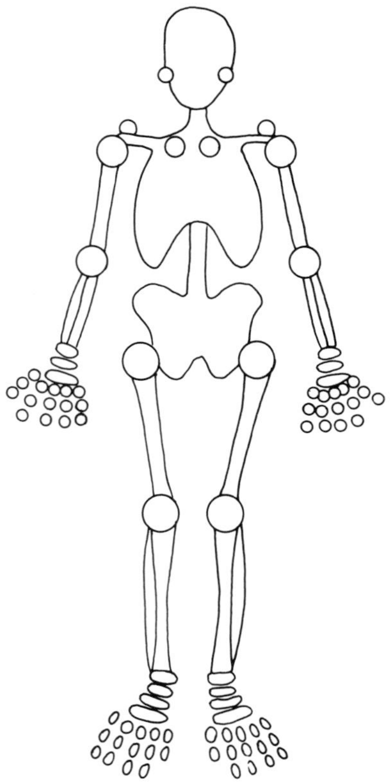

Arthritis Treatments

Most arthritis specialists recommend a building block approach for the treatment of rheumatic disease. The treatment is progressive and additive, using many different methods and involving the entire treatment team, including its most important member—you. You and your health care team build on basic strategies—education, self-management, and pain or anti-inflammatory medications. If your arthritis does not respond, then you and your health care team can add more intensive treatments. As figure 18.2 indicates, basic self-management approaches are the building blocks of arthritis care.

While this chapter will touch briefly on the treatments administered by other members of the health care team, arthritis self-management skills will be the primary focus. Research demonstrates that people who learn and practice arthritis self-management skills such as exercise, stress reduction, and problem solving report feeling less pain, have positive changes in their health and quality of life, and may have reduced arthritis-related medical expenses. If you become an effective self-manager, you and your arthritis will benefit.

Medication

Many of the medications prescribed for arthritis are used to reduce the pain you experience and the inflammation that leads to that pain. Some medications used are not unique to arthritis and have been described in chapter 12. All medications have potential benefits as well as potential negative side effects. You and your health care provider need to balance these effects. The arthritis medications most commonly used are:

Acetaminophen. This is a nonprescription drug with few side effects. It is known by several brand names and is used to control pain. It has no anti-inflammatory effect and thus is often used to treat OA where pain, not inflammation, is the primary problem.

Nonsteroidal anti-inflammatory drugs (NSAIDs). These medications are used often because they reduce inflammation and pain. It has been shown that a substance called *prostaglandin* leads to the pain that results from inflammation. NSAIDs reduces the amount of prostaglandins produced, thereby decreasing inflammation-related pain. The oldest and most basic NSAID is aspirin. Your doctor may prescribe large doses of aspirin. Don't be fooled into thinking, "This is only aspirin—how can it help?" Aspirin can be powerful medication if taken appropriately. As with all NSAIDs you need to be mindful of side effects such as gastrointestinal problems. Coated aspirin and some NSAIDs may have fewer side effects. Be a good self-care manager and talk to your health care provider if you have questions. Research indicates there is little difference in effectiveness among the NSAIDs. Some NSAIDs have the advantage of requiring fewer pills per day to be effective and thus are more convenient; however, some are more expensive than others. NSAIDs are available in both prescription and nonprescription strength. Different people respond to different types of NSAIDs so you must work carefully with your health care provider to find a medication regimen that balances safety and results.

Corticosteroids (steroids). These are strong drugs that quickly reduce inflammation and pain. Although you may feel better, steroids do not reverse the underlying disease. They may also cause serious side effects such as thinning of the bone, high blood pressure, muscle atrophy, or depression. Steroids are used primarily when other efforts have not been successful. You should never change or reduce the amount of steroids you are taking without talking to your doctor.

Slow-acting antirheumatic drugs. These medications attempt to slow the underlying progress of the disease, although how they work is not well understood. This class of drug is used primarily after trying several NSAIDs. Examples include methotrexate, gold, penicillamine, and antimalarial and cytotoxic medications.

Figure 18.2
Slow-Acting Antirheumatic Drugs
Cytotoxic Medications

Methotrexate		Gold

Physical & Occupational Therapy

Assistive Devices	Assisted Exercises	Advanced Education

Pain & Inflammation Medication

Acetaminophen	Nonsteroidal Anti-Inflammatory Drugs

Self-Management

Education	Exercise	Coping Skills
Weight Loss	Rest	Heat/cold

You need to play a responsible role in using medication to modify your arthritic pain. First, be an active self-manager: know what medications you are on, what the side effects may be, and how often they should be taken. Second, follow the treatment that you have agreed on with your doctor. Missing doses of medicine can increase your pain. Use a worksheet like the one below to keep track of the medication you are taking.

Medication	*How many and how often*	*Side effects*
_____	_____	_____
_____	_____	_____
_____	_____	_____
_____	_____	_____
_____	_____	_____
_____	_____	_____
_____	_____	_____

Exercise and Rest

Exercise and rest are both important in self-management for arthritis. Total body rest is necessary to balance the fatigue associated with some forms of arthritis. Protecting and resting specific joints is helpful in preventing pain. The physical benefits of regular exercise—strength, conditioning, and maintenance of range of motion in the joint—are all helpful in managing arthritis pain. Also important are the benefits of psychological well-being, a sense of purpose, and a feeling that you are helping to manage your disease that exercise can give. The specific exercises that are best for you depend on the type and severity of your arthritis as well as on your overall physical condition. You and your health care team are the best ones to make a decision regarding the proper exercise for you.

General Rest Guidelines:

- Use thirty- to sixty-minute daytime rest periods to offset fatigue.

- Develop good sleep practices. Set regular times for going to bed and rising. Attempt to get eight to ten hours of nighttime sleep. Monitor caffeine, medication, and environmental disturbance if you are having sleep problems.

- Learn proper posture and positioning.

- Develop your ability to use relaxation techniques so you can physically and mentally relax during rest periods.

- Use splints, assistive devices, activity modification, and environmental changes to protect specific joints that are painful or inflamed. Consultation with a physical or occupational therapist can be helpful in learning to use these devices and practices.

General Exercise Guidelines:

- If you are being treated by a health care provider for arthritis (and you should be if you have active rheumatic disease), talk with that person before beginning your exercise program.

- Range of motion, strengthening, and endurance exercises are all important. A good program will balance all three. You can use both dynamic and isometric exercises.

- Begin at a comfortable level for you and stick to your program regularly. If you have pain for two or more hours following an exercise, reduce that particular exercise. Be capable of eight to ten repetitions of an exercise before you add more resistance or more repetitions.

- It is best to exercise when you have the least pain and stiffness and are not tired.

- In general, avoid any exercise that puts extra pressure on an inflamed joint.

- A particularly excellent type of exercise for people with arthritis is swimming (or other water-based exercise programs). Water exercise involves many of the typical exercises done on land, however, the buoyancy of the water supports your muscles and joints so that you feel lighter, are able to move easier, and run less risk of injury. The water also provides gentle resistance, much like light weights, so that you are strengthening your muscles and improving your endurance while you work out in the water. Check with your local Arthritis Foundation for the location of a water exercise program in your area.

1. *For fingers.* To help increase movement in the joints of the fingers, start with joint 1 at the tip of the finger. Slowly bend with other hand till you reach joint 7. Continue gradually applying pressure through joint 3. You can reverse this process, starting with joint 3 and working up. Do this exercise as many times in the day as feels comfortable, but at least once a day.

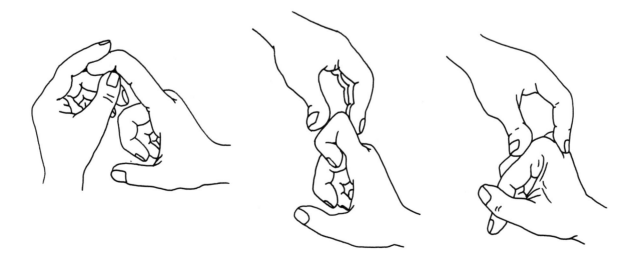

2. *For wrists.* To increase flexibility and movement in the wrists, place palms together with fingers interlaced. Slowly apply pressure by pushing the palms on one side and then the other. Push to the point of discomfort, then just a little bit beyond. Repeat as many times as feels comfortable, but at least once a day.

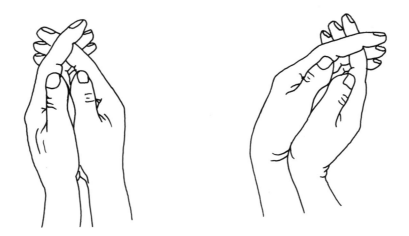

3. *For elbows.* Place palms and fingers together, bringing arms to right shoulder. Now press downwards on a diagonal toward your left knee, straightening both arms. Go slowly and push just a little beyond any discomfort. Repeat on the other side. Repeat as many times as feels comfortable, but at least once a day.

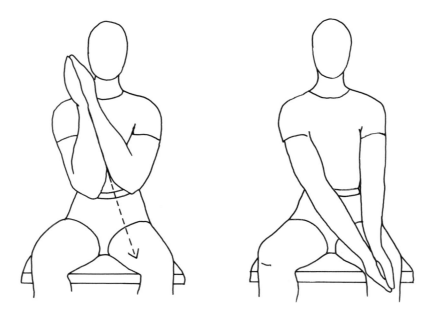

4. *For shoulders.* Clasp your hands behind your neck. Slowly pull your elbows as far back as you can, then bring them forward and touch them together if you can. This exercise rotates your shoulder to help increase movement and also stretches out your chest muscles. Repeat three to five times.

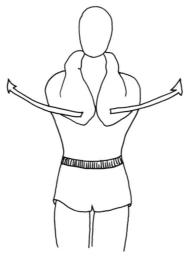

5. *For calves and ankles.*

(a) Using a stable object such as table or wall, lean into the object with both hands. Bend your left knee as you lean forward and stretch your right leg behind you, straightening the leg as much as possible. Make sure both feet are pointed straight ahead to get the right stretch. You should feel a good stretch in your calf if your heel is as flat to the floor as possible. Hold twenty seconds. Switch to other side and repeat with left leg.

(b) Now place both legs back together as you lean into the table or wall. Slowly raise up on the balls of your feet and back down, pushing your heels flat to the floor. Repeat ten times. This exercise is excellent for promoting flexibility and movement in the calves and ankles.

6. Other suggested exercises for the rest of the body. (Please refer to chapter 3 for a full description of these exercises.) Once you get started, all of the exercises in chapter 3 are good for promoting overall body strength and flexibility. But for beginning exercisers with arthritis, do the exercises here first because they are low-stress, low-load range of motion exercises (moving the joints through all positions).

a. *Hip flexor stretch* (exercise I.3). Promotes movement and flexibility in the hips as well as a stretch for the lower back. Start with the easier exercise first, lying flat, and work up to the harder exercise where you tuck your chin towards your knee at your chest. As you get better at this exercise you can also straighten the non-chest leg.

b. *Cross leg rotation stretch* (exercise II.1). Good for hip rotation and stretching lower back and sides. Keep shoulders on the floor or bed.

c. *Lower back stretch and roll* (exercise III.2). Also good for hip rotation and lower back stretch. Keep shoulders on the floor or bed.

d. *Neck stretches and strengtheners* (exercises III.4 and III.5). Neck stretches are good for promoting flexibility in neck and shoulders. Neck hold promotes strength in muscles in front and back of neck. Be gentle. If you feel sharp pain in your neck or down your arm stop and consult your health care provider.

Physical and Occupational Therapy

Physical therapists teach you how to perform exercises and help you to carry out exercises that you may not be able to do alone or may require special equipment. They can also train you to use pain relief methods such as heat and cold treatments or transcutaneous electrical stimulation (TENS). In arthritis, TENS is most successful in reducing pain if the pain is localized in a specific joint. Occupational therapists can teach you ways of protecting your joints and techniques to conserve energy. They can also provide adaptive devices and aids to help with your daily activities. Ask your doctor about the ideas and techniques reviewed below if you feel that they would be helpful.

Heat and cold. Either of these two pain management techniques may be helpful with arthritis pain and stiffness. For some people with arthritis heat works best, for others cold. You may also want to try a combination of heat and cold. This *contrast bath* involves soaking the inflamed joint in warm water, then in cool water, and then in warm water again. Repeat this cycle every three to five minutes for a total of twenty minutes. Physical and occupational therapists can tell you more about the use of heat and cold.

Joint protection and energy conservation. Taking care of your joints and yourself are key principles in preventing arthritis pain. The Arthritis Foundation lists eight principles for protecting your joints and conserving your energy:

1. Respect pain. If you have pain for two or more hours after doing a task, you have done too much.

2. Become aware of your body position. Avoid activities that involve a tight grip or put too much pressure on your fingers.

3. Control your weight.

4. Avoid staying in one position for a long time.

5. Use your largest and strongest joints and muscles for the task. For example, carry your purse on your shoulder or elbow rather than with your hand. Lift with your larger leg muscles rather than your weaker back muscles.

6. Balance activity with rest. Listen to your body's signals.

7. Simplify your work by planning ahead and managing your time.

8. Ask for help.

Surgery

Many people who have arthritis will never have surgery. Each individual's case needs to be decided by you and your doctor. However, a few points are worth remembering. The primary reasons for surgery are for joint repair, joint replacement, and removal of joint lining (a *synovectomy*). These surgeries are seldom urgent, so you will have time to consider the decision. Think it over and get multiple opinions if possible. Remember that surgery cannot replace good self-management skills. In fact, you will have better results from surgery if you are in good physical and mental condition. You will also need to plan on a rehabilitation program to maximize your benefits from the operation.

Relaxation Training

Many people with arthritis, along with many scientists, realize that physical and emotional stress increases the amount of pain you experience. Pain and stress have similar effects on the body. Muscles become tight, breathing becomes faster, and blood flow is restricted. Learning methods to relax can help you combat the pain and physical and emotional stress related to arthritis. Relaxation is more than just sitting back, reading, or watching television. It is a skill involving learning ways to calm and control your body and your mind. Relaxation does not come easy if you are in pain or have a chronic disease such as arthritis. It must be practiced like any other skill.

Several methods can be used to develop the relaxation response. These include progressive muscle relaxation (PMR), autogenic training, imagery, self-hypnosis, and biofeedback. Follow the instructions for performing these relaxation exercises given in chapters 4 and 5. Here are a few hints for using these techniques when you have arthritis:

- *Progressive muscle relaxation* can place excessive strain on inflamed joints if done too strenuously. A more passive relaxation method such as autogenic training or imagery may be more helpful. If you choose to use PMR, be sure not to strain your joints excessively.

- *Autogenic training* may be a helpful exercise to begin with, as it will not strain your joints. It also allows you to focus the relaxation on particular parts of your body.

- *Imagery* can be extremely useful when you have hot, inflamed joints. You might picture your pain as a setting sun—hot, red, and bright. As the sun slowly sets in your mind, you feel your pain going down with it. You can picture the sun setting again and again until you feel cool and relaxed.

- *Self-hypnosis* is deep relaxation created by focusing your attention internally. See chapter 5 for instructions and a sample induction that you can adapt to fit your condition. Not everyone has the knack of using hypnosis successfully, so don't be discouraged if it takes some time for you to develop this self-regulation skill.

- *Biofeedback* can help you learn to relax if other techniques are difficult for you. With the assistance of biofeedback you can develop an awareness of when you are becoming tensed. While biofeedback is not necessary to learn relaxation it is helpful to some individuals.

Learning relaxation skills can aid in the management of arthritis pain and can help you develop a reassuring sense of control over your body. It may be necessary to seek some professional assistance or join a self- help or pain management group to develop these relaxation skills.

Other Self-Management Tools

Weight loss and diet.   Maintaining appropriate weight is helpful in preventing OA and assists in the management of other rheumatic diseases. This is done through proper exercise and diet. Good nutrition is important for everyone, and particularly important for anyone who has a chronic disease. But note that no diet or food has been proven to prevent or cure any type of arthritis except gout. People with gout should avoid foods that contain high levels of purines such as organ meats, peas, beans, and shellfish, and should work with their health care professional to develop an appropriate diet. Other types of arthritis require a balanced diet that includes portions from each one of the four basic food groups: meats, vegetables and fruits, milk products, and grains. Use a common sense approach to any diets you hear about. If they totally avoid any of the basic food groups, they may be harmful.

Self-massage.   Massage increases blood flow and brings warmth to the painful area. This technique may be useful for arthritis pain. To perform self-massage, you need only devote some time and patience to it. Some people have found that using a menthol gel provides a comfortably warm or cool sensation that can ease the arthritis pain. (Be certain to remove the gel before using heat, or you may burn yourself.)

Cognitive Coping Skills

Identifying and changing negative thoughts that can grow out of chronic pain and disease is an important self-management tool. How do you think about your pain and arthritis? Often people have automatic negative thoughts such as, " I am hurting and there is nothing I can do about it" or "I am never going to get better." How you think about your pain and life situation has a great deal to do with how you feel. People who concentrate on their pain are more likely to say that their pain is severe than people who think less frequently about it. Here are a few tips to develop positive coping skills:

- *Develop a constructive way to distract yourself.*   Your distraction could be reading, talking to others, watching television, prayer, or seeing a movie. Pick something positive to do that will take your mind off the pain and focus it on something pleasurable or rewarding.

- *Begin to see pain as a signal to begin a constructive pain management strategy.*   Pain should become a cue from your body to take a break, and perhaps practice relaxation, or use heat or cold.

- *Put your pain in perspective.* Remind yourself of times when the pain has passed, and what you did to help yourself—what you have, instead of what you don't have. Think of what you can do, as opposed to what you can't do. Identify negative thoughts regarding pain and replace them with positive images.

See chapter 6 for discussion of psychological techniques you can adapt for the management of arthritis pain and building your coping skills.

Other Psychosocial Issues

Depression. It is common for people with a chronic disease to experience depression. Major signs to watch for are sadness, a change in sleep habits, poor appetite, withdrawal from others, and crying spells. If you feel that you are depressed, try using some of these self-help strategies. If the symptoms persist seek help from your health care provider.

- One effective way to control depression is to control negative thinking (see chapter 6) and to cope with feelings of helplessness by developing a sense of control through self-management.

- Keep a positive events diary. Each day write down two or three activities that give you pleasure—a call from a friend or family member, a nice meal, a good movie. (Reading this book and trying some of these exercises is a positive event!) When you are depressed you need to remind yourself of the parts of your life that still feel meaningful and rewarding.

- Many people who have arthritis find that sharing their experiences and learning new self-management skills within a support group of others in similar situations makes coping easier. Ask your doctor or contact local arthritis organizations for information about groups in your community.

Sleep problems. Disturbed sleep patterns will contribute an additional burden to your pain. Practicing relaxation techniques at bedtime can often help improve your sleep. Using self-hypnosis or an hypnosis tape is often especially helpful. Ask your doctor for other suggestions to improve your sleep.

Sticking with the program. Managing your arthritis will require you to do many self-care activities—keeping up your medication regimen, exercising, learning about your disease, practicing stress management, and attempting to maintain home, work, and social responsibilities. You may get discouraged and feel that it's just too much to do all of these activities on top of the burden of your arthritis pain. To help yourself cope, set up a daily diary. List the activities that you will do to manage your arthritis pain. Begin with one new activity and add others once one healthy habit is established. Check off each activity that you do each day. For an extra boost, treat yourself to something special when you start the program. Once you get started, do something special for yourself for each week that you stick to your program.

Lifestyle Changes

A chronic disease like arthritis requires you to change your life in many specific ways. For some individuals, these changes will touch every aspect of their lives—leisure, work, and family activities. For others the changes will be less dramatic. You'll need to draw on the skills listed in this chapter, as well as others in this workbook, including assertiveness (see chapter 7). Keep in mind that you are not alone. Others who have arthritis are also trying to cope with their pain, and a health care team is ready to back you up. You may find additional helpful information in the suggested readings below. Keep in mind that you are the primary health care worker when it comes to taking care of your arthritis. You need to be educated and should reward yourself for doing an important job.

Kate Lorig and James Fries have written an excellent book called *The Arthritis Helpbook,* which provides information on additional exercises and self-help strategies useful for arthritis. For more information you may wish to contact the Arthritis Foundation, which has a national office and local chapters around the country. The local chapter can direct you to doctors and clinics in your area, provide educational materials, offer volunteer opportunities, and provide information on self-help classes and exercise programs. You may contact them at:

The Arthritis Foundation
1314 Spring Street, N.W.
Atlanta, Georgia 30309
(800) 283-7800
(404) 872-7100

Further Reading

Coping With Arthritis Pain. Atlanta, GA: Arthritis Foundation.

Fries, J. F. 1986. *Arthritis : A Comprehensive Guide*. Reading, MA: Addison-Wesley Publishing Co.

Lorig, K., and J. Fries. 1986. *The Arthritis Helpbook*. Reading, MA: Addison-Wesley Publishing Co.

The Primer on Clinical Care in the Rheumatic Diseases. 1996. Atlanta, GA: American College of Rheumatology.

Online Information Can Be Found At:

http://www.arthritis.org/

http://www.netshop.net/~nsardy/dancer/asmp.html

http://www.nerdworld.com/nw783.html

19

Irritable Bowel Syndrome

by Kimeron Hardin, Ph.D., and William Stewart, Ph.D.

Irritable bowel syndrome, also known as IBS, is a complicated pain disorder of the gastrointestinal (GI) tract (your stomach and intestines). IBS is not a rare disorder—it occurs in as much as 10 to 15 percent of the adult population. One study estimated that about 75 percent of patients seen at a gastrointestinal specialty clinic report symptoms of pain, and in about half of these patients, pain was likely due to IBS.

Doctors are working to standardize the criteria used to diagnose IBS, but because there is no known physiological abnormality underlying the disorder, health professionals will usually define IBS by describing the symptoms associated with it. The proper diagnosis of IBS is made more difficult if you take multiple medications with strong gastrointestinal side effects (such as heartburn, gas, or constipation) or if you have other complex conditions such as myofascial pain syndrome (see chapter 15) or fibromyalgia (see chapter 14). This chapter will describe commonly observed symptoms of irritable bowel syndrome, and will suggest ways to manage the pain and other distress associated with it. While IBS may sound frightening, and is indeed both chronic and uncomfortable, it is neither life threatening nor contagious.

Symptoms of Irritable Bowel Syndrome

There are three basic forms of IBS. The first group of patients tend to have chronic, intermittent diarrhea, usually without pain. Some research suggests that this particular group may actually be a separate disorder altogether. A second group however, has complaints of chronic abdominal pain and constipation that may be referred to as *spastic colitis* or "spastic colon." Finally, the last group consists of patients who have features of both previous types, with alternating episodes of diarrhea and constipation. Other symptoms of IBS include sensations of an overpowering urge to go to the bathroom, presence of mucus in the stool (but no blood), increased sensitivity to certain foods, weight loss, fatigue, a sensation of not being able to completely eliminate stool during a bowel movement, and nausea. Each individual's particular set of symptoms may vary from one to all of the above, which again explains why IBS is so difficult to diagnose.

Your doctor will confirm a diagnosis of IBS by excluding the presence of other physical diseases through a medical examination and testing, which will be discussed later in this chapter. The absence of signs of physical disease is an important part of making the diagnosis and should never be overlooked.

A person with IBS may have loose stools or watery diarrhea chronically for months or years, with the diarrhea usually worse in the mornings. After several "loose" stool bowel movements upon awakening or after breakfast, the IBS sufferer may feel perfectly fine for the rest of the day and evening. Some people have long periods of time where they resume normal bowel habits in between IBS bouts and some may never have a recurrence following one or several initial episodes. Constipation and abdominal cramps are also symptoms of IBS. Sometimes the cramps are relieved by passing gas or having a bowel movement.

In order to understand more about this complex problem, you must first learn about how the gastrointestinal system works.

The Lower Gastrointestinal System

Of the twenty-eight feet of the human digestive tract, the *large intestine* (also known as the *colon*) makes up the last six feet. The large intestine consists of three distinct parts (see figure 19.1). The *cecum* is a small pouch that connects the lower small intestine (*ileum*) to the colon via the *ileocecal valve*. It starts in the lower right area of the abdomen and merges with the *ascending colon* which extends upward toward the liver. The next part of the colon, called the *transverse colon*, drapes across the abdomen, toward the left side. Here the large intestine turns downward toward the pelvis. The final segment, the *descending colon*, merges into the *sigmoid colon* (with S-shaped turns) and ends at the *rectum*. The primary functions of the colon are to absorb water from fecal material and to store feces until it is eliminated.

Activity in the Colon

Health professionals claim that IBS is not only a disorder of the motor activity of the intestines, that is, how the intestines move fecal matter through the system, but also involves the pain

Figure 19.1

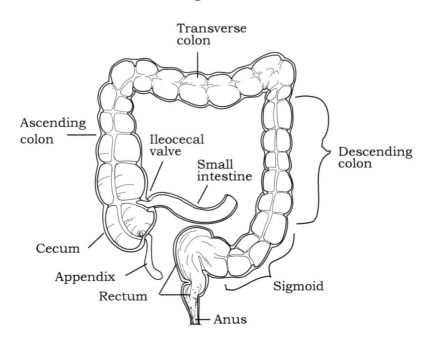

sensory system and the central nervous system. The colon's movements serve to *mix* its contents and *move or propel* these contents along its route to the rectum. Mixing occurs when the ringlike muscles contract at specific points along the colon. Movement occurs when areas of the transverse or descending colon contract or squeeze contents of the bowel along the downward route, followed by a series of similar contractions that eventually push the contents toward the rectum and out of the body. A similar process occurs when you push toothpaste from a tube or when you see a snake swallow a large meal. These contractions usually occur only a few times a day, most commonly during the hour following the morning meal.

Pain and Sensation in the Colon

Many IBS patients report abdominal pain that is usually below the navel and can be either "dull and achy" or "sharp and sudden." You feel pain in your internal digestive organs (or *viscera*) in different ways than you feel pain in other parts of your body. For example, if you were to puncture your skin with a nail, you would usually feel sharp pain. Gastroenterologists tell us, however, that the viscera can be cut, torn, or crushed and humans will rarely feel any pain. This does not mean that the nerves in our digestive organs cannot feel pain, but that the nerve endings that transmit pain from the smooth muscle walls of the gut are primarily sensitive to rapid stretching or *distention*. Pain can also be a result of inflammation of the digestive tract due to a bacterial infection, exposure to chemicals, food allergies or milk intolerance, spasm of the smooth muscle in the intestines, the buildup of metabolic waste products due to poor blood circulation, or stretched ligaments in the abdominal cavity.

The abdominal pain of IBS is most likely the result of several factors: spastic contractions, excessive stretching and distention (bloating) from gas and stool in the bowel, or oversensitive nerves in the intestines reacting to normal stretching and distention. Recent research has also shown that spasms can occur spontaneously in the small bowel due simply to stress. In other words, the internal functioning of a person with IBS is no different than others without symptoms of IBS. You differ only in that you seem to experience more pain and contractions due to multiple factors including stress, diet, lack of exercise, genetics, and greater sensitivity to the normal stretching of the bowel.

Loss of more than 5 percent of your body weight in the past year, the presence of blood in the stool (except from hemorrhoids or small tears around the anus), fever, anemia, a positive lactose tolerance test (milk intolerance), evidence of intestinal parasites in a stool culture exam, or the suggestion of inflammatory bowel disease on barium enema X rays are all signs of problems beyond IBS. Note that abdominal pain is a prime symptom for many serious diseases. If you feel a distressing abdominal pain that you have never experienced before or has never been medically evaluated, you should *consult your doctor immediately.*

Ongoing abdominal pain must also be medically evaluated, since it may be a sign of a condition other than IBS. Lower right abdominal pain may occur chronically but recurrently and still be appendicitis, which is a medical emergency. The following conditions may give rise to frequent, recurrent lower abdominal pain and warrant immediate medical attention: diverticulitis (inflammation of a normal or abnormal pouch opening out from the intestinal tract), inflammatory bowel disease (IBD), pelvic disease (including a ruptured ovarian follicle), painful menstruation, and carcinoma of the colon. Other diseases that can cause pain in the abdomen and require medical management include: gallbladder disease, Crohn's disease (a chronic inflammatory disorder affecting the lower part of the small intestine), peptic ulcer, pancreatic disease, angina, dyspepsia, esophagitis (heartburn), endometriosis, and aortic aneurysms.

Because IBS shares some common symptoms with other types of disorders, many people with IBS wonder if their problems will turn into, or predispose them to, more harmful conditions like the ones mentioned above. To try to answer this and other questions about the course of IBS, researchers at the Mayo Clinic examined the records of 112 patients during their treatment over an approximate thirty year period. Interestingly, they found that after the initial diagnosis of IBS was made, only 10 patients were later diagnosed with an organic gastrointestinal disease (about 9 percent). Also interestingly, a positive patient-physician relationship appeared to be related to fewer return visits over time. In such a relationship, a patient asks questions and follows recommendations and a physician works with you in providing an accurate diagnosis, talks with you about your concerns, and helps you develop an individual treatment program. In other words, you need to develop a positive and open working relationship with your doctor, as you should with any personal health care professional.

Diet

Because IBS affects the GI system, where you process food, it is logical that you should explore your diet as a potentially important factor in managing IBS. One therapeutic approach that has often been encouraged is to increase dietary fiber intake. The idea behind this therapy is that fiber shortens the time it takes for a meal to travel through the intestinal tract and thus increases stool bulk, which some consider helpful for constipation ("hard stools") and diarrhea. Too much fiber can actually irritate IBS, so you need to find your own balance.

Many people with IBS recognize that certain foods aggravate their symptoms. As a result, it has been popular to encourage a person to eliminate foods or chemicals that could irritate the gastrointestinal tract, such as caffeine, alcohol, and tobacco. However, a clear relationship between specific dietary factors and IBS has not been well-established. One recent study compared the diet of women with and without IBS-like symptoms and found that women with GI distress symptoms consumed more refined carbohydrates (processed sugars) than women who were symptom-free, while other types of food intakes were relatively similar.

Many people with IBS experiment to see if certain foods have an effect on their symptoms. Generally, most start by eating a limited bland diet for a three- to five-day period. As symptoms improve, they add a new food every day or so, while paying careful attention (by keeping a diary) to see if this food stimulates IBS symptoms. In this way, they determine which foods may trigger flare-ups of IBS. Examples of foods that often trigger symptoms include pepper and spices, chewing gum, raw vegetables, and dairy products.

You should always discuss a new diet with your doctor before beginning. Certain specialists, including gastroenterologists and allergists, may in fact, have more detailed guidelines to help you with this process. It may also be important to consult a nutritionist or registered dietician if you have a particularly difficult case of IBS to insure that you get the vitamins, minerals, and other essential nutrients you need to stay healthy.

It's important for you to know that there is a difference between an allergic reaction and "intolerance" to certain foods. A classic food allergy is defined as having typical "allergic" reactions caused by certain foods, such as wheezing, runny nose, throat swelling, and so on. A food that increases diarrhea, abdominal pain, or other GI distress alone is therefore not considered an "allergy," but is generally referred to as "intolerance."

Stress and IBS

The idea that our thoughts and feelings impact the way our "insides" function is an old one. We've all felt, or heard of someone feeling, a "nervous stomach." Or maybe you've heard someone talk about the "butterflies" in his or her stomach before a speech or an exciting event. Many researchers have reported a relationship between psychological stressors and the onset or worsening of IBS symptoms. It is estimated that between 50 to 80 percent of IBS patients have reported noticing this relationship themselves. People with IBS often report a wide variety of psychological stressors including worries about work and family; the loss of a parent or spouse, which can be accompanied by unresolved grief; and life changes that demand many social and personal adjustments, such as separation or divorce, being fired or hired, or moving to a new home.

The most common psychological symptoms that occur along with IBS include fatigue, low mood, irritability and other symptoms of depression, anxiety, oversensivity in relationships, and being overly concerned with, or excessively focused on, bodily functions. Studies using psychological tests show that individuals with IBS tend to report less general psychological distress than psychiatric patients, but more distress than the average (nonpsychiatric) population. Most authorities, and people with the condition, agree that stress and other psychological factors play a significant role in irritable bowel syndrome.

Medical Treatments

W.G. Thompson (1984) wrote:

> Satisfactory management of the irritable bowel syndrome demands much of the art and science of medicine. It is a common experience that lasting cures are unusual . . . Thus the physician's duty is to help the patient to understand and cope with his symptoms and to avoid any therapy which might be harmful.

As you see from these remarks, better understanding of this disorder will only become possible within a consistent, trusting, and open relationship between you and your doctor. This can be difficult to achieve due to managed care, hectic schedules, and rapidly changing information. Nevertheless, you can prepare to develop such a relationship by seeking out a physician with whom you can talk easily and by taking stock of both your feelings and stress levels at home and at work. A good physician will be prepared to explain the condition to you and will listen to and calm your fears about whether your symptoms indicate serious conditions such as colitis or cancer.

As we discussed before, an accurate diagnosis of IBS involves ruling out other types of similar diagnoses by various procedures such as physical examination, history, symptoms, and often, medical tests. Medical tests may include barium X rays, stool cultures, blood work, and even sigmoidoscopy/colonoscopy (procedures that allow the physician to see inside the GI system, entering from either the mouth or the rectum). All, some, or none, of these medical testing procedures, may be used by your particular physician, depending on your unique situation. After the diagnosis is established, frequent X rays and endoscopies are usually not necessary, but general physical examinations, blood work, and stool examinations for occult (not present in large amounts) blood may be performed at regular intervals.

As much as you may wish for a quick cure for your IBS, surgery is never an appropriate option for the benign pain of IBS. There is nothing you can "cut out" or "sew up" to fix IBS and alleviate the symptoms. In fact, surgery may actually make the problem worse by causing scar tissue. Due to the complex interweaving of psychosocial factors, IBS is best managed with nonmedical treatments, such as diet, stress management, and the other suggestions in this chapter.

Various medications have also been tried with mixed results. Most IBS patients do not seem to benefit from trials of drugs called "antispasmodics," prescribed by physicians to try to relax the "overactive" smooth muscles of the colon, although it may be worth a try if your physician recommends it due to persistent pain following meals.

A study in 1994 (Clouse et al.), which reviewed the outcome of the use of antidepressants by patients with IBS, suggested that low doses of antidepressants appeared to improve symptoms in a majority of the patients, particularly those with pain as a primary symptom. It also found that in many cases, when the first antidepressant was ineffective or had too many side effects, a later trial with a different antidepressant appeared to be beneficial. While the authors suggested caution in interpreting these results because it was study based on a review of records versus a clinical study, there was enough positive evidence to suggest more research is needed on antidepressants and IBS. Another recent study of antidepressants and IBS found that tricyclic antidepressants improved small intestinal motor function in people who have diarrhea-predominant IBS.

Anti-anxiety medications, such as the benzodiazepines Valium and Xanax, have been prescribed in some cases, but they have not yet been shown to have a direct beneficial effect on the symptoms of IBS. Benzodiazepines can also become addicting after long-term use (see chapter 12), causing other problems such as sleep disturbance and depression. If these are prescribed, you should consider them as supplements for *short-term use only*, and should begin finding other, nonpharmacological ways of managing stress and anxiety (see chapters 4 and 5).

Finally, there are several "over-the-counter" or nonprescription medications that help alleviate IBS symptoms. Products containing symethicone for gas and heartburn have recently been suggested as helpful for IBS, particularly if taken regularly as directed by your doctor. Several recent studies are also examining the effects of drugs that may reduce the sensation of bowel distention common in IBS patients, but as yet, none have proved consistently effective.

Psychological Treatments

Several studies about IBS and stress by Whitehead and Schuster (1985) clearly show that how a person reacts to stress, what they learned in their families of origin, and whether or not they have a diagnosed psychological problem are all factors that can influence the course of IBS.

Given that most patients with IBS recognize that stress frequently increases before, during, or after a flare-up of their symptoms, people with IBS would clearly benefit from learning some stress management strategies.

Several studies over the past decade have suggested that various psychological treatments, including progressive muscle relaxation, hypnosis, biofeedback, and assertiveness training (see chapters 4, 5, and 7), are all superior to monitoring symptoms or routine medical care alone. Learning to relax easily and deeply can be accomplished by motivated individuals who can visualize fairly well by listening to an audiocassette tape. Perhaps the best approach, however, is to work closely with a qualified behavior therapist (licensed psychologist or therapist, or certified biofeedback therapist) in a chronic pain or stress center. Learning meditation procedures for relaxation and focusing is another potentially beneficial option. Most recently, Green and Blanchard (1994) found that individualized cognitive therapy over an eight-week period, as is described in chapter 6, produced significant improvement (fewer IBS symptoms) in 80 percent of the patients, whereas only 10 percent of the IBS patients who learned only to monitor their symptoms with a diary (no therapy of any kind) improved. They also found that the improvement appeared to be stable over several months. Cognitive therapy involves changing the way you think about your stress and your illness and is most often accomplished with the help of a licensed psychotherapist (including psychologists, psychiatrists, and social workers) with cognitive-behavioral training and experience.

A brief course of general psychotherapy (seven to ten sessions) may also be helpful. Accepting and adjusting to any chronic condition means not only learning what to do for yourself physically, but also avoiding "burning out" family and friends with complaints or worries (see chapter 7). In a recent study in Sweden, half of a large sample of people with IBS participated in brief psychotherapy, along with routine medical management. The other half of people with IBS received only routine medical management. The therapy, adjusted to each individual's needs and personal strengths, focused on finding new solutions to old problems, recognizing and modifying maladaptive behaviors, and learning better styles of coping with stress and emotional tension. Both groups had improved at three months, with the people who had received therapy showing the most improvement. At a one-year follow-up, the patients who had received therapy reported still greater improvement in physical and emotional distress, while the untreated patients, true to the natural course of IBS, had some relapse. It appears that IBS patients can readily make the emotional adjustments that lead to reduced abdominal pain and other gastrointestinal symptoms by briefly involving themselves in problem-resolution psychotherapy. The study suggests that a holistic treatment benefits those with IBS who are motivated to explore the role of psychological stress in their lives. If you consider counseling or psychotherapy for IBS management, you will find that when you keep an open mind and participate with your counselor, you will make greater progress in managing your IBS. It's easy to get stuck in your ways of thinking about your disease. Common complaints are "This will never change," "I'm a victim," and so on. This kind of closed-mindedness in your thinking only keeps you from exploring options and potentially feeling better. Counseling can help you explore ways to break out of old, ineffective patterns if you give it an honest try.

What You Can Do

Irritable bowel syndrome can be a painful and chronic condition. While you might be grateful that properly-diagnosed IBS is benign in nature, you still must face the challenge of adapting to the syndrome. With increasing evidence, there is hope however, that personal adjustments within your control can influence the natural course of the condition for the better.

You need to establish a cooperative dialogue with your physician where you feel free to ask questions and you can listen to his or her feedback. Your physician should have a good understanding of IBS and be prepared to take a longer-term, management perspective, rather than a short-term, "Band-Aid" approach. The more positive the relationship between the two of you, the better. You also may consider, with the advice of your physician, consulting with another specialist such as a nutritionist or psychologist.

You must examine your attitude about your condition. You will need to accept the fact that your IBS is likely a chronic condition with periodic remissions and worsenings, but that you can adjust the factors that influence it.

You will also need to examine your lifestyle and personal relationships for excessive strain and tension. You can learn to better manage stress and emotional strain through regular deep relaxation exercises and other stress management procedures.

Finally, consulting a qualified psychotherapist and investing yourself in a brief course of therapy or counseling can lead to greater personal resiliency, stronger coping skills, and better problem-solving skills, which, in the long run, can help you ultimately feel more empowered and "in control" of your life and your IBS symptoms.

Further Reading

Cunningham, C. 1995. *The Irritable Bowel Syndrome (I.B.S.) and Gastrointestinal Solutions Handbook.* Leucadia, CA: United Research Publishers.

Drossman, D. A. 1994. "Irritable bowel syndrome." *Gastroenterologist*, 2(4), 315-326.

Greene, B., and E. B. Blanchard. 1994. "Cognitive therapy for irritable bowel syndrome." *Journal of Consulting and Clinical Psychology*, 62(3), 576-582.

Howard, N. 1995. *The Natural Way with Irritable Bowel Syndrome.* Rockport, Mass.: Element.

The Irritable Bowel Syndrome & Gastrointestinal Solutions Handbook. United Research Publishers, 103 N. Highway 101, Dept. RS-41, Encinitas, CA 92024. Send $12.95 plus $3.00 postage and handling.

Jarrett, M., M. M. Heitkemper, E. F. Bond, and J. Georges. 1994. "Comparison of diet composition in women with and without functional bowel disorder." *Gastroenterology Nursing*, 16(6), 253-258.

Nicol, R. 1995. *Irritable Bowel Syndrome: A Natural Approach.* Berkeley, CA: Ulysses Press.

Owens, D. M., D. K. Nelson, and N. J. Talley. 1995. "The irritable bowel syndrome: long-term prognosis and the physician-patient interaction," *Annals of Internal Medicine*, 122(2), 107-112.

Shimberg, E. 1993. *Relief from I.B.S.: Irritable Bowel Syndrome.* New York: Dorset Press.

Thompson, W. G. 1984. "Progress report: the irritable bowel," *Gut, XXV*. 305-320.

Information Regarding Support and Education for People with IBS Is Available Through:

IBS Self Help Group
3332 Yonge Street
P.O. Box 94074
Toronto, Ontario
Canada M4N3R1

Online Information Can Be Found At:

http://www.ibsgroup.org/

http://128.197.93.205/cduchome.html

20

Neuropathic Pain

by Robert W. Allen, M.D.

When you prick yourself with a pin or step on a nail, you probably feel a sharp, brief pain. This kind of pain signals that the nerve endings in the skin are activated, but not necessarily damaged. On the other hand, you may sustain an injury caused by a trauma, surgery, or infection that damages the nerve, leaving you with chronic, persistent pain. This type of pain is called *neuropathic pain*, meaning the damaged nerve itself produces pain. Also known as *neuralgic pain*, neuropathic pain can be worse than the pain of the original injury. We still do not understand why and how it occurs to the extent that it does in some people and not in others, making it a difficult condition to treat.

Recent research suggests that neuropathic pain may develop because of chemical changes that occur in the nerve fiber at the site of injury and in the spinal cord and brain. For this reason medications are usually used to help change some of the electrical and chemical activity of pain nerve fibers in order to reduce pain levels.

A few of the more common neuropathic pain conditions include peripheral neuropathy (due to diabetes, AIDS, or chronic alcoholism), post-herpetic neuralgia, trigeminal neuralgia, complex regional pain syndrome (formerly known as reflex sympathetic dystrophy), spinal cord injuries, and traumatic nerve injuries. This chapter covers some of the typical symptoms and treatment options for the more common neuropathic pain syndromes. For each condition, I will describe the general types of medications used in treatment, but you can find more detail about medications in chapter 12.

Common Neuropathic Pain Syndromes

Peripheral Neuropathy

Peripheral neuropathy is a term used to describe a painful condition that primarily affects the nerves of the feet and hands. *Peripheral* means "away from the center" (as in limbs away from the center of the body) and *neuropathy* means "damage to the nerves." If you have this disorder you will often experience the pain as "numb or tingling" or sometimes as "burning." You may also experience your pains as "shooting" and "stabbing." The pain is especially bothersome at night, when you're trying to get to sleep. While the symptoms may be similar for most peripheral neuropathies, the underlying causes can range from such illnesses as diabetes, AIDS, and chronic alcoholism to, more rarely, exposure to toxic chemicals.

Many patients with diabetes, AIDS, and chronic alcoholism eventually suffer from painful burning feet or hands. Studies show that the elevated blood sugars in diabetics leads to damage to small, peripheral nerves in the hands and feet, and thus the pain of *diabetic neuropathy. AIDS neuropathy* may occur because the virus which causes AIDS damages the nerves directly. A second theory about how AIDS neuropathy develops is that the doses of medications HIV-positive patients take to fight the virus are so high that the medications themselves damage the nerves. *Alcoholic neuropathy* may be due to nutritional deficiencies in alcoholics.

Medications such as tricyclic antidepressants and anticonvulsants are used to reduce the irritability of nerves and thereby reduce the level of pain you experience due to peripheral neuropathy. Some examples of frequently used medications for peripheral neuropathies include amitriptyline (Elavil), nortriptyline (Pamelor), and carbamazepine (Tegretol).

Other interventions that have helped patients include transcutaneous electrical nerve stimulation (TENS) (see chapter 2), and biofeedback (see chapter 5) for pain control and stress management. You may also consider using a combination of these methods.

Shingles or Postherpetic Neuralgia

Shingles is the common name for the pain that occurs when you have the herpes zoster virus (brought on by the reactivation of the virus that causes chickenpox). The virus infection enters your pain nerve fibers and damages them, resulting in the severe, burning pain of shingles. In some patients, the damage may be so severe that pain continues even after the virus infection has healed. This persistent pain is called *postherpetic neuralgia* and can be so severe that it is considered the number one cause of suicide in the elderly. The area affected can be so sensitive that even lightly touching the skin with clothes or bed sheets causes an extreme flare-up of the pain. Stress or emotional upset will also increase the level of pain.

Treatment for shingles includes multiple trials of medications (including the antiviral medication Acyclovir), and in some cases, anesthetic nerve blocks. If nerve blocks are used, early treatment is absolutely essential. Once the pain has been present for more than two months, the success of anesthetic blocks appears to decrease dramatically. These blocks are usually performed by an anesthesiologist with special training and involve placing anesthetics around the painful nerves with a needle to obtain pain relief.

Other medications that are used in the treatment of shingles include antidepressants such as amitriptyline (Elavil) and anticonvulsants like carbamazepine (Tegretol). Other interventions include transcutaneous electrical nerve stimulation (TENS), which is discussed in chapter 2. The surgical "ablation" (meaning cutting and destroying) of painful nerves has not proven to be very effective and in some instances has resulted in increased pain. Because of the potential for increased pain, you should discuss all benefits and potential risks with your doctor prior to having surgery for this pain. The role of using steroids in the management of acute shingles remains unclear, but most studies suggest that steroids are of little benefit in chronic postherpetic neuralgia pain.

The nonmedical therapies that have been helpful for postherpetic neuralgia pain include progressive relaxation and imagery, which are discussed in chapters 4 and 5. Some patients have also reported success with acupuncture, but there is not enough scientific data to make any conclusions about the usefulness of this technique with postherpetic neuralgia.

Trigeminal Neuralgia

Trigeminal Neuralgia (also known as *tic douloureux*) is a stabbing, shooting pain along the side of the face that begins without warning and is described by some as feeling like an electrical shock. Some people with this condition feel that there are certain "triggers" that lead to this pain, such as eating or brushing their teeth, but others find it unpredictable. The attacks of pain are typically brief, but may occur many times a day. This pain has been treated most successfully with the anticonvulsant carbamazepine (Tegretol). Typical doses begin at 100-200 mg per day and may be increased to 1500 mg per day. Unfortunately, you may experience side effects from the Tegretol that are more uncomfortable than the pain itself. Typically these side effects include dizziness, sleepiness, and nausea. In very rare cases the medication may also cause *aplastic anemia* (a drop in your red blood cell count). Your doctor monitors for this side effect by ordering blood cell counts every three to six months for as long as you are taking the medicine. Because of the success with this medication in treating trigeminal neuralgia, this treatment is worth a try. Sometimes the side effects can be avoided by beginning at very low doses and slowly increasing to an effective level. Patients often take a month or more to reach an appropriate dose.

As with postherpetic neuralgia, some patients have found pain relief with acupuncture, cognitive-behavioral therapy, progressive muscle relaxation or a combination of the above. However, if medications and all other techniques have failed to provide adequate pain relief, a neurosurgeon may consider surgery on the *gasserian ganglion*, which is the underlying nerve believed to be causing the pain. Unfortunately, as with all surgical procedures, there are risks, such as unpleasant facial sensations or numbness.

Complex Regional Pain Syndrome (formerly known as Reflex Sympathetic Dystrophy or RSD)

Complex regional pain syndrome (CRPS) has many symptoms similar to other types of neuropathic pain and typically begins after a trauma. The trauma is most often to the arm or leg, and may be severe, such as with a "crush" injury, or very minor, such as with a minor sprain. CRPS is probably the least understood of all chronic pain syndromes. Symptoms include a sensation of burning pain, temperature changes in the affected area (either hot, cold, or alternating), skin changes (shiny appearance, hair loss), swelling, and reduced flexibility of the joints.

Experts believe there are two separate types of CRPS. One type seems to be maintained by activity of the *sympathetic nervous system*, the part of the nervous system that increases the heart rate, raises the blood pressure, and constricts the capillaries in response to a stressor. The other type of CRPS seems to have similar symptoms but does not involve the sympathetic nervous system.

Some researchers believe that CRPS may affect both the sympathetic and nonsympathetic nervous systems. When sympathetic nerves are involved, early intervention with anesthetic nerve blocks seems most effective. These blocks involve placing anesthetics around the sympathetic nerves with a needle to achieve pain relief. If anesthetic blocks fail to provide relief or are not appropriate, then the oral medications listed in the previous sections for neuropathic pains are considered, such as anticonvulsants and tricyclic antidepressants.

A great deal of controversy still surrounds the diagnosis of CRPS in the medical community. It was initially referred to as reflex sympathetic dystrophy (RSD) because clinicians felt that the symptoms were due to the overactivity of the sympathetic nervous system. In very early CRPS, this does seem to be the case and anesthetic blocks of the sympathetic nerves may be helpful in controlling the pain. However, there are many patients who have almost identical symptoms with apparently no input from the sympathetic nervous system. Clinicians are therefore attempting to move away from the term "RSD."

One of the problems in diagnosing CRPS is that patients may complain of symptoms similar to other types of neuropathic pains. Examples of common symptoms include pains described as "burning," "shooting," "electrical," and "stabbing." Both patients with CRPS and patients with other types of neuropathic pains may experience pain when clothing or bed sheets touch their skin. Typically, for both types of patients, cold makes the pain worse. It is sometimes hard for physicians and pain specialists to make a conclusive diagnosis because of the many similarities. Patients have been labeled inappropriately with RSD or CRPS and have therefore been treated with inappropriate and unsuccessful interventions. Research continues in the area of sympathetic nervous system pain in an effort to distinguish between the various types of neuropathic pain and subtypes of CRPS.

In any case, physical therapy is absolutely mandatory in cases of CRPS. Any effort you make at increasing the use of your arm or leg is beneficial. The less you move your affected arm or leg, the more likely it is that the limb will become nonfunctional. Physical therapy for CRPS often involves gentle exercises to increase flexibility as well as prevent stiff joints and osteoporosis due to lack of movement. Therapists may also use special techniques to reduce swelling associated with CRPS such as retrograde massage, coban wrapping and gloving, and neuromuscular electrical stimulation (NMES). NMES promotes your muscles' natural pumping action, which, in turn reduces fluid buildup. Sometimes physical and occupational therapists can help decrease the affected limbs' sensitivity to touch by using a variety of techniques like "light touch" rubbing, hot and cold water baths, and vibration. They also may offer assistance in pain management by helping you learn special positioning, by splinting, or by using of a TENS unit, as mentioned earlier this chapter.

As with the other neuropathic pains already mentioned, techniques such as biofeedback and progressive muscle relaxation training can be beneficial in providing you with tools for managing the pain of CRPS more effectively.

Successful Management of Neuropathic Pain

You cannot completely treat your neuropathic pain without attending to your emotional needs, as with most pains discussed in this book. You may find that the "wear and tear" of coping on a daily basis makes you feel tired and frustrated. You may even find yourself seriously depressed or agitated because of the limitations you now live with due to pain. What makes living with neuropathic pain, and in particular CRPS, especially difficult is the fact that most physicians do not yet understand these conditions, and you may have lived without a proper diagnosis or treatment for quite some time. You may read some frightening literature about the progression of the syndrome or you may have faced the spread of the pain into other parts of your body. You may even find a direct relationship between psychological stress (in the forms of anger, fear, or frustration) and increases in your pain.

Because of these and other emotional features of pain, it is crucial that you consider the addition of a psychotherapist to your treatment plan. As mentioned above, biofeedback techniques and progressive relaxation exercises are traditionally provided by mental health specialists and can be especially helpful with management of both acute flare-ups of pain and with overall stress management. Individual psychotherapy can be helpful in reducing feelings of depression and hopelessness, as well as in providing you help with anger and stress management. Self-hypnosis (see chapter 5), within the context of an individual psychotherapy session, may also be helpful. Supportive group therapy can also be useful by providing a safe outlet to express your feelings to other people with pain who can understand you and provide support. Sometimes, support groups are combined with education to provide you with more tools for coping with pain.

Finally, family therapy or counseling can be highly effective in reducing stress at home and helping spouses or children understand more about how they can help you manage your pain. Often, family members "stand by" when you hurt, feeling helpless and unable to do anything about your pain and yet feeling awkward about going on with their own lives. While they may not be able to take your pain away directly, family members can learn to help motivate you to stay on your daily activity schedule. Or they can simply learn how to respond to your emotional needs. When you are in pain and focused on your treatment, it may seem to family members that you don't care about them or are avoiding or ignoring them. Family therapy can help you learn to express yourself to your family more directly, so that all of you can provide emotional support for each other.

With proper diagnosis and treatment, you'll be on your way to easing your pain. These nonmedical treatments can help further you along that path.

Further Reading

Gordon, N. F. 1993. *Diabetes: Your Complete Exercise Guide.* Leeds: Human Kinetics.

Janig, W. F., and M. Stanton-Hicks, eds. 1995. *Reflex Sympathetic Dystrophy: A Reappraisal.* Seattle: IASP (International Association for the Study of Pain) Press.

Jeffcoate, W., and R. MacFarlane. 1995. *The Diabetic Foot: An Illustrated Guide to Management.* New York: Chapman & Hall Medical.

Lee, J. J., and C. A. Gauci. 1994-95. "Post-herpetic neuralgia: current concepts and management." *British Journal of Hospital Medicine,* 52 (11); pp. 565-570.

Lefkowitz, M., and R. A. Marini. 1994. "Management of postherpetic neuralgia." *Annals of the Academy of Medicine,* 23 (6 suppl.); pp. 139-144.

Rovit, R. L., R. Murali, and P. J. Jannetta. eds. 1990. *Trigeminal Neuralgia.* Baltimore: Williams & Wilkins.

Williams, R. 1995. *RSD: Reflex Sympathetic Dystrophy.* Bethesda, MD: American Occupational Therapy Association, Inc.

Zakrzewska, J. M. 1995. *Trigeminal Neuralgia.* London: Saunders.

Information Regarding Support and Education Is Available Through:

Reflex Sympathetic Dystrophy Syndrome Association of America (RSDSA)
116 Haddon Avenue
Suite D
Haddonfield, NJ 08033
(609) 795-8845

Trigeminal Neuralgia Association
Claire W. Patterson, President
P.O. Box 340
Barnegat Light, NJ 08006
(609) 361-1014

Online Information About Trigeminal Neuralgia Can Be Found At:

http://neurosurgery.mgh.harvard.edu/tna/

http://www.lib.umich.edu/chdocs/support/chronic.html#trigem

21

Relapse and Recovery

It is not unusual for episodes of chronic pain to flare up from time to time, tempting you to feel like you are right back where you started. John had entered a pain clinic program with the set expectation that after a certain period of time his pain condition would completely disappear. He did enjoy a tremendous decrease in pain while participating in the program, until after about eight weeks when a muscle spasm incapacitated him for several days. He felt despondent at the thought that all the skills he had learned were of no use. He was sure that his pain was returning in full force, never to be controlled again.

By now you are familiar with the ideas presented in this book, and you have probably already identified the errors in John's thinking that led him in unproductive directions. First, he had an unrealistic expectation at the start of the program that his pain would *never* return. Second, at the first sign of pain, he "catastrophized" his setback into a disaster and honestly convinced himself that all he had learned before was useless. Third, by letting his anxiety levels escalate, he experienced increased physical tension. This made his painful spasm worse and made it harder for him to practice his skills.

But for all his doubts, John stuck with it. He learned to control his catastrophic thinking so that the next time he had a pain episode, he was prepared. Every time the negative thoughts surfaced, he reminded himself that he "controlled the pain, the pain didn't control him." He learned to religiously follow his doctor's orders about proper medication use and exercise. Staying consistent in the face of intermittent flare-ups and discouragement required real tenacity. But he gained confidence in his ability to use the relaxation skills and programmed himself to use them immediately upon the first sign of pain.

Probably the most important factor in John's comeback was his introduction to a way of thinking about pain relapses that was used by Dr. Ian Wickramesacra, a behavioral medicine psychologist at Eastern Virginia Medical School in Norfolk, Virginia. Dr. Wickramesacra explains that whenever you make major behavioral changes, there are inevitably some setbacks. But if you sincerely want to cope better, you cannot let those set backs dictate the rest of your life. Put them into perspective. Accept the fact that there will be times when you cannot cope as well as you'd like, and that you may need to pull back and regroup. Dr. Wickramesacra devised the graph on the next page to illustrate his point.

As you make your way along your coping road, you know that you will have "up times" and "down times." The double Os on the graph are those up times, when you feel bursts of energy, well-being, and mastery. But sometimes the pain causes you to slip down to where the double Xs are

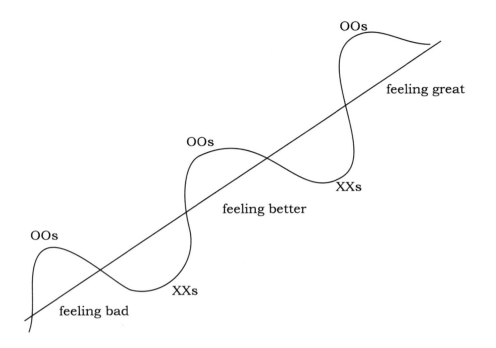

on the graph. These are the times when things are not going so well, when you may have a pain relapse and feel depressed and frustrated.

The trick here is to have a plan to get you through those low periods. You might pull out the plan of action contract you started at the beginning of this book and review it. Have you strayed from any of your goals and activities? Are there any outdated goals you could now replace with goals that are more appropriate? Or perhaps you simply need a boost of support from your friends or counselors. Make an appointment to see your doctor or health care professional who you know will be supportive. If you've tried biofeedback, hypnosis, or another type of pain control program, now might be a good time to make an appointment for a refresher session.

Remember that everything you learn and do adds another coping skill to your repertoire and takes you a step further along the road to recovery. Remind yourself that you do have the stamina to get through any difficult period and that you will eventually improve again. When you tell yourself that, believe it! Getting better means holding on to your commitment to healing yourself. The doctors and health care practitioners are only resources. You are the real healer, the one who marshals the helping resources, learns the essential skills, and keeps on working through the grim days of pain until you gain control of your body and your life again.

Appendix

by Richard Gevirtz, Ph.D.

How to Make a Personalized Relaxation Tape

Many fine commercial tapes are available to help with relaxation training. Most are based on principles developed by Edmund Jacobson in 1938. Several years ago I was about to give one of the commercial tapes to a client when I realized that I had exhausted my supply. Out of desperation, I recorded a version of the procedure onto a blank cassette and sent the client off to practice. At the next session, I offered her the commercial tape, which she tried but gave back, claiming that she liked her "personalized" tape better. I had been worried about the tape I had made because my voice didn't sound very "professional" and because there was no real script. As it turned out, these "drawbacks" offered certain advantages.

Since this accidental discovery, I have made personalized tapes for clients while observing psychophysiological indications of arousal (skin temperature, electrodermal response, muscle tension, heart rate, and pulse volume). I have discovered that almost all clients can produce a "cultivated low arousal" with the help of a personalized short tape (twelve to eighteen minutes). People also seem to practice more with personalized tapes and become more inventive in the ways that they use them. These tapes can be adapted to special circumstances and seem to promote generalization better than commercial tapes. Each tape can reflect the physiology and imagination of the specific client. With small cassette recorders so readily available, many applications are possible. I have used tapes for:

- General relaxation training
- Presurgical calming, coping, and relaxation
- Coping with panic attacks while driving
- Coping with agoraphobic fears
- Desensitization of dental phobias
- Prevention of nighttime bruxing
- Test anxiety
- The production of optimal performance in sports or other performance settings
- Hand warming for Raynaud's Syndrome (cold hands)
- Muscle relaxation for chronic muscle bracing
- Facial postures for muscle contraction headaches
- Relaxation focus for various other disorders

- General stress management

As you can see, this technique can be a versatile tool to be used with biofeedback and clinical stress management, or by itself.

Troubleshooting

Very few people experience problems with tape-assisted relaxation training, but occasionally a few difficulties can occur.

1. Parasympathetic rebound. On rare occasions clients using a relaxation procedure may report nausea, dizziness, and general malaise upon completing a session of relaxation. This response has been documented in the literature as *parasympathetic rebound,* the overreaction of the part of the autonomic nervous system that usually controls digestion and body conservation. This reaction is more likely to occur if the training does not include any active muscle tensing. A simple solution is to include muscle tensing and relaxing in the exercise.

2. Disturbing thoughts. Some people experience an uncontrollable flood of thoughts as soon as they begin a relaxation session. It is important not to make these individuals feel "put down" for this. Instead, instruct them to "step back" and observe the thoughts happening to them. I often use the phrase, "What you resist will persist" to convey the essence of "passive volition," or learning to purposely "let go."

But note that a person with a serious thought disorder may experience something disturbing and need special care. Caution should be taken with anyone diagnosed as schizophrenic or as having manic-depressive disorders. (I have found, however, that even quite disturbed individuals usually seem to benefit from this sort of training.)

3. Fear of failure. Some clients will see their training as an arena of success or failure and it will not work if seen as a competitive activity. Great care must be taken to help these clients accept the essentially passive nature of the relaxation response. Biofeedback is more useful with competitive, goal-oriented people, since they can only make the numbers decrease by learning to "let go."

4. Giggling or self-consciousness. Some people can't seem to stop giggling while listening to relaxation instructions. Once the tape is made, however, they usually settle down well on their own. If clients are self-conscious because you are watching them, have them practice when they are alone with the tape.

5. Diabetic problems. There are rare reports of diabetics having problems with their usual insulin intake because they have lowered their need for the insulin by using relaxation techniques. Be sure to have your diabetic clients monitor their insulin levels carefully after beginning a course of training.

6. Extreme drowsiness. Some people become profoundly relaxed and need a transition period to get back into normal functioning. You can build such a period into the tape.

7. Sleeping. Some people fall asleep while listening to the tape. If they enter deep sleep, they may not experience the full benefits of the training. One solution is to build in periods of lighter, alerting instructions, along with deepening, relaxing ones. With experimentation you can usually keep the person from going into a deep sleep.

Making a Tape

Have the person for whom you are making the tape relax in a recliner-type chair. While narrating the tape, observe his or her breathing patterns and general demeanor. Be sensitive to any environmental distractions or uncomfortable positions. Observe facial muscle patterns. If possible, monitor physiological parameters. This can be accomplished by using a measure as simple as a little thermometer taped to a finger or as complex as a biofeedback display. Watch breathing. Respiration rates vary but should show some slowing (fewer than twelve breaths per minute).

If you are a pain sufferer making this tape for yourself, you will probably find it difficult to monitor your physical reactions while you speak. But you can check your temperature, notice your breathing and check for overall relaxation while listening to your first tape. Later you can modify the tape to emphasize what seemed to relax you most—lengthening or shortening sections, repeating or deleting phrases, depending on your reaction.

The following script can be used by professionals, but can also be adapted for use by those making tapes for their own use. Speak slowly. Let your voice drop into a low, relaxing cadence.

Sample Script

1. Breathing. Start the relaxation by focusing on your breathing patterns. You're striving for diaphragmatic or "belly" breathing, rather than thoracic or "chest" breathing. Take each breath in deep down into your abdomen, so that your belly expands when you breath in and contracts when you breath out. *(Demonstrate this.)* Take each breath deep down while keeping your chest fairly stable. Imagine that you are breathing in beautiful, clean, pure mountain air and breathing out all the particles of tension in your body. With each breath you purify and relax your whole mind and body. *(Breath deeply while instructing client.)* Now let your breathing slow down and become automatic, but still work to release all the tension in your body. *(Observe breathing patterns and wait for a stable pattern.)*

2. Autogenic phrase. As you settle down to a safe and relaxed state, repeat this phrase over and over again to yourself. You don't have to really believe it or work at it, just let the words repeat silently in your mind: "My arms and legs are heavy and warm, my whole body is calm, quiet, and relaxed." *(Repeat four or five times. Other phrases can be incorporated for individual uses, such as "My jaw muscles are loose and relaxed" and so on.)*

3. Progressive muscle relaxation. Now I want you to concentrate on your muscle tension. To start, tense your left calf and foot tightly for five seconds *(one thousand, two thousand, and so on. Be sure to count this with the client.).* Now relax. Let the tension go. Carefully notice the contrast between a tight muscle and a loose one. Notice a pleasant sort of burning that occurs as the muscle relaxes. Now make that muscle even more relaxed. Notice you can *let go* even more. Let the chair hold up your leg completely. Now try the other leg. Tighten the calf and foot for five seconds *(one thousand, two thousand, and so on).* Now you can move to the quadricep, or thigh muscle. First, the left leg; tighten *(one thousand, two thousand, and so on); relax. Notice the dramatic flow of tension from this large muscle. There's a warm, comforting feeling as the muscle loosens and relaxes. Arms and legs are heavy and warm, the whole body is calm, quiet, and relaxed. *(Repeat for the other thigh muscle.)*

Now concentrate on your lower back. Imagine opening up the lower back and pelvic muscle, sinking deeper in the chair. Focus on letting go of all the muscles in the lower back, pelvis, and abdomen. Feel yourself sinking, slipping, sinking into the chair, as you let the lower portion of your body relax completely. Monitor all the tension in your legs and back, and let go even more.

Begin feeling the relaxed feeling in your legs and back spreading, slowly, to your upper back and chest. First, focus on your shoulder blades. Imagine the distance between them. Now *slowly* feel that distance increase and expand. Slowly feel your shoulders move apart, spreading down and back, down and back. Take a deep breath and let go of the tension in your shoulders as you exhale. With each breath feel calmness in your shoulder, neck, and chest muscles. Let go of any remaining tension and let your shoulders go back and down, back and down. Arms and legs are heavy and warm, whole body calm, quiet, and relaxed.

Let your jaw become relaxed. Imagine that you are on the verge of a smile. Make your face smooth and relaxed. Imagine every muscle in your face smoothing and relaxing with your jaw loosely relaxed. Now let all the muscles in your shoulder, neck, and back let go a bit more. Breathing in beautiful, pure, relaxing air, and letting go of all the tension in your body. As you breathe slowly and deeply, let go of any tension left over in any muscles in your body. Let yourself slip into a calm, quiet, relaxed state.

Recording a Visualization Scene

Before you start the exercise, you should interview the client to determine the optimum scene for that individual. Many people find the following beach scene relaxing, but great individual differences exist. For example, a fair-skinned person may imagine being sunburned on a beach. Be sensitive to your client's unique characteristics. Whatever scene you use, try to involve all the senses, including the proprioceptive sense of muscle and joint position. Try to include the person in the scene in one of two ways: (1) from the client's point of view ("Look around you and see the white sand . . .") or (2) from a third person's perspective ("See yourself lying on the sand with no one around you . . .") Use the pretraining interview to determine ahead of time which of these approaches to use.

If you are making the tape for your own use in relaxation and pain relief, simply choose a scene, either real or imagined, where you feel deeply relaxed. Describe the scene on tape using an approach similar to the beach scene below.

Visualization scene. Imagine yourself on a deserted Caribbean beach. It is a crescent-shaped beach with a reef so that the water is calm and clear. There's no one around, the beach is yours. The sand is white and very clean and pure. The water is very warm and a beautiful aqua-blue color. The wind is warm and gentle, cooling you from the warmth of the sun. There's nowhere to go, nothing to do. You can see yourself settle back and enjoy the peace and calm, the sound of the wind in the trees, the gentle lapping of waves on the shore, the sweet salty sea air, the warmth and quiet. See yourself as totally relaxed, quiet, peaceful, with nowhere to go, nothing to do, your whole body calm, quiet, and relaxed. As you lay back and enjoy the serenity, see a person totally at peace, totally safe, totally relaxed. *(Continue the scene to the desired length.)*

Now let your mind drift back to the present. As you emerge from your deeply relaxed state, feel yourself become alert and refreshed. Your body remains completely relaxed, but with each breath, your mind becomes more alert. I will count five breaths. With the fifth breath, your eyes will open and you will feel very refreshed and relaxed, alert, but calm. One, two, three, four, five.

Debriefing

Make sure that the client is alert enough to drive. Inquire about hand warmth and muscle relaxation. Find out if anything on the tape was disturbing or distracting. If any problems exist, correct them or do another tape. Remember that it's only twelve to eighteen minutes. If all is well, begin to work out the logistics of when, where, and how the tape will be used. Adherence to a practice regimen is the biggest problem that many clients face. Work as a colleague, not a parent, and find a workable schedule.

Index